P9-BIH-409

THE RISE OF ESOTERIC BUDDHISM IN TIBET

THE RISE OF ESOTERIC BUDDHISM IN TIBET

EVA M. DARGYAY

MOTILAL BANARSIDASS
DELHI :: VARANASI :: PATNA

Indological Publishers and Booksellers
Head Office : BUNGALOW ROAD, JAWAHAR NAGAR, DELHI-7
Branches : 1. CHOWK, VARANASI-1 (U.P.)
2. ASHOK RAJPATH, PATNA-4 (BIHAR)

ISBN 0 8426 0889 3

First Edition : Delhi, 1977

Price $14.00

Printed in India

BY SHANTILAL JAIN, AT SHRI JAINENDRA PRESS, A-45, PHASE-I, INDUSTRIAL AREA, NARAINA, NEW DELHI-28 AND PUBLISHED BY SUNDARLAL JAIN OF MOTILAL BANARSIDASS, BUNGALOW ROAD, JAWAHAR NAGAR, DELHI-7

FOREWORD

The study and appreciation of Tibetan Buddhism is a comparatively recent development. There are many reasons for the fact that an immensely important field in the history of ideas has been neglected for such a long time. The remoteness and inaccessibility of Tibet has tended to shroud what the Tibetans thought, and on what they built their civilization, in mystery, and the myth that Tibetan literature is but a mass of translations from Sanskrit and Middle-Indian vernaculars, perpetuated by academics in the East and the West alike and re-endorsed by a certain segment of the Tibetans themselves that recognizes only Indian sources, prevented people from looking deeper. It shall not be denied that much of Tibetan literature has been translated from Indian sources and that Tibetan Buddhism is deeply indebted to Indian Buddhism, but in the life of a people the important point is not so much the fact that texts were translated but what these translations achieved by stimulating the minds of the people who were eager to absorb and assimilate new ideas. As a matter of fact the indigenous literature that developed in the wake of the translations far exceeds the translations and it is a sad state of affairs that hardly anything of it is known outside Tibet. Moreover Tibetan Buddhism has traits of which no Indian origin is known.

By its geography Tibet was exposed to different influences, if by this term we understand a recasting of ideas rather than a mere superimposition. To the west it was a country of vague definition, known as Shang-shung (*zhang-zhung*). Its capital to the west of Mount Kailas was until recently a favourite place of pilgrimage for Hindus. The country seems to have had contacts with the neighbouring Indian regions of Kulu and Jalandhar by passes which are still used today. But it also seems to have had close contacts with Kashmir, noted as a great Buddhist country, attracting visitors from as far away as China, especially from the 5th to the 8th centuries. According to Tibetan tradition Shang-shung is the home of the Bon religion which shows both Buddhist and even Iranian influences and which must be credited to have paved the way for the ready acceptance of new ideas. But before Tibet proper emerged as an Asian power and established formal contacts with its neighbours, Nepal and India in the South and China to the East, its main cultural link has been with the Ch'iang tribes on China's north-western borders, who lived within the reach of the trade routes that linked China with India, Iran, and, ultimately, Byzantium and along which all kinds of cultural ideas and artistic motifs found their way into Tibet.

Dr. Eva Dargyay's book deals with the formative period of Tibetan Buddhism and centres round the tradition of the 'Old School' which may be said to have kept the spirit of Buddhism alive, since it was less interested in power politics and mere scholastic debates on problems of philosophy. This school frankly admits that some of its leading figures came from China and that they played an important role in the formation of its way of thought which, for political reasons, had to go 'underground', not only figuratively but quite literally. The period of the so-called 'Religious Kings of Tibet' marked a growing emphasis on the Indian contribution which, philosophically speaking, was noted for its interest in epistemology and its almost total rejection of metaphysics. But metaphysics is the life of philosophy; it has lived on in the 'Old School' which had to 'conceal' its texts in face of the changed intellectual and political climate. Later on, when the connection with Chinese Buddhist thought had been mostly forgotten, these texts were 'rediscovered'. Of course, 'rediscovery' implies 're-interpretation' as well as continuity.

Dr. Eva Dargyay thoroughly investigates the many problems connected with the 'Old School'. Thereby she is able to throw new light on the rather enigmatic personality of Padmasambhava.

Students of early Tibetan history and thought will no doubt be grateful to Dr. Eva Dargyay for having undertaken this arduous task of unravelling the traditions and their intricate interrelationships, of one of the most fascinating ways of thinking.

University of Saskatchewan
Saskatoon, Sask.
Canada

HERBERT V. GUENTHER
Professor and Head of the Department of Far Eastern Studies

ACKNOWLEDGEMENTS

I wish to express my deep gratitude to the Hierarch of the Old School, bDud-'joms Rin-po-che, who generously presented me his work on The Rise of the Old School (*rNying-ma'i chos-'byung*), and to my husband, dGe-bśes bLo-bsang Dar-rgyas, who guided me through the history and the tradition of Old School thought and theories.

I am also greatly indebted to Dr. Herbert V. Guenther, Professor and Head of the Department of Far Eastern Studies of the University of Saskatchewan, Saskatoon (Canada) for his encouragement of my work, for his unselfish readiness to answer my questions, and for writing the Foreword.

The Publishing House, Motilal Banarsidass, deserves well of bringing forth this study.

Also, I have to thank the Prussian State Library in Berlin for having put the Rin-chen-gter-mdsod at my disposal, and to the Insdological Institute of the University of Münich for granting me permission to use its library.

E.D.

LIST OF ABBREVIATIONS

DC	Gangs-ljongs rgyal-bstan yongs-rdsogs-kyi phyi-mo snga-'gyur rdo-rje-theg-pa'i bstan-pa rin-po-che ji-ltar byung-ba'i tshul dag-cing gsal-bar brjod-pa lha-dbang gyul-las rgyal-ba'i rnga-bo-che'i sgra-dbyangs
DD	bKa'-brgyad bde-gśegs-'dus-pa cycle
DM	Tshal-pa deb-dmar by Kun-dga'-rdo-rje
DNg	Deb-ther-sngon-po (see Roerich, Blue annals)
GR	rGyal-rabs-gsal-ba'i me-long (ed. by Kusnetzov)
GT	Grub-mtha' thams-cad-kyi khungs-dang-'dod-tshul ston-pa legs-bśad śel-gyi-me-long by Thu'u-bkvan Rin-po-che Chos-kyi-nyi-ma
JA	Journal Asiatique
KD	bKa'-babs-bdun-ldan (see Grünwedel, Edelstein-mine)
KhG	Chos-'byung mkhas-pa'i-dga'-ston by Karma-pa dPa'-bo-gtsug-lag (ed. by L. Chandra, New Delhi 1959-62)
MBT	Minor Buddhist texts (see G. Tucci)
PJ	dPag-bsam-ljon-bzang by Sum-pa-mkhan-po Ye-śes-dpal-'byor (ed. by S. Ch. Das Calcutta 1908 and Sarnath n.d.)
PK	Chos-'byung padma-rgyas-pa'i-nyin-byed by Padma-dkar-po
SCD	DAS, S. Ch. Tibetan-English Dictionary
TM	Rin-chen-gter-mdsod (mTshur-phu edition, 63 vols.)
TPS	Tibetan Painted Scrolls (see G. Tucci)
TTP	Tibetan Tripitaka, Peking Edition (ed. by Suzuki)
ZDMG	Zeitschrift der Deutschen Morgenländischen Gesellschaft
ZG	Dzam-gling-rgyas-bshad (see T. Wylie)

CONTENTS

PART I

THE BEGINNINGS OF THE OLD SCHOOL OF TIBETAN BUDDHISM
(4th century—10th century)

1. THE OLD SCHOOL IN ITS HISTORICAL STARTING POSITION

1.1. THE GEOGRAPHICAL ZONE OF TIBET

Like so many European countries, Tibet was fated to accept constantly changing state borders; the exact lines of these cannot always be defined precisely because local kingdoms often were only loosely connected with the central empire, the zone of cultural influence is clearly distinguishable from the political one. Cultural influence often penetrated far into India and China. The language zone is the third component in the term "Tibet"; this component is tightly interlaced with that of culture.

In the reign of the kings of the Yar-klung dynasty (7th-9th century A.D.), the central empire of Tibet reached its pinnacle of power. At that time the political borders of Tibet expanded far beyond the territory of the cultural and language zone.[1] These political borders were, however, eclipsed by the influence Tibet exercised on the surrounding countries. Already in the Tibetan middle age the political territory started to dwindle away, and its shrinkage continued into modern times. Thus the Autonomous Region of Tibet, which is now under the rule of Communist China, is only a very modest remainder of the former empire of the Yar-klung dynasty kings—just as the Federal Republic of Western Germany comprises only a miniscule part of what was once the Holy Roman Empire of German Nations. For a long time then, the zone of Tibetan culture and language included large areas that had not been a political part of it. Recently Tibet's scope of influence was extended to areas which never before had come in contact with Tibetan culture.

When the term "Tibet" (which can be understood in many different ways) is used in the following study, it refers to the area ruled by the Yar-klung dynasty, but only insofar as it is identical with the zone of Tibetan culture and language. When areas, culturally belonging to Tibet, were not clearly under the rule of the Yar-klung kings or their successors in central

Tibet, we term them "border regions" without defining their political status. Areas settled predominantly by non-Tibetans even though they were part of the Yar-klung dynasty's domain are not considered Tibet proper.

1.2. TIBET'S FIRST CONTACTS WITH THE BUDDHIST WORLD

The native tradition as well as European scholars differ as to the time of Tibet's encounter with Buddhism. The Tibetan sources furnish the following picture: The whole dynasty of Yar-klung is divided into three periods : pre-Buddhist, Buddhist, and gLang-dar-ma's. He, however, was not regarded as a legitimate king. Buddhist authors only recognize the pre-Buddhist and Buddhist periods. King Lha-tho-tho-ri[2] is referred to be the first Buddhist king during whose reign some sacred objects were presented by an Indian embassy. The very lineage starting with Lha-tho-tho-ri is called the Happy Generations (*skyid-pa'i-gdung-rabs*)[3]. During the lifetime of king Lha-tho-tho-ri there fell a golden stūpa, a Buddhist book and a wish-bestowing jewel from heaven upon the roof of the castle Yum-bu-bla-sgang, and a voice was heard from heaven to declare: "After five generations One shall appear who will understand their significance !" Thus we are told in a Tibetan legend. In the historical tradition of the Tibetans the king to come is identified as Srong-btsan-sgam-po. Although apparently a mere legend, this account undoubtedly indicates the fact that Buddhist scriptures and sacred objects were brought to Tibet generations before Srong-btsan-sgam-po, but remained unread and unintelligible until his time. As to the historical reality of Lha-tho-tho-ri, the study of Tibetan pre-history adduces many reasons for considering him a real person.[4] The source material for this examination of the ancient history of Tibet is widely scattered. Therefore, the attempts to characterize Tibet's encounter with Buddhism at the time of Lha-tho-tho-ri as mere legend are to be viewed with some reservations.

As to the Tibetan border regions there are indications that not only Buddhist texts and sacred objects were present but also that Buddhist teachings were already known. East Tibetan tribes infiltrated into China already in the 4th century A. D.: "The proto-Tibetan Ti and Ch'iang tribes from the Lop-nor region and western Kansu, had infiltrated from the West and were living in great numbers in eastern Kansu, Shensi, and Ssuch'uan."[5] Further it is said in the same work:[6] "T'an-i[7] one of Tao-an's disciples who was of 'Tibetan'[8] origin, had become abbot of the important Ch'ang-sha[9] monastery at Chiang-ling." This happened at the end of the 4th century A.D.[10] T'an-i is also described as being wealthy, and having supported poor monastic students,[11] a habit well-off Tibetan monks continued up to modern times. It is hard to believe that an individual enthusiast of the teachings of Buddha, coming from an environment averse to higher culture and civilization, should become abbot of such an influential monastery. One should rather start with the premise that T'an-i came from surroundings in which Buddhism, as a religion, was influential. To substantiate this premise, it may be pointed out that Tibetan noble families are mentioned as patrons of the Buddhist scholar, Hui-yuan.[12] Kumārajīva (born 350 in Kucha), the famous translator and renewer of Chinese Buddhism, lived from the year 401 under the protection of the Tibetan ruler who conquered the Later Liang and whose name Chinese sources give as Yao-hsing.[13]

From these data one can justifiably conclude that, at least in Eastern Tibet, there existed during and after the time of Lha-tho-tho-ri a solid knowledge of Buddhism and that the upper classes of the people were faithfully devoted to it. But the border regions in the north and west probably had also come into contact with Buddhism long before the time of Srong-btsan-sgam-po. Buddhist teachings reached China via a route along the western and northern borders of the Tibetan culture and language zone; the same route was travelled by Indian Pandits and Chinese pilgrims in their endeavor to bring this Indian religion to China.[14] There used to be contacts with the Tibetan population in these border regions. It is possible that the knowledge gained from these encounters was spread by merchants over large areas of Tibet. Thus, when Srong-btsan-sgam-po succeeded to the throne of Tibet in the year 627, the country was ready for a systematic missionary drive under royal patronage.[15] During his reign Jo-khang and Ra-mo-che, the two main temples of Lha-sa, were built. King Khri-srong-lde-btsan (755-797) continued to spread Buddhism with great enthusiasm and devotion. The crowning of all his efforts was the construction of bSam-yas (755), the first Tibetan monastery; in this seven Tibetan monks (*sad-mi mi-bdun*) lived under the guidance of Indian Buddhist scholars.[16] In addition King Khri-srong-lde-btsan had called famous masters of contemporary Buddhism to Tibet: among those were Śāntarakṣita, Padmasambhava, Vimalamitra, Śāntigarbha, Viśuddhasiṃha, Dharmakīrti, Jinamitra, Dānaśīla, Kamalaśīla, Hva-śang Mahāyāna[17]. Padmasambhava and Vimalamitra are most important to us. The person of Padmasambhava, the Old School master of sometime dubious repute, poses many problems; the sources which clarify the Padmasambhava dilemma are too heterogeneous and voluminous as to be even mentioned here. We shall, however, show that his person is only of peripheral interest to our concern, the elucidation of the beginnings of the Old School (*rNying-ma-pa*).

However, the relationship of King Khri-srong-lde-btsan with Padmasambhava is present in all our sources, especially in the hagiographies of the Discoverers of Concealed Teachings (*gTer-ston*). In these works the king is rarely called by his name; mostly he is identified by his title only: "The king who complied with the Buddha-Dharma" (*Chos-rgyal*). It is to be noted, however, that apart from this special circle of the Old School literature, all Yar-klung kings starting with Lha-tho-tho-ri had a right to this title.

1.3. THE INTELLECTUAL TENDENCIES OF TIBETAN BUDDHISM FROM THE 7TH TO THE 9TH CENTURY

In respect of the Old School (*rNying-ma-pa*), comparisons may be made, to some extent, with the development of occidental Christianity. Just as the Roman Catholic Church can only be understood as such in its opposition to the Protestant Church; the Old School followers (*rNying-ma-pa*) understood themselves as such only when Atīśa came to Tibet in 1042,[18] introduced some reforms according to the Indian teaching tradition, and when the followers of these reforms called themselves The New School (*gSar-ma-pa*). After this development, the previous, partly heterogeneous, traditions were gathered uniformly under the term The Old School (*rNying-ma-pa*). Just as little as one can deny the continuity of the Roman Catholic Church beyond Luther, one cannot deny that the *rNying-ma-pa* form the oldest Buddhist school in Tibet.

The exceedingly stormy history of the first Buddhist missionary period (*snga-dar*) has been described repeatedly, most recently by Tucci.[19] In this work stress is laid for the first time on the continued interlacing of political group interests with religio-dogmatic ambitions. A brief sketch of the various intellectual tendencies will be of some help.

The Indian pandits, represented mainly by Śāntarakṣita, Kamalaśīla, and his disciple Ye-śes-dbang-po, form a known group. These scholars were all defenders of the *Madhyamaka* school, which is based upon Nāgārjuna's teachings. First of all, however, they taught the ten rules of behaviour of the Buddhist ethics (śīla) and a summary of the teachings according to the canonic Sūtras of the Mahāyāna, as well as the virtuous works of the six *pāramitās*. These exercises are supposed to lead, in a long seemingly endless way, to the gradual ascent to the acquisition of higher intellectual abilities finally culminating in Buddhahood. This trend was intensified after the debate of bSam-yas had taken place in the years 792 to 794;[20] the exact outcome of this debate is still debatable.[21]

Current ideas among the Indian Siddhas penetrated Tibet; Padmasambhava and Vairocana are representing some of these ideas. The teachings of these Siddhas are difficult to grasp because they were transmitted secretly "from the mouth of the teacher to the ear of the disciple"; however, texts such as the KD, the hagiographies of the masters of the *bka'-brgyud-pa* School,[22] and the works of other mystics of the Siddha tradition (in which the hagiographies of the Discoverers of Concealed Teachings are included) give us certain hints.

Scholars with a knowledge of Buddhist texts were called to Tibet not only from India, as overemphasized in some places, but also from China,[23] Khotan[24] and other surrounding Buddhist countries. As has been pointed out above, Kumārajīva had close contacts with Tibetan princes who were his patrons (*sbyin-bdag*, *dānapati*). Kumārajīva has presented the *Madhyamaka* doctrine to the Chinese in a much clearer form than previous translators had been able to do. His principal disciple was Seng-chao (died in 414),[25] of whom it is said : "Seng-chao was still a bridge between Taoism and Buddhism. His fondness for Lao Tzu and Chuan Tzu had a lasting influence on him. The Taoist ideas of vacuity and the sage having to deliberate mind of his own have a prominent place in his philosophy. In this way he not only incorporated Taoism into his system but also harmonized the *Madhyamaka* philosophy with the wisdom (*prajñā*) movement which aims at achieving the wisdom of realizing that things in their own self-nature are unreal."[26] In Liebenthal's treatise, Seng-chao is characterized as a mystic who received his philosophical schooling in the *Madhyamaka* doctrine, and who, in his search for a direct and indelible experience of noetic being (*chos-sku, dharmakāya*) had visions of reality which he formulated in paradoxes similar to those expressed by the followers of *Ch'an* Buddhism;[27] in this he and the *rDsogs-chen*, the Absolute Perfection and Completion, meet on common ground. "Stimulated by the lively atmosphere in Ch'an-and the discussion with his fellow students and opponents he feels that he must tell of the truth he has found. This truth is a vision; it is not in the words of the text-books themselves but lies behind the words. It cannot be learned but must be experienced. It is discovered in moments of 'ecstatic acceptance' of Life; it is hidden in the seemingly paradoxical statements of the *Madhyamaka* philosophy, which tells of the One in whom opposites meet."[28] It is further said : "Chao's paradoxes must not be understood as sophisms or expressions of scepticism, but, as I shall try to prove in my analysis, they reflect the experience of a mystic. They revealed to Chao in moments of ecstasy; and which takes the form of arguments, in some cases condensed to syllogisms, are in fact restatements or paraphrases of this one invaluable experience."[29] Hva-śang Mahāyāna, the Chinese scholar present at the debate of bSam-yas, maintained that he advocated the *Madhyamaka* doctrine; Kamalaśīla, his Indian adversary rejected this assertion, insinuating that this Chinese opponent adulterated the *Madhyamaka* doctrines, and that he (Kamalaśīla) alone advocated the pure and true form of it.[30] According to statements concerning the developments within the *Madhyamaka* School, we may presume that Hva-śang advocated the Chinese version of that school, interspersed with terms of Taoist mysticism; Kamalaśīla, on the other hand, advocated the Indian interpretation of the same school. The texts which

Hva-śang hid when he left Tibet were later unearthed by the followers of the Old School (*rNying-ma-pa*) and handed down as Concealed Teachings (*gter-ma*). In this lies the explanation of the Taoist influence which is felt in some of the *rNying-ma-pa* texts:[31] "...that some books of his school were buried by Hva-śang as *gter-ma*, just as were the books of the *rNying-ma-pa*, and, as we shall see, by the survival of some of their views in the *rDsogs-chen* branch of the *rNying-ma-pa* sect." We do not share Tucci's opinion that Hva-śang and his adherents were Ch'an-Buddhists and that the doctrines of Ch'an-Buddhism have survived in Tibet as *rDsogs-chen*. Rather we would put forward the working hypothesis that Hva-śang was an adherent of the school of Seng-chao; what separated him from Kamalaśīla was the Taoist element which had found its place in Seng-chao's school as well in Ch'an-Buddhism.

However, Tucci is correct when he suggests survival of Ch'an ideas in Tibet within the *rNying-ma-pa* traditions. The passages from the *bKa'-thang-sde-lnga*[32] show this plainly. Certainly there is more than one book handed down within the compass of the *rDsogs-chen* that manifests tendencies which allow it to be counted within Ch'an-Buddhism. The *rDsogs-chen* teachings are, in all probability, not based on one single Chinese school but on several of them, mixed with elements of Indian systems. As stressed in the introduction, Guenther suggests that the *rNying-ma-pa* teachings show strong similarities to the Hua-yen School which was founded by Fa-tsang (643-712) and the earlier *Mahāyānaśraddhotpāda*.

In conclusion, it seems almost certain that in addition to the Indian school of the *Madhyamaka* and Siddha tradition several Chinese schools, first of all Hua-yen, Seng-chao's School, and Ch'an pursued missionary activities in Tibet at the time of the first spread of Buddhism (*snga-dar*). The monks who immigrated into Tibet from Central Asia and who for the most part belonged to one of the many Hīnayāna schools should be excluded from the missionaries under consideration. Only the scrutiny of the Old School's Tantras (*rgyud-'bum*), their colophons and the catalogues (*dkar-chags*) belonging to them will show in particular which tendencies flowed into the great melting pot of the Old School.

All these clerical hierarchies, scholars and mystics were

advisors as well as religious tutors at the court of the Tibetan kings, and their influence on politics was significant. Gifted sons of the noble families became clerics, but they did not relinquish their group interests as members of one of the feuding factions of the nobles. The dispute about the new religion and the new cultural and social tendencies raged fiercest in the upper social classes. The conservative nobles and their followers counteracted Tibet's "new learning" with the magic of *Bon*-religion and popular belief.

1.4. THE CONSEQUENCES FOR THE OLD SCHOOL

After the *rNying-ma-pa* were certain of their royal patronage, they had to include into their missionary efforts the reactionary and lower classes of the people. By this process the *Bon*-religion and the popular belief were, as far as it was considered justifiable, incorporated into the frame of Buddhism in changed form. This is probably the explanation of the statement that Padmasambhava placed the native spirits under oath (*dam-can*) to serve Buddhism in the future and that they fulfilled their oath. This assimilation of the *Bon*-religion and the popular belief continued, although scholars of the Old School fought against excessive assimilation. An overly close merging of the Old School ideas of the *Bon* and the popular belief, gave birth to the pseudo *rNying-ma-pa*; they devoted themselves to the fulfillment of the needs for magic of a society of farmers and cattle raisers. These pseudo *rNying-ma-pa*, unfortunately, often became more famous than the learned representatives of the school, who as true Yogis remained silent and stayed in seclusion, and unlike the *dGe-lugs-pa* School, did not criticize these excesses in their own school.

A further problem consisted in mastering the many and often very different systems that had been brought into Tibet from the surrounding countries during the first missionary period (*snga-dar*). This proliferation of philosophical teaching, opinion and mystic practices needed some checks to insure a balance. Even today it cannot be said to what degree such a balance was actually achieved. However, as was pointed out in chapter 1.3., remains of these different school traditions are noticeable in many instances. Thus the *rNying-ma-pa* preserved teachings which other schools had long ago eliminated or adjusted because they seemed to be contradictory.

Within the framework of this school, the translators had to master the difficult task of putting philosophical texts in Sanskrit and Chinese into the newly created "High Tibetan," which lacked a philosophical terminology. They very often chose a way which differed from that of the later translators,[33] who depended largely on the work of Atīśa and his disciples. Here a gap separates the first missionary period (4th cent.—10th) from the second one (*phyi-dar*) beginning in the 11th century and reaching into modern times. As transmitters of the textual tradition of the first missionary period (*snga-dar*), the Old School adheres to the "Teachings of the Earlier Translations", while the *dGe-lugs-pa* and *bKa-gdams-pa* Schools recognize, above all, the translations of the second missionary period. Both traditions alternatingly polemicize against each other; yet, their respective philosophical systems were and are studied by members of the other branch.

The fall of the Yar-klung dynasty also ended the Old School's influence on political events in Tibet. In contrast to most of the other schools, they devoted themselves completely to mysticism and also insisted at least outwardly, on poverty. Through this isolation the religious forces were deeply divided.[34] This isolationist attitude explains the completely unpolitical hagiography of the fifth Dalai Lama, which will be discussed in the second part of this treatise. However, as it will be shown later, the *rNying-ma-pa* have preserved their religious vitality to the present time.

2. THE OLD TRANSMISSION OF THE "PRONOUNCEMENTS" (*ring-brgyud bka'-ma*)

2.1. THE FOUNDATION IN THE TRANSCENDENTAL

If one examines Buddhism from the purely historical point of view, typical for the western approach, one tends to see Gautama Buddha, the scion of the Śākya clan, as the founder of Buddhism. However, no religion bases itself in the transitory sphere of temporal history. Every religion first creates a transcendental system of relationships, into which the historical manifestations which can claim reality are then imbedded. Thus Buddhist tradition, although not denying the fact that Gautama was a real person, views this historical reality as only the expression of a higher reality. This higher reality is represented as a concentration of all components of reality, termed noetic being (*chos-sku*). The central importance of the term *chos-sku*, requires a short explanation. In the *Doha-skor-gsum-gyi ti-ka sems-kyi-rnam-thar ston-pa'i me-long* Karma-phrin-las describes *chos-sku* as follows : "Noetic being (*chos-sku*) is a priori awareness, the aesthetic perception of everything perceptible, non-dual, and devoid of the extremes of eternalism and nihilism are the formulated fictions of affirmation postulating existence and of the negation postulating non-existence."[35] In this connection one should not stress the innumerable incarnations (*sPrul-pa*) which are met as historical persons in the hagiographies of the Discoverers of Concealed Teachings (*gTer-ston*); rather, one should emphasize the primary *sPrul-pa*, the authentic beings, who form the link between noetic being and the world as it appears, Saṃsāra. These authentic forms of the intellectual world ensure the tradition of the wisdom of noetic being, the primary wisdom (*ye-śes*).

The special wisdom, which comprises the whole of being and which is reserved for the Buddhas alone (*rnam-pa-thams-cad-mkhyen-pa'i ye-śes* abridged *rnam-mkhyen*, Skr. *sarvajñā*), presents itself in its totality as Kun-tu-bzang-po. This is the point where the converging lines of space and time meet in the coordinate field of Saṃsāra, which is permeated by discrimination-appreciation (*śes-rab*). This perceptiveness forms the process of intellectual maturation (*lam*), which often is translated as "path". Through this perceptiveness, which expands into infinity, the coordinate field of Saṃsāra coincides in the zero point, and thus proves itself as the open dimension of Being in general (*stong-pa-nyid*). The converging line of time meets in Kun-tu-bzang-po, who is the discrimination-appreciation (*śes-rab*) of all the Buddhas who have appeared in all times (*dus-gsum*); and in all the ten directions of the compass; the converging line of space also meets in Kun-tu-bzang-po, since it comprises the process of intellectual maturation (*lam*), the wisdom which encompasses all being. In other words, Kun-tu-bzang-po teaches the Pronouncements (*bka'-ma*).[36] This allegoric mode of expression does not describe a primitive mythology, but must be translated into the rational language; only then can its contents become intelligible to modern man. These Pronouncements are essentially timeless, since Kun-tu-bzang-po, the primary wisdom of noetic being, is unchanging and eternal.

Since *bka'-ma* literally means "word", it would be easy to indulge into speculations about similarities found in the Gnosis and the Logos doctrine of the West. At this point, it would be premature to put forward any hypothesis concerning any possible influence by, or relationship of the Pronouncements (*bka'-ma*) with the Gnosis, since up to now hardly anything is known about the Old School, and the central texts of the Pronouncement literature (*bka'-ma*) have not yet been translated and studied. Therefore I shall render the word *bka'-ma* by "Pronouncements", add the Tibetan word in parenthesis, and use it in this work only as the name of a certain type of literature.

In another source, the beginning of the *bka'-ma* in the transcendental is pictured more explicitly.[37] The element designated above as the field of coordinates or Saṃsāra is called in this text the first of all Maṇḍalas (*dkyil-'khor-kun-gyi gtso-bo*). In it there exists, like in a palace for gods (*gzal-yas-khang*), the five-fold light of the objectified sphere of Being (*chos-dbyings*). The first Maṇḍala is not located anywhere in space (*rgya-chad phyogs-lhung dang bral-ba*); as stated above, it is in the point of convergence of space and time, and is omnipresent in this point. There, at this point of convergence, is the center of the Buddha

Kun-bzang Che-mchog Heruka.[38] He is surrounded by his emanative aspects, the peaceful and the fierceful powers (*zi-ba's* and *khro-bo'i lha*). From *Kun-bzang Che-mchog Heruka*, as the very voice of the very nature of the things (*chos-nyid*)[39] spring the five general Tantras, the five special Tantras, and the many very special Tantras (which particular Tantras were included in these groups could not be determined from the text). This tradition manifested in the transcendental is called "The Tradition of the Buddha's Intentionality" (*rgyal-ba-dgongs-pa's brgyud-pa*).[40]

The PK[41] also confirms that at the beginning the Pronouncements (*bka'-ma*) rested in the intellect of *Kun-tu-bzang-po*. He caused a Maṇḍala of the fierceful powers (*khro-bo dkyil-'khor*), encompassing all intellectual intentions of the Buddha (*bźed-pa*)[42] to appear to facilitate the education (*'dul-ba*) of the disciples.

2.2. THE TRANSMISSION OF THE PRONOUNCEMENTS THROUGH THE INTERMEDIATORS OF THE SPIRITUAL WORLD (*rig-'dsin-brda'i brgyud-pa* and *mkha'- 'gro gtad-rgya'i brgyud-pa*)

We are still not in the sphere of the temporal, historically comprehensible, world. *Kun-tu-bzang-po* forms his intellect into Rig-'dsin rDo-rje-chos-rab, said to be *Kun-tu-bzang-po's* own force or the effort of his intellect (*thugs-kyi rang-rtsal*).[43] Rig-'dsin rDo-rje-chos-rab compiles in a Tantra the primary wisdom (ye-śes) of *Kun-tu-bzang-po*, including the allegorical picture of *Che-mchog*. Thus, Rig-'dsin rDo-rje-chos-rab becomes, as it were, a Buddha himself. Here is probably one of the few instances where even the native tradition itself admits that some of these Tantras were written down by some other person, even though they rested in the wisdom of noetic being, and are concurrent with the intentions of the Buddha. Rig-'dsin rDo-rje-chos-rab in turn creates many Wisdom-Holders (*Rig-'dsin*), who put this Tantra into words; later they teach the Tantra and the five Tracts of Oral Tradition (*lung-gi chos*), and write them down with molten lapis lazuli. The Wisdom-Holders entrust these books to the mKha-'gro Las-kyi-dbang-mo-che.—According to PK[44] the function of the intermediator is fulfilled by the absolute and unchanging Being (*rang-byung rdo-*

rje-sems-dpa'), which is personified and born in a lotus flower analogous to Padmasambhava's birth story.

TM[45] reports a further variation of the tradition: the Buddha assumed the form of a "terrifying, all-conquering lord of the secret" (*gSang-bdag dregs-pa kun-'dul*), and revealed the Tantra in the cremation ground Śītavana,[46] and other locations. He entrusted the text of the Tantra to the Wisdom-Holders (*Rig-'dsin*). This is called the Transmission of Symbols through the Wisdom-Holders (*rig-'dsin brda'i brgyud-pa*); the symbols contain the meaning of the Tantra.

TM-DD places the transmission of the literature of Pronouncements (*bka'-ma*) even further into the sphere of spiritual go-betweens. In view of the subsequent part of the tradition, the above statement has to be modified to some extent. The circumstances described point to the extra-human sphere, but the fact that concrete literal works are not mentioned point to the opposite. However, at the end of the passage in question we find the following sentence: "After that came the time to educate the human world." Because of this sentence we decided to count the Transmission through the Spiritual Beings (*mKha'-'gro*) among those of the Intermediators of the Spiritual World.[47]

The *mKha'-'gro-ma* bDe-ba'i-dngos -grub descended from the sphere of the evidence of Being (*chos-dbyings*), out of pity for man who was to be instructed, and hid all the Tantras of the Developing Stage (*bskyed-rim*) and the Fulfilment Stage (*rdsogs-rim*) in the stupa bDe-byed-brtsegs-pa, which is located in the cremation ground Śītavana. The following is the description of the respective parts of the stupa in which the books were hidden.[48] In the foundation, the *sGyu-'phrul-sde-brgyad* was hidden; in the middle, the bulge of the stupa (*bum-pa*), the *bDe-gśegs-'dus-pa* was hidden. In the four intermediate directions of heaven, the special Tantras were put (*Bye-brag-sgos-rgyud*); in the flute of the stupa, the *gSang-ba-yongs-rdsogs*; and in the rim of the umbrella (*chos-skor*), the Tantra *Rang-byung-rang-śar*.[49] In the middle of the umbrella, the *Sangs-rgyas-mnyam-sbyor*[50] was hidden, and in the tip of the stupa were sealed the *Yang-gsang-bla-med-yang-ti-nag-po* from the central doctrine of the *rDsogs-chen* philosophy. Ye-śes-mkha'-'gro, Las-kyi-mkha'-'gro, 'Jig-rten-skyong-ba'i dPa'-bo and Ḍākinī were charged with guarding the stupa. This is the Tradition of the

Sealed Texts, which had been entrusted to the Spiritual Beings (*mkha'-'gro gtad-rgya'i brgyud-pa*), and it is the end of the Transmission of the Pronouncement Doctrine (*bka'-ma*) through the intermediators of the spiritual world in its two modifications.

2.3. THE PRINCIPAL TRADITION OF THE "GREAT PERFECTION" DOCTRINE (*rdsogs-chen mthur-thug-gi chos- kyi brgyud-pa*)

The transmitters of this tradition belong to the entire history of Tantrayāna, of which, however, only fragments are known to us. Even native scholars tackle this theme only with caution. Tāranātha writes in the 43rd chapter of his *History of Buddhism in India*:[51] "Now, I find some conceited people who, in spite of being full of doubts, consider themselves to be extremely ambitious. However, their muddled view of the different origins of the Mantra-yoga, needs to be examined.... It is well known among the scholars that Śrī Dhānya-kaṭaka was the place where Mantra-yāna was originally preached. But what is written in the glosses by some older Tibetan scholars in defiance of this, is unknown in India. To write that this place —the name of which should be known even to the foolish Tibetans—was called Saddharma-megha-viśālagañja (chos-bzang-sprin-gyi-yang-rdsong) is due only to a bias for what is baseless and to the tendency of placating (the older scholars). This is nothing but the way in which fools befool other fools. Sensible persons do not take it as a serious statement at all .... The origin of the Mantra-yāna is to be understood on the basis of its *śāstra-s* and by compiling the original account coming from their traditions. All these are briefly stated in my *Rin-po-che'i byung-gnas-lta bu'i-gtan* (i.e. our KD) which should be consulted."

To begin with, a survey of the structure of the entire Tantrayāna should make it easier to classify the *rDsogs-chen* system within the Tantrayāna. The Tantrayāna is arranged in three major parts:

1. Tantras dealing with ritual acts (*bya-rgyud* or *kriyā-tantra*)
2. Tantras dealing with ritual acts and meditational practices equally (*spyod-rgyud* or *caryā-tantra*)

3. Tantras for the spiritual transformation (*rnal-'byor-pa'i rgyud* or *yoga-tantra*)

These three steps comprise the secret tradition of the Tantra-yāna (*gsang-sngags*);[52] they are part of all Buddhist schools of Tibet, and in their entirety form the basis and the background for the following discussion. A description of these three lower steps of the Tantrayāna, as they are seen from the Old Schools' point of view, would be advantageous, but, fortunately, there exists now the translation of the passage in question of Mi-pham 'Jam-dbyangs-rnam-rgyal-rgya-mtsho's Summary of Philosophical Systems as detailed in the *Yid-bžin-mdsod* (*Yid-bžin-mdsod-kyi grub-mtha' bsdus-pa*),[53] so I may refer to this lucid explanation.

The last step, the Tantra for spiritual transformation (*rnal-'byor-pa'i rgyud*), is the most widely spread Tantra. It, in turn, is subdivided into three steps:

3.1. The Great Yoga of development (*bskyed-pa mahā-yoga*)

3.2. The Anu-yoga of accomplished meditation (*rdsogs-pa anu-yoga*)

3.3. The Ati-yoga of the Great Perfection (*rdsogs-pa-chen-poa-ti-yoga*)

Together these three steps comprise the *rDsogs-chen* philosophy. *rDsogs-chen*, which we shall always leave in its original, means literally the Great, Ultimate Perfection. Each of the three steps has its own line of tradition, the transmitters of which were especially concerned with the spread of this system. In additon, there is a general *Dsogs-chen* tradition,[54] which names the most important masters of this system. The special traditions, which will be discussed shortly, form the branches on the main trunk of the tree. At first, we shall sketch their relationship according to the PK;[55] then we shall give the more detailed reports of the DC. The DC reports in this chapter are very close to those of the KhG; this can be seen from the footnotes. The KhG generally uses a shorter, more condensed style, and often omits the names of persons and localities; whenever names are mentioned, however, they are identical with those of the DC. The KhG often gives years, and this is an additional aid in the reconstruction of the historical process.

As we have already stated in the previous chapter, *rDo-*

rje-sems-dpa', the Indestructible Cognitiveness, is the beginning of the *rDsogs-chen* tradition. Its personification inspired dGa'-rab-rdo-rje, who three times beheld the countenance of the Indestructible Cognitiveness (*rDo-rje-sems-dpa'*), heard his sermon (*gsung*) three times, and perceived his intellect (*thugs*) three times. dGa'-rab-rdo-rje is the first of all Wisdom-Holders (*Rig-'dsin*); in bKra-śis-khrigs-sgo in China, he taught 'Jam-dpal-bśes-gnyen, who in turn taught Śrīsiṃha, who was born in the town of Źo-śa'i-gling in China. In the forest Sing-nga-la Śrīsiṃha found the true spiritual potency (*siddhi*). In the cremation ground Śītavana in India he instructed Vimalamitra, who was born in the western part of India. Again in bKra-śis-khrigs-sgo in China, Śrīsiṃha instructed the Indian Jñānasūtra. He in turn instructed Vimalamitra. This is called the Transmission of that Doctrine which leads to the Final Goal of the *rDsogs-chen* (*rdsogs-chen mthar-thug-gi chos-kyi-brgyud-pa*).[56]

Although the circles o the Indian mystics (*Siddha*) are discussed by 'Gos Lo-tsā-ba in the DNg, as well as in Tāranātha's KD, the masters of this particular tradition discussed here are rarely mentioned. As to 'Jam-dpal-bśes-gnyen, the KD reports only that he gave many Tantras and commentaries to the Brahman Jñānavajra.[57] This reference is made within the framework of the life history of Sangs-rgyas-(dpal)-ye-śes, alias Buddha-(śrī)-jñāna, who however, is mentioned only incidentally in the *rDsogs-chen* transmission.[58]

In discussing the influence of Chinese Buddhism on Tibet, Tucci merely relied on the *bKa'-thang-sde-lnga*.[59] It is apparent that the transmission presented here, even if it cannot yet be fixed historically, contributes to the solution of the problem. It must be left undecided in which part of the Chinese empire the localities referred to were situated. It is conceivable that Źo-śa (according to the PK) or So-khyam (according to the DC) was located in Central Asia. The name Śrīsiṃha can hardly be a Sanskritised Chinese name.[60]

Without discussing further the separate personalities of this line of tradition, I wish to add the more detailed versions of the KhG and DC, in which short biographies of the masters of the main *rDsogs-chen* tradition are contained. Even though one cannot yet arrange the particulars of the stories into an unbroken historical connection, I consider them valuable material for the knowledge of the history of the Tantrayāna. The content of historical truths in these texts should be estimated as high, because dPa'-bo-gtsug-lag (born 1503), the author of the KhG, proved himself a very reliable historian.[61] His reports of wonderous occurrences do not minimize the value of his account although from the viewpoint of hard facts they may be irreconcilable with historical truth.

The Lord of Secrets (*gSang-ba'i-bdag-po*)[62] instructed the Holders of Wisdom (*Rig-'dsin*) in Dhanakośa in Uḍḍiyāna, the contemporary Swat valley. There was a large temple, called bDe-byed-brtsegs-pa; it was surrounded by 1608 smaller chapels. King Uparāja, and Queen sNang-ba-gsal-ba'i-'od-ldan-ma[63] resided there. They had a daughter called Sudharmā; she took the novice vows, and soon afterwards the full monastic vows. Sudharmā, together with her maidens, stayed on an island and meditated about the Yoga Tantra (*rnal-'byor-gyi rgyud*). One night the Bhikṣuṇī Sudharmā dreamed that a white man had come, who was utterly pure and beautiful. He held a crystal vessel in his hand which had the letters oṃ ā hūṃ svāhā engraved upon it. Three times he set the vessel upon the crown of her head, and light then shone from it. While this happened, she beheld the threefold world perfectly and clearly. Not long after this dream the Bhikṣuṇī gave birth to a true son of the gods. She, however, was very ashamed and thus had bad thoughts: "Since the child was born without a father the whole world will regard it as a spectre." Thereupon she decided to throw the infant boy on the dust-heap. But light and music sprang from the heap; when this continued for three days and the child had not yet died, the Bhikṣuṇī believed the infant an incarnation (*sPrul-pa*) and took him back into the house. All the gods and spirits came to pay respect to the infant and offer gifts to him. When the boy was seven years old he asked his mother to be allowed to dispute with the Paṇḍitas, the scholars. The mother rejected his request because of his tender age. However, after he had repeated his request, he stepped in front of the five hundred scholars, who were guests at the royal court, and conquered them all in the disputation. Prostrate on their knees, now the scholars honoured the boy and gave him the name Prajñābhava, "The One Whose Being is

Wisdom." The king, who was very pleased with this occurrence, gave him the name sLob-dpon dGa'-rab-rdo-rje; under this name he became famous. Because his mother had once thrown him on the dust-heap, he was also known as Ro-langs-bde-ba or Ro-langs-thal-mdog, "Who rose Happy from the Dust" or "The Ashy-pale One who rose from the Dust." In terrible mountain ranges and solitudes where the hunger spirits (*Preta*) appear in hordes, he meditated for thirty-two years. When the earth trembled seven times, the heretic and infidel *mKha'-'gro-ma* called: "He injures the Hindu belief!" The Hindu king then wanted to hold dGa'-rab-rdo-rje responsible, but the latter ascended into space. Because of this event the king and his entourage became very religious.

This legend has some similarity with the legend of Sophia and the story of Christ's life. We, however, do not want to speculate as to whether reciprocal influences and dependencies exist beyond the parthenogenesis,[64] or whether we deal with a polygenesis in this cycle of legends.

After these ascetic exercises,[65] dGa'-rab-rdo-rje knew the exoteric and the esoteric path, and most of all, the sixty-four by a hundred thousand verses of the *rDsogs-chen*. *rDo-rje-sems-dpa'*, the Being of Unchangeability,[66] whose emanation dGa'-rab-rdo-rje was, now gave him in addition a special empowerment (*dbang-bskur*).[67] Together with the three *mKha'-'gro-ma* he compiled an index (*dkar-chags*) of the sixty-four by a hundred thousand *rDsogs-chen* verses; this task took three years.[68] After that he went to the cremation ground Śītavana, where many frightful creatures lived.

Mañjuśrī gave 'Jam-dpal-bśes-gnyen[69] the following prophecy: "If you want to attain Buddhahood go to the cremation ground Śītavana!" 'Jam-dpal-bśes-gnyen followed this advice, and met dGa'-rab-rdo-rje there. For seventy-five years 'Jam-dpal-bśes-gnyen listened to dGa'-rab-rdo-rje's instructions in the *Dharma*. After having given all traditions to 'Jam-dpal-bśes-gnyen, dGa'-rab-rdo-rje died. At the death ceremony the Teacher dGa'-rab-rdo-rje appeared in the middle of a mass of light, surrounded by Spiritual Beings (*mKha'-'gro-ma*). He handed 'Jam-dpal-bśes-gnyen a golden box which contained the *rDsogs-chen* verses.[70] He divided these sixty-four by a hundred thousand verses[71] into the Three Sections of the *rDsogs-*

pa-chen-po (*rDsogs-pa-chen-po sde-gsum*) : the Spiritual Section which relates to firmness of mind (*sems-gnas-rnams-la sems-sde*); the Section of Infinity of Dynamic Being (*klong-sde*),[72] which is related to effortlessness (*bya-bral-rnams-la klong-sde*); and the Section of Instructions (*man-ngag-sde*), which is related to the most important essence (*gnad-gtso-bo-la man-ngag-sde*). He arranged the latter section into the Transmission of what was Heard (*Snyan-brgyud*),[73] and the Transmission of what was Explained (*bśad-brgyud*). For the main text of the first part, *bśad-brgyud-snying-gi-bka'*, he found no suitable disciple, and thus he hid the scriptures east of Bodh Gaya underneath a rock, which was sealed with a double *vajra*, so that no one could detect them. 'Jam-dpal-bśes-gnyen himself went to the west of Bodh Gaya, the cremation ground So-sa-gling. He stayed there for nine hundred years,[74] absorbed in meditation.

Sangs-rgyas-ye-śes-źabs (Buddhaśrījñāna)[75] was the disciple of 'Jam-dpal-bśes-gnyen. He had already heard the secret tradition of the Tantrayāna (*gsang-sngags*) from Jalandharipa,[76] Līlāvajra, the Teacher from Uḍḍiyāna, and from the Yoginī Gu-ni-ru.[77] For nine years he heard the *'Dus-pa'i rgyud*[78] eighteen times from Palitpapa, the Teacher from Konkani, without understanding its contents. He then asked his teacher, who confessed that he himself did not understand it. The material which follows corresponds roughly to the story which Grünwedel translated from the KD.[79] The KD, however, has a lack of clearness in its text: the "house keeping Ārya" was not *Mañjuśrī* himself, but 'Jam-dpal-bśes-gnyen, who was an incarnation (*sPrul-pa*) of *Mañjuśrī*.

Since the chain of transmission (*brgyud-pa*) does not go beyond Sangs-rgyas-ye-śes-źabs, whom the KD calls (as stated above) Buddhaśrījñāna, it is unnecessary here to report his further fate.—According to the DC, some say that he also had the name Śrīsiṃha. However, bDud-'joms Rin-po-che justifiably considers this to be improbable; the KhG contains no reference to this matter.

Whatever the case may be, it is certain that at the time under consideration, in China in the town So-khyam (according to the PK Źo-śa'i-gling), a son full of the preferences and gifts was born to a virtuous father and his wife who were of clear intellect; this son was the Teacher Śrīsiṃha.[80] At the age of fifteen he studied grammar and logic and the other usual disciplines with the master Haribhala. When, after three years, he had become a great scholar, one night in the town of gSer-gling *Avalokiteśvara* appeared to him and prophesied: "If you really aspire for the Buddhahood, then go to India to the cremation ground So-sa-gling!" The Teacher Śrīsiṃha put his trust in this word. Since he thought that the other Tantra should also be studied, he went to the Wu-tai-shan, and there he studied the exoteric and the esoteric Tantra with the Teacher Bhelakīrti. Śrīsiṃha took the vows of a monk, and for three years practised asceticism according to the *Vinaya*-system (i.e. rules for the conduct of monks). Admonished by a prophecy repeatedly given by *Avalokiteśvara*, he set out to India. Because of his spiritual potency (*siddhi*) he encountered no pain and hardship on the way. Thus he came safe and sound to the cremation ground So-sa-gling, where he met the great Teacher 'Jam-dpal-bśes-gnyen, who, because of Śrīsiṃha's entreaties, accepted him as student. For twenty-five years the Teacher gave him the instructions and subcommentaries belonging to it, till finally the master dissolved in a mass of light.[81] When Śrīsiṃha was engaged with the death lamentations, the form of the master appeared in the sky and instructed him bodily. He gave Śrīsiṃha a little box made of jewels, which contained the Six Meditation Experiences (*sGom-nyams-drug-pa*). After the death of his master, Śrīsiṃha practised this doctrine and realized the absolutely real (*don-gyi-gding*).

Then in the west of India, in gSer-gyi-brgyan-pa'i-gling, sLob-dpon 'Jam-dpal-bśes-gnyen was miraculously reborn without physical parents.[82] This incarnation had the name 'Jam-dpal-bśes-gnyen, the younger (*phyi-ma*) who instructed sLob-dpon Padmasambhava in all the exoteric and the esoteric Tantra (*sngags-phyi-dang-nang*). He ('Jam-dpal-bśes-gnyen, the younger) also taught the sLob-dpon Āryadeva[83] the *rDsogs-chen*, whereupon the latter renounced the five categories of the animated world (*phung-po lnga*), his worldly, intellectual and physical being, which are afflicted with the three primary distortions (*nyon-mongs, kleśa*). Later, Śrīsiṃha went to Vajrāsana (i.e. Benares) and took out the *rDsogs-chen* Tantra concerning the Section of Instruction (*man-ngag-sde*) which 'Jam-dpal-bśes-gnyen had hidden there. Śrīsiṃha divided the whole

Section of Instruction into four parts: the Exoteric Cycle (*phyi-skor*), the Esoteric Cycle (*nang-skor*), the Secret Cycle (*gsang-skor*), and the Cycle of the Highest Secret (*gsang-ba bla-na-med-pa skor*). He appropriated the first three cycles to the outer sphere, still tainted by propositions (*spros-bcas-kyi don*), and hid them in the garret floor of the temple Byang-chub-źing. According to the prophecy of the *mKha'-'gro-ma* he—making a wishful prayer (*smon-lam*)—concealed the fourth part, the Cycle of the Highest Secret, in a column of the temple bKra-śis-khri-sgo. Śrīsiṃha went to the cremation ground called bSil-bying. There the demonic beings honoured him; and he taught them the *Dharma* and stayed there in meditation.

At this time, in the west of India in a locality called gLang-po'i-sgang, a son, Vimalamitra, was born to the householder bDe-ldan'khor-lo and his wife bDag-nyid-gsal-rigs-ma. At the same time in the east of India, in a village in the eastern part of the land Kama-si-la, a *Caṇḍāla* called Źi-ba'i-lag-pa and his wife dGe-ba'i-sems-can-ma had a son named Jñānasūtra (Ye-śes-mdo). Thus both of them were in India at the same time. The Being of Unchangeability (*rDo-rje-sems-dpa'*) actually came and gave them a prophecy: "You sons of good families! For five hundred generations both of you will be reborn as *Paṇḍita* and practise the venerable *Dharma*. But since you attained no result formerly you shall attain none now. Therefore if in this life you want to renounce the five categories of the animated world (*phung-po lnga*) which are afflicted with the three primary distortions (*nyon-mongs, kleśa*) and reach Buddhahood, go to the temple Byang-chub-źing in China!" Upon this statement Vimalamitra took his alms bowl and started for China. There he met the Teacher Śrīsiṃha, and for twenty years he (Śrīsiṃha) gave him the complete instructions in the three sections of the oral transmission, that is in the Exoteric, the Esoteric, and the Secret Cycle (*snyan-brgyud phyi-nang-gsang gsum-gyi gdams-pa*).[84] Śrīsiṃha, however, did not give him the books of these cycles. Nevertheless, Vimalamitra was completely satisfied and returned to India, where he met Jñānasūtra and reported everything to him.[85]

With great zeal the two of them started together for China, and as it was said in the prophecy of the Spiritual Beings (*mKha'-'gro-ma*),[86] in the cremation ground bSil-bying they met the master Śrīsiṃha. For three years Śrīsiṃha tried to be an exemplary master. At the end of this period, his two disciples brought him a cosmic *Maṇḍala* made of gold and begged him for further instructions. During the following nine years he gave them the instructions of the Oral Transmission (*snyan-brgyud*),[87] together with the books. They were very satisfied and prepared to leave when their master asked: "Are you satisfied?"—"Yes, we are satisfied!" they answered. The *bLa-ma*, however, said: "I gave you nothing!" When he said this, the concept-free direct awareness (*rtogs-pa*)[88] of the *rDsogs-chen* rose in Jñānasūtra and he begged: "Now give me the whole profound instruction!"—"For this you need an empowerment (*dbang-bskur*)!" replied the bLa-ma. Later Śrīsiṃha gave his disciple Jñānasūtra an empowerment which still was connected with propositions (*spros-bcas-kyi dbang*),[89] for three years he taught Jñānasūtra in the Instruction of the Highest Secret (*gsang-ba bla-na-med-pa'i man-ngag*). After this Jñānasūtra begged Śrīsiṃha to show him the exercises belonging to it. The master gave him an empowerment independent of propositions (*spros-med-kyi dbang*). On the mountain peak of the Ri-bo-ko-sa-la he gave him the Yoga exercise for the separate meditation on *Saṃsāra* and *Nirvāṇa* (*'khor-'das-ru-śau-dbye-ba'i-spyod-pa*). Then the master gave him an empowerment which was even beyond any possibility of propositions (*rab-tu-spros med-kyi dbang*). After this empowerment Jñānasūtra meditated for sixteen years on the practice of this empowerment. Śrīsiṃha showed him first of all various forms of ways of actions (*spyod-pa*).

At another time Śrīsiṃha was invited by the King of Khotan (Li-yul).[90] Seven days after he had gone there, wonderous signs were seen and voices heard. Jñānasūtra saw the master appear in the sky and knew that he had passed on. He therefore intoned the mourning lamentations. He then received the will called *gZer-bu-bdun-pa*,[91] which is said: "The books of the Secret Instructions of the *sNying-thig* (*sNyig thig gsang-ba'i ngag*) are in the column of the temple bKra-'is-khri-sgo. After you have taken them out, go to the cremation ground Bha-sing!"[92] After Jñānasūtra had taken out the secret books, he journeyed to the cremation ground Bha-sing in India. There he preached the secret doctrine of the *sNying-thig*[93] to the worldly and super-worldly Spiritual Beings (*'Jig-rten dang 'jig-rten-las-'das-pa'i-mKha'-'gro dang mKha'-'gro-ma*), and stayed for some time.

At this time Vimalamitra was occupied with Yoga exercises, and he received the prophecy of the Spiritual Being (*mKha'-'gro*): "You, talented one, if you desire the earlier, profound *sNying-thig* instructions , go to the cremation ground Bhasing !" Following the prophecy, he started on his journey and met Jñānasūtra. He begged him to be taught in the great profound instructions. Jñānasūtra showed Vimalamitra various wonderous ways of action (*spyod-pa*) and gave him an exoteric and esoteric empowerment (*dbang*), and also further empowerments, just as Śrīsiṃha had given Jñānasūtra. After the third empowerment, there appeared on Vimalamitra's nose tip the letter AH , white and as if it wanted to fall down. After the fourth empowerment, he saw Mind itself in all its nakedness (*sems-de-nyid rjen-par*).[94] In continuation of the empowerment Jñānasūtra gave him, in its entirety, the four cycles of the *rDsogs-pa-chen-po*, including the books. For ten years Vimalamitra became more and more absorbed in these exercises; then the Teacher Jñānasūtra dissolved into a mass of light.[95] Vimalamitra intoned the mourning lamentations. Later he saw the figure of the master, which gave him a little box made of the five treasures and which was called *bźab-thabs-bźi-pa*. Thus, after the passing of his master he received the entire, delusion-free, complete truth (*don*) and attained the goal (*gding thob-pa*). Vimalamitra then proceeded eastwards to the town Kama-ru in which King Seng-ge-bzang-po (Siṃhabhadra) ruled, and as court chaplain stayed there for twenty years. Afterwards he went to the west, to the town Bhirya ruled by King Dharmapāla, where he became a monk who was subsidized by the king (*mchod-gnas*). Later he journeyed to the large cremation ground Rab-tu-snang-byed, where he practised magic (*brtul-źugs*) which surpassed everything that ever was in this world and taught the *Dharma* to the demonic beings. He copied the most excellent secret books three times. He hid one copy on the "island in the ocean, where the golden sand is scattered" (*rgya-mtsho gser-gyi bye-ma-gdal-bai 'gling*) in Uḍḍīyāna.[96] The second copy he hid under a rock called gSer-gling in Kashmir,[97] the last copy was hidden on this cremation ground as an aid to the religious fervor of the *mKha'-'gro-ma.* The Teacher won the spiritual potency of the Body of the Rainbow (*'ja'-lus*); that is, he found the innermost value of human existence, which manifests itself as a light, and in its being is wisdom, if one wants to express the Tibetan term intelligibly in the language of existential philosophy.[98] Vimalamitra wandered all over India, and later he went to Tibet.[99]

The material reported above must be supplemented by special studies of other Tibetan sources, and the result of such studies must be compared with the Chinese material. Both tasks go beyond the scope of this work. It is to be noted that, according to the PK, dGa'-rab-rdo-rje taught his student Jam-dpal-bśes-gnyen in China; according to the KhG and the DC however, he taught on the cremation ground Śītavana in India. The books of the *rDsogs-chen* doctrine, in any event, were given to the disciples only in China, even though they had been hidden at first in India. In China the *rDsogs-chen* tradition hinges on the temples bKra-śis-khri-sgo and Byang-chub-śing. If one were to consider the PK as reliable, the origins of this system would lie in China. Yet, I prefer the traditions reported in the KhG and DC, especially as the KhG in the chapters so far studied have turned out to be very reliable. It seems that the initial impetus came from India but its final form originated in China, so that from then on these teachings could be traced as books. Jñānasūtra's revelatory experience, which was triggered by the master's paradoxical statement "I have given you nothing" after years of intensive teaching, shows that this system, concerning its religious practices, has certain similarities with *Ch'an* Buddhism. One could call this a *satori* experience.[100]

The following charts illustrate the chain of transmission from master to disciple:

CHARTS OF THE PRINCIPAL TRADITION OF THE RDŚOGS-CHEN DOCTRINE (Chapter 2.3)

I. According to the DC

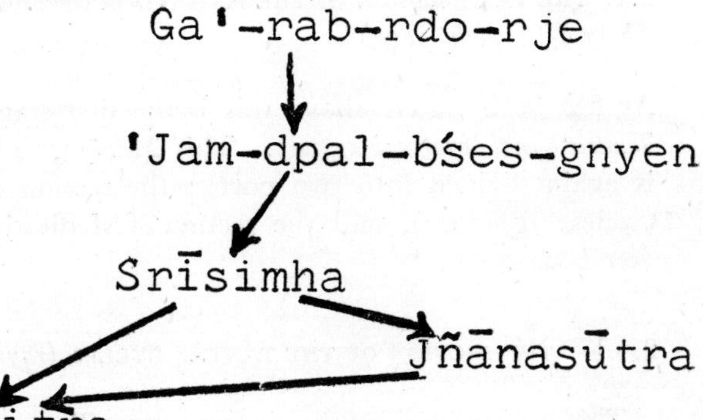

II. According to the KhG

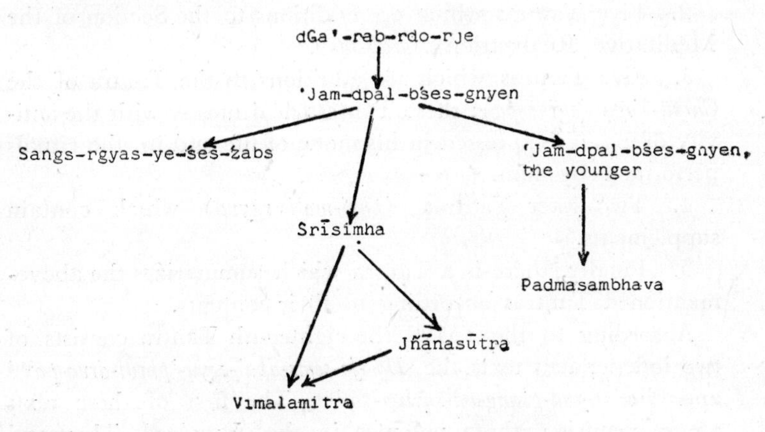

III. According to the PK

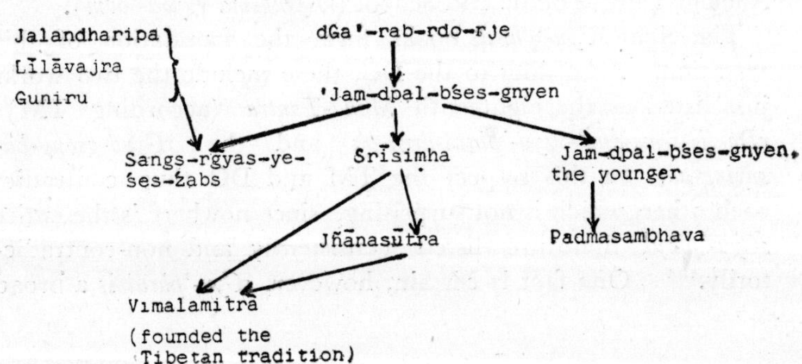

2.4. THE TRANSMISSION OF THE MAHĀYOGA OF THE DEVELOPMENT (*bskyed-pa mahā-yoga*)

As has been stated above this is the first stage of the *Yoga-Tantra* (*rnal-'byor-gyi rgyud*). This *Mahāyoga* of Development is again divided into two parts : the section of the Tantra Cycles (*rgyud-sde*), and the section of Meditative Realization (*sgrub-sde*).

2.4.1. THE SECTION OF THE TANTRA CYCLES (*rgyud-sde*)

This section contains the eighteen great Tantras in general,[101] and may be divided as follows :

1. The five basic *Mahā-Tantras*: the *sKu-*, *gSung-*, *Thugs-*, *Yon-tan-* and the *Phrin-las-kyi rgyud*; i.e. the Tantras which concern themselves with existence, communication, mind, value, and performance of Buddhahood.[102]
2. Five Tantras which are additions to the Section of the Meditative Realization (*sgrub-sde*).
3. Five Tantras which are additions to the Tantra of the *Caryā-Yoga* (*spyod-pa*); these Tantras deal mostly with the activity of man as expressed in his mode of life and in the rituals performed by him.
4. Two later Tantras (*phyi-ma'i rgyud*) which contain supplements.
5. Finally, there is a Tantra which summarizes the abovementioned Tantras according to their contents.

According to the TM[103] the eighteenth Tantra consists of two independent texts, the *rDo-rje-sems-dpa'-sgyu-'phrul-drva-pa*[104] and the *rGyud-gsang-ba-snying-po*.[105] The first of these texts alone comprises three volumes in the Hundred Thousand Ancient Tantras of the Old School (*rNying-ma rgyud-'bum*).

The eight *sGyu-'phrul* books form the foundation of this tradition. According to the DC, these include the two works just listed as the eighteenth *Mahā-Tantra* (according TM): *rDo-rje-sems-dpa'-sgyu-'phrul-drva-pa* and the *rGyud-gsang-ba-snying-po*. In this respect the TM and DC thus contradict each other, which is not surprising, since nowhere is the entire *sGyu-'phrul* literature listed consistently and non-contradictorily.[106] One fact is certain, however, *sGyu-'phrul* is a broad classification of literature. The DNg, too, gives only separate names of works which supposedly belong to this division without clarifying their inner relationship and classifications.[107] Like all other problems of *rNying-ma-pa* literature, this one too can only be solved after the Hundred-Thousand Ancient Tantra (NGB) had been analysed and studied thoroughly. Presently we must be content with sporadic references.

The texts of this tradition which belong to the Developing Stage (*bskyd-rim*), as listed above, were handed down in two lines of tradition. The first starts with Vimalmitra; the second begins with Padma-'byung-gnas, as the famous Padmasambhava is called in Tibetan. The line of the tradition which is traced back to Vimalamitra is designated as the Transmission of Instruction (*man-ngag-gi brgyud-pa*) or as the Transmission of the Pronouncements Hidden at mChims-phu (*bka' mchims-phu*).[108] The major concern of Vimalamitra's student rMa Rin-chen-mchog was the translation of the texts which Vimalamitra had brought from India. Žang rGyal-ba'i-yon-tan spread the doctrine in dBus, gTsang, and Khams, i.e. the both central Tibetan provinces and East Tibet.

CHART OF THE TRANSMISSION OF INSTRUCTION (*man-ngag-gi brgyud-pa*)

(chapter 2.4.1. according to DC)

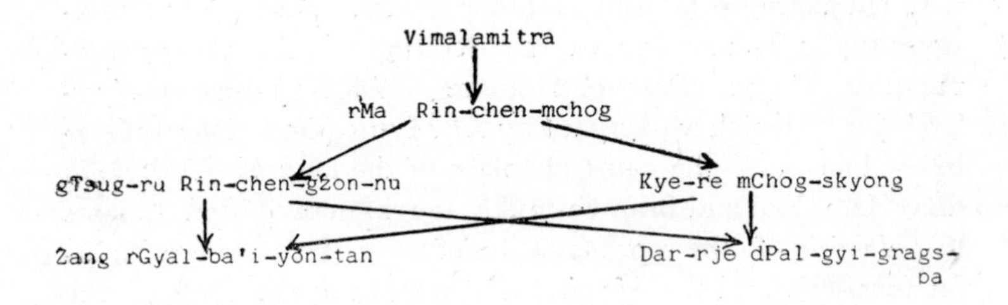

The tradition which goes back to Padmasambhava is known as 'the line similar to the one of instruction' (*man-ngag-lta-bu'i phreng-ba*)

CHART OF THE LINE SIMILAR TO THE ONE OF INSTRUCTION (*man-ngag-lta-bu'i phreng-ba*)

(chapter 2.4.1. according to DC)

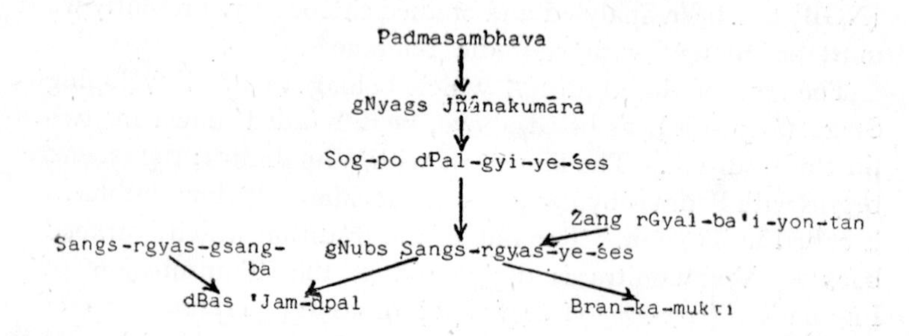

At Gangs Ti-se, the holy Kailāsa mountain, sLob-dpon Sangs-rgyas-gsang-ba instructed the two disciples dBas 'Jam-dpal and Bran-ka-mukti in the basic Tantra (*rtsa-rgyud*) of the *gSang-ba-snying-po* cycle[109] and in the *sGyu-phrul-lam-rnam-bkod*, which is the most important commentary of this Tantra. He conveyed to them the *Guhya-samāja* Tantra according to the system of sLob-dpon rDo-rje-bźad-pa,[110] which is based on Viśvāmitra's commentary; in addition he taught them the *Sangs-rgyas-mnyam-sbyor*;[111] i.e. the basic doctrine of the *rDsogs-pa-chen-po*, together with the commentaries of Ku-ku-ra-ja[112] and Hūṃkara,[113] as well as other cycles. sLob-dpon Sangs-rgyas-gsang-ba also spread the doctrine of the great commentary of the *rDsogs-chen* system, *Sangs-rgyas-mnyam-sbyor-'grel-chen*,[114] which was written by the Mystic (*Grub-thob*) brGya-byin-sdom-po,[115] the court chaplain of the king of Uḍḍiyāna. dBas 'Jam-dpal and Bran-ka-mukti taught many gifted students the *Maṇḍala* of the representation of noetic being as the frightful (*khro-bo*), and the *Maṇḍala* of *Hayagrīva* as the circle of the protectors (*yi-dam-gi skor*).[116] King Khri-srong-lde-btsan also practiced the realization of *Hayagrīva* (*rTa-mgrin*) himself, so that, when his endeavours had success the whole world echoed with the neighing of horses.

The statements in the chapters 2.3. and 2.5. support the tradition of Vimalamitra historically. He directly continues the Principal Tradition of the *rDsogs-chen* Doctrine, or—as it is called in Tibetan—'the tradition of the doctrine which leads to the end goal of the *rDsogs-chen*' (*rdsogs-chen-mthar-thug-gi brgyud-pa*). —The tradition of Padmasambhava seems to be less reliable, since he was instructed by an incarnation of 'Jam-dpal-bśes-gnyen and (according to the PK) "was taught by other Wisdom-Holders (*Rig-'dsin*)." According to the literature listed in that tradition sequence—excluding the works about the famous *gSang-ba-snying-po* and the *Sangs-rgyas-mnyam-sbyor-* Padmasambhava's tradition seems to have been formed, as a variation of the Tradition of Meditative Realization (*sgrub-sde brgyud-pa*). Even its name points to the premise that this line was formed after already existing samples of other tradition lines : 'The line similar to the one of instruction' (*man-ngag-lta-bu'i phreng-ba*). Here, the word 'instruction' (*man-ngag*) is naturally understood as the Tradition of Instructions (*man-ngag-gi brgyud-pa*) founded by Vimalamitra. The Padmasambhava tradition is only similar to Vimalamitra's; i.e. it was added later to make Padmasambhava also master of the tradition of the Instructions (*man-ngag-gi brgyud-pa*).

2.4.2. THE SECTION OF MEDITATIVE REALIZATION (*sgrub-sde*)

The Section of the Tantra Cycles (*rgyud-sde*) comprises the dogmatic, canonic teaching texts; the Section of Meditative Realization (*sgrub-sde*) contains, first of all, the practical instructions for meditation and spiritual exercitium.[116a] These instructions are contained in the text group of the Eight Pronouncements (*bka'-brgyad*). They constitute the eight main doctrines of Padmasambhava. The names of the separate sections follow : *gŚin-rje-snying-thig*, *Padma-snying-thig*, *Yang-dag-thugs-kyi-snying-thig*, *bDud-rtsi-yon-tan-snying-thig*, *Phrin-las-phur-pa-snying-thig*, *rBod-gtong-ma-mo'i-snying-thig*, *Rig-'dsin-bla-ma'i-snying-thig*, and *Jig-rten-dregs-pa'i-snying-thig*. Occasionally two more Pronouncements (*bka'*) may be added : *Dregs-sngags-dmod-pa'i-snying-thig* and *sPyi-dril-snying-po'i-snying-thig*. The names of these secret doctrines transmitted by literature do not lend themselves to a meaningful and concise translation.

For the content of these texts, I refer to the publications listed in the footnotes.[117] These Eight Pronouncements contain the most important teachings of the *rDsogs-chen* system as to its practical application. In many particular instances these teachings correspond with those of the Chinese Buddhist schools which were mentioned earlier, i.e. *Ch'an*, *Seng-chao*, and *Hua-yen*. This is not surprising, many of the early hierarchs of the Tibetan Old School (*rNying-ma-pa*) received their education in China and brought texts from there to Tibet, where they were translated into Tibetan.[118] At the time of the expulsion of Chinese Buddhists, many of these texts were hidden and later unearthed as the Concealed Books (*gter-ma*). Ratna-gling-pa's hagiography makes this connection evident.

The Tibetan tradition agrees that the doctrine of the Eight Pronouncements (*bka'-brgyad*) was brought by Padmasambhava to Tibet. It indeed seems that these doctrines originated from him, that is, from the circle of the eight great Ācārya (*sLob-dpon chen-po brgyad*), who are also called the eight Wisdom-Holder (*Rig-'dsin brgyad*). These eight Ācāryas lived, taught and meditated in the cremation ground Śītavana, which is said to have been in the vicinity of Bodh Gaya. These doctrines are legitimized by the fact that Padmasambhava is *Kun-tu-bzang-po's* incarnation, and thus perceived in himself the doctrine in the direct path of inspiration. The above statement does not, however, explain the manner in which the *rDsogs-chen* teachings were incorporated into the Eight Pronouncements (*bka'-brgyad*), because at the time of the first dissemination of Buddhism the *rDsogs-chen* tradition was still strictly separated from the teachings of Padmasambhava. Upto this time the *rDsogs-chen* tradition was only upheld by Vimalamitra and Vairocana who both belong to the lineage of 'Jam-dpal-bśes-gnyen and Śrīsiṃha. As we shall see in the chapters 2.5. and 2.6. there does not exist any linkage between these two distinct currents of mystic Buddhism. There is not a single passage within the historical reports which could claim a reliable relationship of Padmasambhava with the *rDsogs-chen* tradition. It was only in the second phase of dissemination of Buddhism that the two currents of tradition merged.

The following question arises: How could Padmasambhava formulate thoughts which are typical for the *rDsogs-chen* system and its related Chinese schools ? Or, how could it have happened that these thoughts were attributed to Padmasambhava ?

Unfortunately, since the life of Padmasambhava is still awaiting a critical study, and since the evaluation of the sources up to now available, has yielded only few passages confirming the historical relationship between the circle of Padmasambhava and the main tradition of the *rDsogs-chen* or the related Chinese schools, it is with considerable reservation that I prefer the second question, to which a cautious answer fitting the historical situation, can be given.

2.4.3. THE DISSEMINATION OF THE TEACHINGS OF THE EIGHT PRONOUNCEMENTS (*bka'-brgyad*) IN TIBET[119]

The first cycle, called *gSin-rje-gśed-gyi snying-thig*, was taught and spread by sLob-dpon Śāntigarbha; *bDud-rtsi-yon-tan-snying-thig*, in contrast, was disseminated by sLob-dpon Vimalamitra and gNyags Jñānakumāra. After the urgent entreaties of King Khri-srong-lde-btsan, Padmasambhava taught these Eight Pronouncements (*bka'-brgyad*) to the king and eight of his vassals in bSam-yas mChims-phu, which then was a flourishing hermitage.[120] The master gave these nine Tibetans the religious empowerments (*dbang-bskur*) necessary for the exoteric, esoteric, and secret *Maṇḍala* (*phyi-*, *nang-*, *gsang-ba'i dkyil-'khor*) of these great meditation exercises (*sgrub-sde*). In addition, he gave them instructions in the meditative realization (*sgrub-thabs*) of the divine powers (*lha*)[121] which they had visualized in the empowerment ceremony, so that they themselves could perform the exercises and finally realize the divine power in meditation.

The King Khri-sron-lde-btsan propitiated *Che-mchog*, the main divine power of the Eight Pronouncements (*bka'-brgyad*). Through a special meditation (*ting-nge-'dsin*) the king gained a special knowledge of this divine power. This knowledge is the basis of the treatises about *b Ka'-yang-dag-pa'i-tshad-ma*. Nam-mkha'-snying-po practised the cycle *Yang-dag-thugs-kyi-snying-thig*, and as a sign of successful meditation he rode on a beam of the sun. Sangs-rgyas-ye-śes practised the *gŚin-rje-snying-thig*, the divine power (*lha*) of which is *Mañjuśrī*; as a sign of successful meditation, he thrust a ceremonial dagger (*phur-bu*) in a rock. rGyal-ba-mchog-dbyangs practised the *Padma-snying-thig*, and on his head appeared the head of a horse, and neighing was heard. mKhar-chen-bza' mTsho-rgyal, who was one of the wives of the King Khri-srong-lde-btsan,[122] practised the *Phrin-las-phur-pa-snying-thig* and was able to resuscitate the dead. dPal-gyi-ye-śes meditated on the *rBod-gtong-ma mo'i-snying-thig*, and the *Ma-mo*[123] served him as maids. dPan-gyi-seng-ge meditated on the '*Jig-rten-dregs-pa'i-snying-thig*, and the eight frightful gods (*sde-brgyad*)[124] became his servants. Vairocana practised the *Dregs-sngags-dmod-pa'i-snying-thig*, and he gained the eye of wisdom and power over magic capacities (*rdsu-'phrul*). gNyags Jñānakumāra made water flow from a dry rock. These eight religious persons from the entourage of the king are included in the 'twenty-five religious persons, i.e. the king and his twenty-four vassals' (*rje-'bangs nyer-lnga*); in the following description they are counted as transmitters of these doctrines.

We shall list the names of the 'twenty-five religious persons, the king and his entourage' as they are given in the DC which shows a few discrepancies as regards the one given in the *bTsun-mo-bka'-thang*:[125] rGyal-mo gYu-sgra-snying-po, sNa-nam rDo-rje-bdud-' joms, Ācārya Ye-śes-dbyangs, Sog-po Lha-dpal, sNa-nam Żang Ye-śes-sde, mKhar-chen dPal-gyi-dbang-phyug, lDan-ma-rtse-mang, sKa-ba dPal-brtsegs, Śud-bu dPal-gyi-seng-ge, 'Bre rGyal-ba'i-blo-gros, 'Brog-ban Khye'u-chung Lo-tsā-ba, O-bran dPal-gyi-dbang-phyug, rMa Rin-chen-mchog, Lha-lung dPal-gyirdo-rje, Lang-gro dKar-mchog-'byung-gans, La-gsum rGyal-ba-byang-chub. In addition female mystics (*Grub-thob*) were listed : Za-hor Mandarāva, mKhar-chen mTsho-rgyal-ma; these two, as incarnation, are identical with *rDo-rje-phag-mo* (*Vajravārāhī*). Tshe-nam-bza' Sangs-rgyas-mtsho, Śel-dkar rDo-rje-mtsho, Tshom-bu-bza' Padma-mtsho, Mal-gon-bza' Rin-chen-mtsho, Ru-bza' Don-grub-ma, Śud-bu-bza' Śes-rab-ma, Yar-rag-bza' Chos-kyi-sgron-ma, O-lce-bza' sKar-rgyal-ma, 'Dsem-bza' Lha-mo, 'Bar-bza' Lha-dbangs-ma, Cog-ro-bza' Byang-chub-sman, 'Brom-bza' sPam-ti-chen-mo, Ron-sman-bza' Tshul-khrims-sgron, Kha-bza' dPal-btsun-ma, and Phrum-bza' Śel-sman. All these attained Buddhahood.

Also part of this tradition of the Section of Meditative Realization (*sgrub-sde*) are the twenty-five Great Mystics (*Grub-thob*, *Mahāsiddha*) of the hermitage mChims-phu; the twenty-five Persons Gifted with Knowledge (*rTogs-ldan*) of Yang-rdsong; the one hundred and eight Yogis, who reached the Body of Light (*'od-lus*)—in other words, they realized the innermost value of being—which shows itself as light and is in its being wisdom, and practised the exercises at Yar-pa and at Chu-bo-ri; the thirty Tantrics (*sNgags-pa*) of Śel-brag; the twenty-five *mKha'-'gro*, which reached the lightlike being; and the uncounted ones which had reached the spiritual potency (*siddhi*).

This tradition of the Section of the Meditative Realization (*sgrub-sde*) is certainly the only one which Padmasambhava had brought to Tibet. A careful analysis of the Eight Pronouncements (*bka'-brgyad*) should show to what degree *rDsogs-chen* thoughts were originally part of this system; today it is completely saturated with them. On the basis of the tradition just discussed, Padmasambhava's position within the Old School was later elaborated more and more, and traditions that had no connections with him were linked to his personality.

CHART OF THE SECTION OF THE MEDITATIVE REALIZATION (*sgrub-sde*) (chapter 2.4.3. —according to DC)

Śāntigarbha Vimalamitra Padmasambhava gNyags
↓ ↓ ↓ ↓ Jñānakumāra

↓
Khri-srong-lde-btsan and his eight vassals
↓
'The twenty-five religious persons'
(*rje-'bangs-nyer-lnga*)

It is not quite clear who belonged to the *Siddha* group of the Eight Wisdom-Holders (*Rig-'dsin brgyad*), or who were the real disciples of Padmasambhava; not even their names have been handed down. The only exception are the well-known groups of the *rJe-'bangs-dgu* and *rJe-'bangs-nyer-lnga*, i.e. the group of the king and his eight and twenty-four followers.

Concerning the foundation of the Section of the Meditative Realization (*sgrub-sde*), or the Concealed Books (*gter-ma*),[126] the PK[127] has some valuable information: The tradition of this section goes back to Rig-'dsin rDo-rje-chos, who entrusted the texts to the Spiritual Beings (*mkha'-'gro-ma*) and to the Eight Frightful Ones (*sDe-brgyad*), who in turn hid them in the Stūpa in the cremation ground Śītavana. The PK continues :[128] "Later when the Eight Great *Ācāryas* (*sLob-dpon brgyad*) were absorbed in meditation, they observed in this large cremation ground wild storms, meteorites, and hail, firy signs, fire and lightning, and many other wondrous events. The Eight Wisdom-Holders (*Rig-'dsin brgyad*) conferred together and decided to find out whether these signs would harbour fortune for the world, such as a new doctrine or treasures, or whether they forbode misfortune, such as evil spells. On behalf of the Spiritual Beings (*mKha'-'gro-ma*) and the Eight Frightful Ones (*sDe-brgyad*), the *Ācārya* made an appropriate worship (*pūjā*). The *Ācārya* preached to them the true teachings and deepened their thoughts. In the seventh night the Protectors of the Concealed Books (*gter-ma*) surrendered, and from the chest which they guarded they gave a golden box to Vimalamitra, a silver box to Hūṃkara,[129] and an iron box to 'Jam-dpal-bśes-gnyen,[130] a copper box to kLu-grub-snying-po, a turquoise box to Padmasambhava, a box crafted out of the skin of rhinoceros to Dhanasaṃskṛta, an agate box to Rong-bu Guhya-devacandra, and an onyx box to Śāntigarbha.[130a] The Protectors put one box, which was crafted out of eight different precious stones in the middle, left it unopened, and hid it again. It is known that Padmasambhava lifted it later."

If one disregards the last sentence (about which even Padma-dkar-po has some reservation), Padmasambhava is only one of the Eight *Ācāryas* and he receives only one-eighth of all texts the Protectors of the Concealed Books (*gter-ma*) handed out.

One must be very cautious as to the persons of the Eight *Ācāryas* if one wants to regard them as an historical factor. The *Siddhas*, just as the Taoist mystics,[131] certainly had unusual long lifespans at their disposal; they retreated into isolation, even invisibility, for long periods of time in order to participate later in the dissemination of the *Dharma*. This circumstance is very difficult to follow historically. According to the 'transmission of the doctrine which leads to the final goal of the *rDsogs-chen* (compare chapter 2.3.), neither 'Jam-dpal-bśes-gnyen, Vimalamitra, nor Padmasambhava were contemporaries. The gathering of the Eight *Ācāryas* on the cremation ground Śītavana and the exorcism of the Protectors of the Concealed Books appears to us as a sign that the Section of Meditative Realization (*sgrub-sde*) comprises the entire meditation practices of the *Siddhas*, which is the method of maturity and liberation characteristic to all of them, and which has been revealed to all of them in ecstasy. Thus, we do not want to consider the gathering of the Eight *Ācāryas* in Śītavana an historical fact, but rather a reality of religious-mystic experience which is to be taken seriously.

As I said before, I doubt that the Eight Pronouncements (*bka'-brgyad*) had been saturated with *rDsogs-chen* thoughts from the beginning. When, after the debate of bSam-yas, the Chinese schools of Buddhism had lost some of their esteem, and when Hva-śang Mahāyāna was expelled from Tibet, the *rDsogs-chen* tradition had also become of somewhat shady repute, since it had too much in common with the Chinese schools as to its doctrine, origin of texts and masters.

It is possible that at that time the followers of the *rDsog-chen* system were not yet distinguished from the related Chinese schools. When Chinese Buddhists were expelled and theirTibetan disciples were regarded with disdain, not only their texts, which included most of the *rDsogs-chen* works, but also the scriptures of the Eight Pronouncements (*bka'-brgyad*) were often hidden in the same locality. Again on the basis of the line of transmission of this tradition, it seems that *rDsogs-chen* philosophy had been incorporated into the Eight Pronouncements (*bka'-brgyad*) at the earliest at the time of Padmasambhava. The titles of the separate Pronouncements (*bka'*) differ from their contents.[132]

At this point a further study of the history of the texts and the teachings of the Eight Pronouncements would be desirable. In the second missionary period (*phyi-dar*), at the time of Atīśa's coming to Tibet (1042 A.D.) when some of the books attributed to the Chinese schools and the *rDsogs-chen* system were unearthed as *gter-ma* or Concealed Books it was repugnant to the ruling groups of that time to attribute these wondrous teachings to the Chinese (who in the meantime had acquired a bad reputation) and their missionary activities in Tibet. Thus the Eight Pronouncements (*bka'-brgyad*) whose author was undisputedly Padmasambhava, and which were found together with the *rDsogs-chen* books, offered a solution. Since at that time the historical connection of the *rDsogs-chen* philosophy with Chinese Buddhism had already been erased from the consciousness of the majority of the religious people, the rediscovered *rDsogs-chen* books were credited to the author of the Eight Pronouncements (*bka'-bragyad*) scriptures, that is, to Padmasambhava. This task was eased by the fact that Padmasambhava was regarded as an emanation of the primary wisdom of all Buddhas, i.e. of *Kun-tu-bzang-po*. Because these texts had been declared to have been written by him, they could now be spread without hindrance. In addition to the transcendental legitimation, an historical legitimation was accomplished by declaring all famous *rDsogs-chen* masters as Padmasambhava's disciples; this is proven by the DC's 'the transmission of Padmasambhava of the Tantra Cycles' (*rgyud-sde*).[133] The *rDsogs-chen* philosophy—as we encounter it in the famous *kLong-chen sNying-thig*—is a mixture of the old *rDsogs-chen* tradition, which was influenced by Chinese schools, and the Eight Pronouncements (*bka'-brgyad*). The common element of these two kinds of literature is that both had been hidden at the time of Khri-srong-lde-btsan (755-797) and gLang-dar-ma (836-842); further, both were later transmitted as Concealed Treasures (*gter-ma*). Inasmuch as the transmission of the *rDsogs-chen* books is always linked to the *gTer-ston*, the Discoverer of Concealed Treasures, the hagiographies of the *gTer-ston* logically follow in part II of this treatise.

2.5. THE TRANSMISSION OF THE ANUYOGA OF ACCOMPLISHED MEDITATION (*rdsogs-pa anu-yoga*)

This transmission has its origin in the Indian movement dominated by the *Siddhas*. Its history is extremely confused; as is evident from a comparison of the sources. There is hardly one statement that is not contradicted by another one. The identification of persons is complicated by the fact that a *Siddha* has several names, and that most *Siddhas* had a range of activities which greatly exceeded the span of a normal human life. The *Siddha's* outward activity is interrupted by periods of isolation in meditation; which may last upto several centuries. It is not always possible to determine whether several persons had the same name or whether the conception of time was distorted.

A solid basis for the discussion of the entire *Siddha* tradition is unfortunately still missing. In the description of the tradition of the *Anuyoga* of Accomplished Meditation we shall follow the DC and correct its data with the help of relevant passages in the KD.

The Lord of Mysteries (*gSang-ba'i-bdag-po*)[134] is a title of *Vajrapāṇi* who gave King Dsa, also called Lung-bstan-rdo--rje, all initiations, so as to enable the king to understand the entire meaning of the *Anuyoga* of Accomplished Meditation (*rdsogs-pa anu-yoga*). Because of pedagogical reasons, however, the king subjected himself to a public instruction by the Wisdom-Holder (*Rig-'dsin*) dGe-bsnyen Li-tsa-bi Dri--med-grags. This *Rig-'dsin* is explicitly described as a human Wisdom-Holder; he gave the king a religious empowerment for the study of the secret doctrine (*dbang-bskur*), and he also gave him an oral explanation of it. Thereupon the king composed many commentaries on the Sūtras as well as other doctrinal explanations (*bstan-bcos*). Then King Dsa handed over these teachings to U-pa-ra-dsa, who had been his friend when he studied with Li-tsa-bi. Dsa gave U-pa-ra-dsa an empowerment for a '*Maṇḍala* of worldly apparitions' (*sprul-pa'i dkyil-'khor*) and the instructions belonging to it (*gdams-ngag*). The king also transmitted this doctrine to his three sons: Śatraputri, Nāgaputri, and Guhyaputri. However, all the Tantras he gave to U-pa-ra-dsa. It is said (according to the DC) that his first son, Śatraputri, was Indrabhūti the Younger.[135] After he had reached the spiritual potency (*siddhi*), he was supposedly also called sLob-dpon Lva-ba-pa.[136] This statement contradicts most known traditions.

In the following passages the DC discusses a Lva-ba-pa who may be identical with Śatraputri. The KD[137] writes about him : "This *Ācārya* was the son of a king." This statement is, however, applicable to many Ācāryas besides Śatraputri. Lva-ba-pa then composed a commentary to the *sahaja-siddhi*[138] *Lhan-cig-skyes-grub-kyi-'grel-ba*[139] and '*Khor-lo-bde-mchog-sdom-pa*.[140] At this point it is said very clearly that Lva-ba-pa used to sleep in front of the gates to a palace which belonged to Indrabhūti the Middle One, who later was converted to Buddhism by the *Siddha*. These statements correspond to the reports of the DC:

Indrabhūti and Lva-ba-pa manifested the signs of successful meditation (*sgrub-rtags*). At the time when Rol-pa'i-rdorje[141] acquired the general spiritual Potency (*siddhi*), Lva-ba-pa and Murundaka competed in magic. The DC says that many stories are transmitted about this occurrence, although neither the KD nor the DNg report a single one. In Uḍḍiyāna Indrabhūti and Lva-ba-pa taught together this instruction, and thus all people who lived there became Wisdom-Holders (*Rig-pa-'dsin-pa*). Indrabhūti (the DC speaks now of the Younger but we assume that he is the same person as the above mentioned Indrabhūti, i.e. the Middle One) gave Seng-ha-pu-tri and Ku-ku-ra-dsa the empowerment (*dbang-bskur*) at the shore of the sea. According to the KD[142] Ku-ku-ra-dsa is identical with Indrabhūti the Middle One; however, according to the DNg[143] Ku-ku-ra-dsa is identical with U-pa-ra-dsa. If we assume that the DC speaks throughout of Indrabhūti the Middle One, and that Ku-ku-ra-dsa is identical with Indrabhūti the Middle One, then Ku-ku-ra-dsa the Younger would be the son of Indrabhūti the Middle One. Later Indrabhūti gave an empowerment (*dbang-bskur*) to the sLob--dpon chen-po Ro-langs-bde-ba and explained the Tantra to him. At this point the DC explains that Ro-langs-bde-ba's incarnation became famous as dGa'-rab-rdo-rje; in contrast, the 'tradition which leads to the final goal of the *rDsogs-chen*' states that dGa' rab-rdo-rje himself had the surname Ro-langs-bde-ba. After he (Ro-langs-bde-ba) had attained the highest spiritual potency (*siddhi*) he edited the work *rNal-'byor-rig-pa'i-nyi-ma*,[144] which has as its content the profound path of the Buddha word (Sūtras) (*mdo'i-zab-lam*). At the banks of the river Sindhu Ro-langs-bde-ba gave his disciple Prabhahasti an empowerment (*dbang-bskur*). After Prabhahasti had taken the monastic vows he had the name Śākya-'od; his students were Śākya-'od the Younger, Śākya-bśes-gnyen, and Śākya-seng-ge. Śākya-bśes-gnyen was well versed in the Tantrayāna and composed a commentary on the *mDo-'dus-pa*, which was called *Ko-sa-la'i-rgyan*,[145] because it was written in the land of Kosala.[146]

Śākya-bśes-gnyen's disciple was Dhanarakṣita, who received instructions in the Sūtras. Dhanarakṣita taught Hūṃkara, alias Hūṃ-mdsad, in the Diamond-Grotto of Padmasambhava (*O-rgyan-gyi-rdo-rje-phug*). Thereupon he wrote the one hundred and seven commentaries to the *Mūlatantra* (*rtsa-rgyud*); further, he wrote the *rNal-'byor-sa'i-sgron-ma* and other instructional works. In the Grotto of the *Asuras* (*A-su-ra'i brag-phug*), situated on the border between India and Persia (Ta-sig), Hūṃkara listened to the teacher Ga-ga-si-dhi. Then Hūṃkara became a Wisdom-Holder (*Rig-'dsin*), who sustained himself by practising the technique called 'taking the essential juices' (*bcud-len*)[147] and then became invisible.

Hūṃkara had given bDe-ba-gsal-mdsad an empowerment (*dbang-bskur*). The latter wrote, among other works, the *mDo'i-yig-sna-bco-brgyad-dang-rnal-'byor-gyi-rim-pa-theg-chen-sgron-ma*. bDe-ba-gsal-mdsad had four principal disciples (*Thugs--sras*) to whom he transmitted the doctrine: Dharmabodhi from Magadha, who was called the Master of the Sūtras (*mDo'i-mkhan-po*) and who wrote the works *mDo'i-dob-bsdu-ba*, *Śes-rab-sgron-ma*, and *bKol-mdo*; Dharmarājapāla, the abbot (*mKhan-po*) of Nalanda, to whom bDe-ba-gsal-mdsad explained the Tantras; Vasudhara, the king of Nepal; and gTsug-lag-dpal-dge. Later Vasudhara also listened to Dharmarakṣita. To these four disciples bDe-ba-gsal-mdsad gave the entire tradition as it was transmitted in the Pronouncements of the Empowerment, of the Explanation and of the Instruction (*dbang-bka'*, *bśad-bka'*, *man-ngag-bka'*). This is the all-compassing chain of tradition.

Later on Vasudhara transmitted the empowerment (*dbang-bskur*) and the Tantra explanations to sLob-dpon Che-btsan-skyes from Bru-śa.[148] sLob-dpon Che-btsan-skyes now invited Dhanarakṣita to Bru-śa to make translations. He tried to translate the *mDo-dgongs-'dus*[149] but could not accomplish the task. He returned to Nepal and told Vasudhara and Dharmabodhi about his experience. Later Dharmabodhi, Dhanarakṣita and the *Ācārya* from Bru-śa, Che-btsan-skyes translated this Sūtra into the language of the land.

Here the tradition of the *Anuyoga* of Accomplished Meditation ends in India; however, it continued in Tibet.[150] Dharmabodhi, the Master of the Sūtras (*mDo-mkhan*), Vasudhara and Che-btsan-skyes, the *Ācārya* from Bru-śa, taught gNubs Sangs-rgyas-ye-śes the doctrine of the *Anuyoga* of Accomplished Meditation (*rdsogs-pa anu-yoga*). He in turn spread this doctrine in Tibet. gNubs Sangs-rgyas-ye-śes wrote, above all, an instruction concerning the *rDsogs-chen* system (*rdsogs-chen gyi man-ngag*), which is called *bSam-gtan-mig-sgron.*[151] The principal disciples of Sangs-rgyas-ye-śes were sPa-gor bLo-chen-'phags-pa, Sru'i-ston-pa Legs-pa'i-sgron-me, Dan Yon-tan-mchog, So Ye-śes-dbang-phyug, and Khu-lung-pa Yon-tan-rgya-mtsho. The last one was the most brilliant of all the students, who spread this tradition. The DNg[152] states that this chain of transmission continued down to Mar-pa (1012-1096), the famous master of Mi-la-ras-pa,[153] to Lha-rje Śangs-pa and sGro-sbug-pa. Then this chain of transmission merged with the *sGyu-'phrul* cycle, i.e. the tradition of the Section of the Tantras of the *Mahāyoga* of Development (*bskyed-pa mahā-yoga rgyud-sde*).

CHART OF THE TRANSMISSION OF THE ANUYOGA OF ACCOMPLISHED MEDITATION (*rdsogs-pa anu-yoga*) (chapter 2.5.—according to DC)

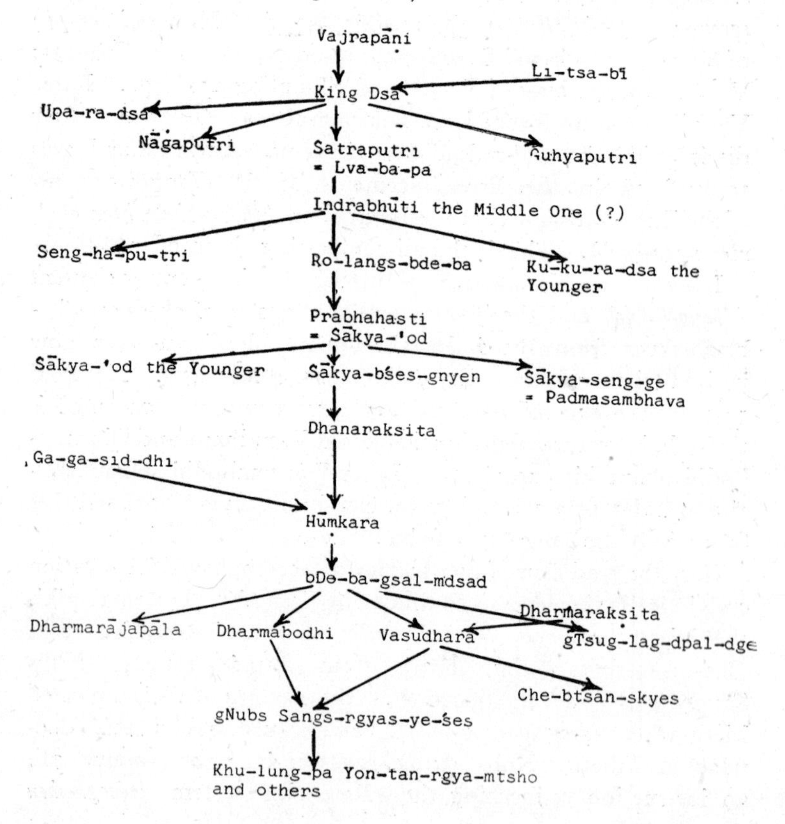

Since the '*Dus-pa-mdo* is the principal text of this line of transmission, 'Gos Lo-tsā-ba names the whole tradition after it. In the DNg, at page 158, it is said: "Now about the text known as the '*Dus-pa-mdo*: ...', then the sequence of transmission given here follows, and at page 160 the paragraph ends with the following words "The chapter of the school of *mDo*." If one compares the previous chart of masters and disciples, which has the name Transmission of the *Anuyoga* of Accomplished Meditation (*rdsogs-pa-anu-yoga*) and was given according to the DC, with the sequence given in the DNg, it becomes evident that the Transmission of the *Anuyoga* of Accomplished Meditation is precisely the "school of *mDo*" in 'Gos Lo-tsā-ba's work translated by ROERICH.

CHART OF THE TRANSMISSION OF THE ANUYOGA OF ACCOMPLISHED MEDITATION (chapter 2.5.— according to DNg)

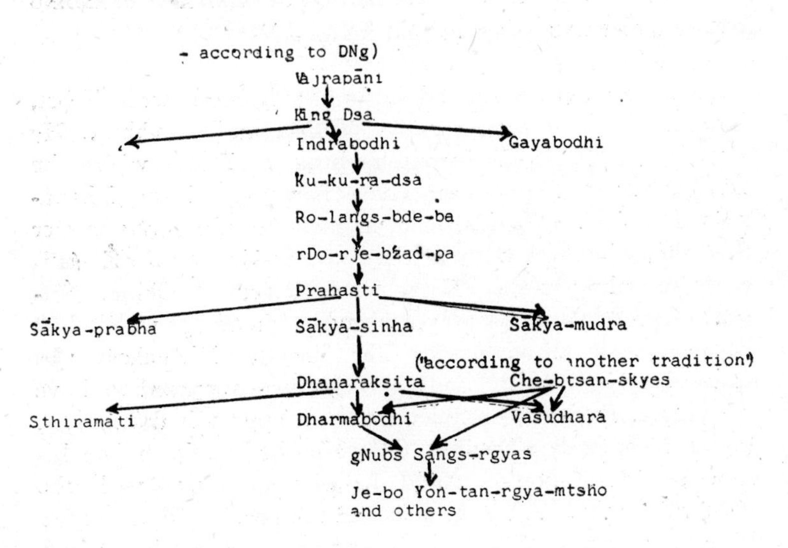

2.6. THE TRANSMISSION OF THE ATIYOGA OF THE GREAT PERFECTION (*rdsogs-pa-chen-po-ati-yoga*)

The third and most sublime stage of the *rDsogs chen* system is again arranged in three sections: the Section of Mind (*sems-*

sde), the Section of the Unending Dynamic of Being (*klong-sde*), and the Section of Instructions (*man-ngag-gi sde*).

For the description of the third stage of the *rDsogs-chen* system, we have used the DC and the DNg as our main sources. As to this chapter, the two sources differ from each other much more than as regards the previous one; thus it seemed advantageous to me to list one source after the other. The differences of the two sources are already manifested in the exterior arrangement: The DC adheres to the known division of three, but combines the Section of Mind (*sems-sde*) with the Section of Unending Dynamic of Being (*klong-sde*). In contrast, the DNg follows only very loosely the division of three and names the separate chains of transmission after their principal texts; in addition, the DNg merges the Section of Mind with the Section of Instructions (*man-ngag-gi sde*).

2.6.1. THE TRANSMISSION OF THE SECTION OF MIND AND UNENDING DYNAMIC OF BEING (*sems-sde* and *klong-sde*)[154]

Both traditions originated in India; their founder in Tibet, however, is Vairocana, a native of sNye-mo-bye-mkhar. He was sent by King Khri-srong-lde-btsan to India, where he finally arrived despite tremendous hardships. Near Dhanakośa, in a forest of sandalwood, he met the *rDsogs-chen* master Śrīsiṃha, who was born in the town So-khyam (or Źo-śa'i-gling according to the PK) which belonged to China. Śrīsiṃha stayed in a nine-storeyed pagoda (*ke'u-tshang*) which had been erected miraculously. The locality Dhanakośa was situated in Uḍḍiyāna,[155] and a great lake was supposed to have been there. Before Vairocana was able to approach the master, he was stopped by a Yoginī. Only after he had shown her his superior psychic powers would she allow a contact with the master Śrīsiṃha. After the gifts had been presented, and after Vairocana had begged to be instructed in a method which required less efforts (*rtsol-med-kyi theg-pa*) than the complicated demands of the Sūtra system, Śrīsiṃha declared he would have to consider this matter for the time being. But the next morning he promised Vairocana to explain the secret, sealed, profound main doctrine. However, since the king in whose domain Dhanakośa was situated had forbidden the spread of these doctrines at the risk of one's life, Śrīsiṃha said that it would be better if Vairocana would study during day time the normal, philosophical doctrines, such as causality (*rgyu-bras*) with other Paṇḍits. During the nights Śrīsiṃha would, however, open the Section of Instructions (*man-ngag-gi sde*) to him. Thus spoke Śrīsiṃha, and he ordered Vairocana to observe strict secrecy. During the night the master wrote the eighteen Instructions of the Section of mind (*man-ngag-sems-sde*) with goat milk on a white cloth. Śrīsiṃha advised : "If this cloth is held over smoke the letters (up to now invisible) will become quite clear. Apart from those here empowered nobody may know about this doctrine because the Protectors of the Doctrine (*bsTan-srung*) watch over its secrecy!"

This episode shows that the secrecy of the Tantra doctrine was taken literally, and that their public spread had been forbidden by the king, the head of the state. In this condition there are probably parallels to the movement of the medieval Anabaptists and other so-called heretics. The reasons for the persecution by the state surely must not be sought in an obligation to maintain a state religion—such a thought is largely irrelevant as to India—but in the fact that the doctrines might upset the social structures of the state. In the Tantrayāna the person of low social rank or the outsider—the 'drop-out'—is the carrier of the highest wisdom. The social hierarchy is intentionally upside down. The rules according to which the good citizen is to model his life are completely disregarded. And thus the whole mechanism of the behavior of the masses toward an 'out-group' comes into play.[156] The cynicism with which the life of the bourgeoisie was mocked in the circles of the Tantrics is shown through the name of Jñānasūtra's father: he was a *Caṇḍāla*, an executioner, and had the name Źi-ba'i-lag-pa, 'the peaceful hand'. Since '*źi-ba*—"peace, quiet"—means also the composure in the state of *Nirvāṇa*, a vast scale of meanings can be read into interpretation. Superficially considered this attitude of the Tantrics seems to be indeed cynical. But if one reflects upon this attitude on the basis of the Tantric theories the cynicism fades out and the knowledge becomes apparently that this hangman is only a momentary manifestation of the all-compassing transitoriness in which the constancy of *Nirvāṇa* is evident. Since the true content and meaning of these doctrines were inaccessible to the masses, their external signs were considered to be abominable. Contemporary times offer parallels to this, if one considers the hippies and the life style they propagate and the public's reaction to it. However, I do not want to presume that the hippies have the perception and enlightenment of the Tantrics, although they may have borrowed some features from the Tantric world. This reference to the social background and to the contemporary time is meant only to draw attention to the fact that the persecution of the Tantrayāna (which consequently advocated secrecy) is not based on a possible oddity of the doctrine, but on the typical attitude of the bourgeois world towards a minority which has its own special tradition of wisdom and an unconventional life style. These observations apply to India as well as China; they were both countries with a rigidly stratified social system into which the Tantrayāna penetrated like a foreign body. However, if Tibet the follower of the Tantrayāna was not a 'drop-out' on society (as in India and China) but the friend and counsellor of the powerful King Khri-srong-lde-btsan, as is exemplified by the highly respected teacher Padmasambhava, Tantrics became respected members of society because it was only at the time when Buddhist influence began spreading that Tibet became a formalized social and political entity. In this formation process the Tantrics had a decisive influence, and the sons of powerful noble families became students of the foreign Tantrics. The results were unavoidable; the secrecy became more and more relaxed. Soon Tantric figures stood in every temple to be viewed by everybody and anybody, and the religious empowerments (*dbang-bskur*) which once had been reserved for the 'chosen' became a general observance.

Our source DC states that Vairocana met his master Śrīsiṃha near Dhanakośa, which was probably situated in Uḍḍiyāṇa. According to the principal transmission of the *rDsogs-chen*, the 'transmission of the doctrine which leads to the final goal of the *rDsogs-chen*' (*rdsogs-chen mthar-thug-gi brgyud-pa*)—chapter 2.3, Śrīsiṃha went only once to India. According to the PK, he stayed at the cremation ground Śītavana; according to the DC, he resided at the cremation ground So-sa-gling, the locality of which is unknown. It must remain undecided whether the name of the Indian locality was transferred to a

Chinese one, or whether Śrīsiṃha stayed at more than one place in India for a longer period of time. The first possibility is supported by a number of parallel cases; we refer only to Ri-bo-rtse-lnga (Wu-tai-shan), which exists both in Tibet and China; to Gośṛnga, a mountain in both Nepal and Khotan;[157] and to the mountain Potala in southern India and Tibet. But even the second possibility is not to be rejected a priori, because according to the PK Śrīsiṃha taught Vimalamitra in Śītavana. Unfortunately, it is impossible historically to trace the person of Śrīsiṃha in an exact manner. At first the DNg[158] mentions a "Siṃha" (so translated by Roerich, who erroneously omitted the prefix 'śrī') who lived as Arhat, and was born in Kashmir and taught King Kaniṣka; the DNg states that these data originate from an Indian document. The same work has two more passages[159] that report a "Siṃha", who had been a student of 'Jam-dpal-bśes-gnyen and who taught the Section of Mind (*sems-sde*) to the scholar Ye-śes-mdo (i.e. Jñānasūtra). The two latter references obviously refer to our Śrīsiṃha; unfortunately they do not furnish any further information. The earlier reference can hardly be applied to the person in question.

But let us return to the DC's report about Vairocana and Śrīsiṃha. At the same time when Śrīsiṃha taught Vairocana, gNubs Nam-mkha '-snying-po[160] was supposed to have studied with Hūṃkara in India.[161] Vairocana was not satisfied with the eighteen Instructions concerning the Section of Mind (*man-ngag sems-sde*)[162] which Śrīsiṃha had given him as a secret document. Thereupon Śrīsiṃha revealed to him all empowerments (*dbang-bskur*) and all the instructions (*man-ngag*) of the sixty Tantra Sections (*rgyud-sde*), and the Section of Unending Dynamic of Being (*klong-sde*) in the three traditional ways: 'black', 'white', and 'multicoloured' (*dkar*, *nag*, *khra*). All these doctrines show Buddhahood as an innate property.[163] Vairocana reached perfection in all these doctrines. However, since he was not yet satisfied, Śrīsiṃha advised him as follows: "The objectified sphere of phenomena (*chos-dbyings*) is without depletion. If one has understood the being-this-or-that (*de-bźin-nyid*) of one phenomenon (*chos*) then nothing is left incomprehensible, everything is perceived. This I promise you!" Śrīsiṃha showed him the three ways in which the instruction is to be sought, the four ways in which he may transmit it, and the four ways in which he may not transmit it.

On the cremation ground 'Place of Smoke' (*du-ba'i-gnas*) Vairocana also met the *Ācārya* dGa'-rab-rdo-rje, the first revealer of the *rDsogs-chen* teachings. From him Vairocana received the sixty-four by one hundred thousand important traditions of the *rDsogs-chen.* Simultaneously he (Vairocana) perceived these teachings and attained the liberation of *Nirvāṇa.* Thus he had apparently reached the highest spiritual potency (*siddhi*). Then Vairocana practised meditative speed running (*rkang-mgyogs*) and thus he reached Tibet.

The episode reported above seems somewhat odd, especially since according to the main tradition of the 'doctrine which leads to the final goal of the *rDsogs-chen*, dGa'-rab-rdo-rje had died after he had taught his student 'Jam-dpal-bśes-gnyen. The above mentioned sixty-four by one hundred thousand *rDsogs-chen* verses are the beginning of the entire *rDsogs-chen* literature.[164] dGa'-rab-rdo-rje, who is an emanation of *rDo-rje-sems-dpa'*, received these verses because of his intuition (*rtogs-pa*).[165] We are of the opinion that Vairocana was later connected with the foundation of the entire *rDsogs-chen* system to emphasize the validity of his teachings. Such an emphasis would not have been necessary, since Vairocana is adequately legitimized through his teacher Śrīsiṃha.

While spreading the *rDsogs-chen* philosophy in Tibet, Vairocana adhered strictly to the instruction given him by his teacher. During the day he taught the King Khri-srong-lde-btsan the general philosophy, consisting above all of the doctrine of causality (*rgyu-'bras*); at night he taught exclusively *rDsogs-pa-chen-po.* He also translated the *Sems-sde-snga-gyur.*

His activities found an early end, however, it had become known in India that the secret doctrines had reached Tibet and that Vairocana was their transmitter. So the Indians plotted against him by spreading rumours.[166] Thereupon the queen Tshe-spong-bza', one of the wives of Khri-srong-lde-btsan,[167] and some of his ministers instigated the banishment of the master to Tsha-ba-rong in the country rGyal-mo-rong, which was at the extreme eastern border of Tibet. This action also expressed the rejection of Chinese culture, because Tshe-spong-bza' belonged to the nationalistic faction of the Tibetan nobles. Vairocana's banishment was not only desirable for religious reasons but had a much higher practical political value.

In rGyal-mo-rong, the land to which Vairocana was banished, his memory had been preserved up to present times. There are many grottos of meditation and memory places which are connected with his name. There, up to the latest Chinese occupation, the tradition of the *rDsogs-chen* and of the entire *rNying-ma-pa* School had been extremely lively. In rGyal-mo-rong Vairocana took as a student gYu-sgra-snying-po,[168] who belonged to the monastery rGyal-rong Brag-la-mgon. For the other inhabitants of the land he also did many good things. In Tsha-ba-rong sTag-rtse-mkhar Vairocana taught gSang-ston Ye-śes-bla-ma[169] in the *rDsogs-pa-chen-po*; in the hermitage Brag-dmar-dgon-rdsong of sTon-khung-rong he taught the old beggar Sangs-rgyas-mgon-po;[170] in central Tibet in the province of dBus, he taught gNyags Jñānakumāra[171] and the Tibetan queen from Khotan (*Li-bza'*), Śes-rab-sgron-ma. To each of these five persons he taught the *rDsogs-chen* verses successively. Later the Tibetan queen from Khotan invited him.[172]

CHARTS OF THE TRANSMISSION OF THE SECTION OF MIND AND UNENDING DYNAMIC OF BEING OF THE ATIYOGA (*sems-sde* and *klong-sde*) (chapter 2.6.1.)

I. According to the DC

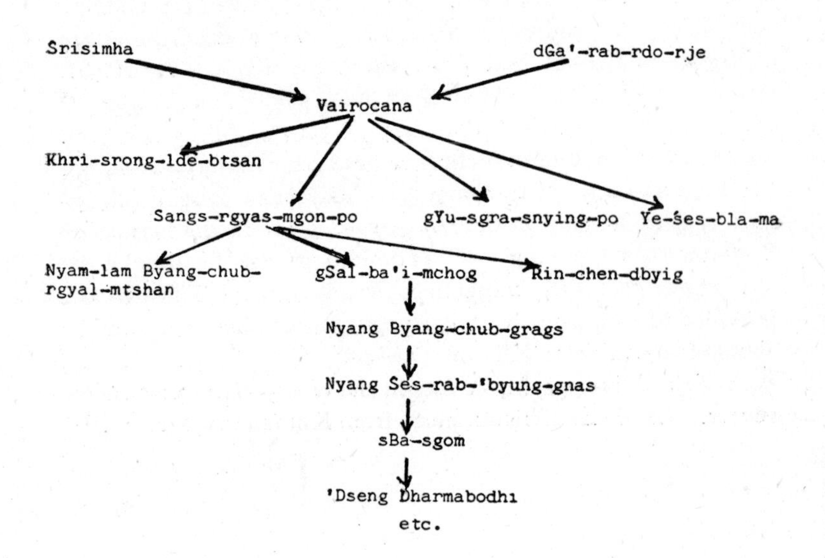

II. According to the DNg (p. 168 and 170) the Section of Mind

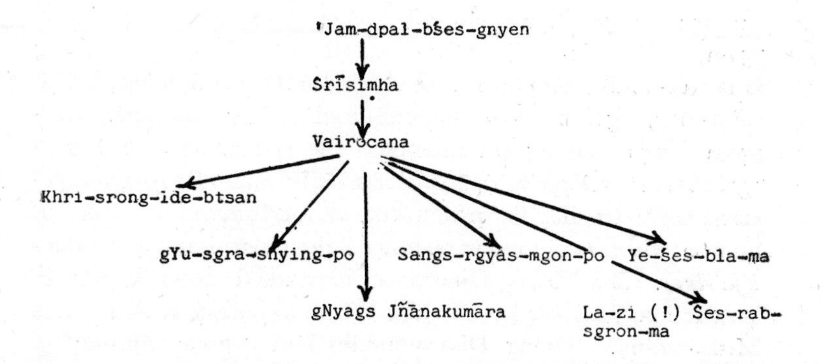

III. According to the DNg (p. 191) the Section of Mind and the lineage of Śrīsimha

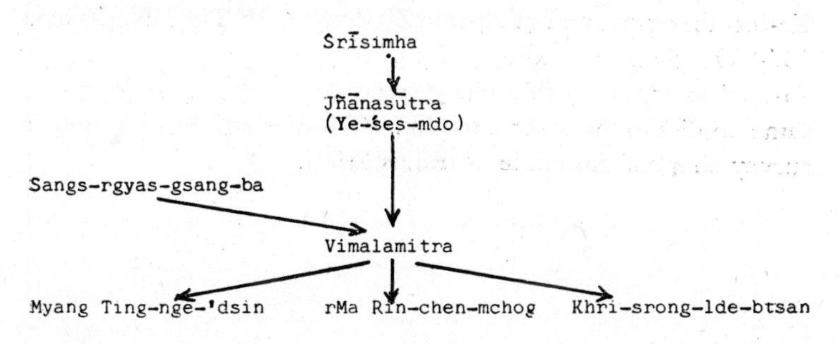

Vairocana's students continued transmitting the doctrine of the Section of Mind (*sems-sde*) and the Section of Unending Dynamic of Being (*klong-sde*) in Tibet. Sangs-rgyas-mgon-po, the old beggar', who was also called sPang Mi-pham-mgon-po, was a direct student of Vairocana.[173] All of Vairocana's disciples attained the being of lightlike perception (*'ja'-lus-pa*). One disciple was Nyam-lam Byang-chub-rgyal-mtshan,[174] who like his teacher reached an age of far more than one hundred years. He taught Za-dam Rin-chen-dbyig, a man from Khams, also Khu-'gyur gSal-ba'i-mchog, who came from the Yar-klungs valley. At their death these three masters dissolved like a melting rainbow; earlier they all had meditated in the same grotto[175] in rGyal-mo-rong. Khu-'gyur gSal-ba'i-mchog taught

Nyang Byang-chub-grags, who then returned to bSam-yas and became famous under the name Nyang Śa-ba-can. He, in turn, taught Nyang Śes-rab-'byung-gnas, who taught sBa-sgom, alias Ye-śes-byang-chub. sBa-sgom taught 'Dseng Dharma-bodhi, who also studied with Dam-pa rGya-gar, A-khu dPal-'bar, gNubs Śangs-po-che and other masters. sBa-sgom taught 'Dseng Dharmabodhi the systems of the *Phyag-rgya-chen-mo*, *rDsogs-pa-chen-po-skor-bdun*,[176] and *rDo-rje-zam- pa-man-ngag*[177] so that he penetrated to the innermost nature of human existence present as an inner light and ultimately wisdom (*'ja'-lus*). But 'Dseng Dharmabodhi studied also many other instructional works; he was also a contemporary of Atīśa and Mi-la-ras-pa. 'Dseng Dharmabodhi had a great number of disciples; particularly : sLob-dpon Kun-bzang, 'Dseng Jo-sras, bTsan-thang-pa, Nyang Dharmasiddha (whom the DNg calls Dharmasiṃha), sLob-dpon gSer-lung-pa, bLa-ma Du rDo-rje-rgyal-mtshan (the DNg reads rDo-rje-rgyan), gZigs Ye-śes-dbang-po, and gYag-ston Zla-'od-zer.[178] The DNg, (pages 187-189) gives the hagiography of the principal disciple Dseng Jo-sras' so explicitly that it is unnecessary to repeat it here; the same applies to the other disciples. Thus I shall furnish only a survey chart of this chain of transmission.

CHART OF THE TRANSMISSION OF THE SECTION OF UNENDING DYNAMIC OF BEING (*klong-sde*)
(chapter 2.6.1.—according to the DC and DNg; DNg names that differ from those in the DC are given in parenthesis)

Dseng Dharmabodhi → 'Dseng Jo-sras

↓

sLob-dpon Kun-bzang

↓

sKye-tshe Ye-śes-dbang-phyug

↓

gZigs Ye-ses-dbang-po

↓

mKhan-chen Ngur-pa (bSod-nams-'od)

↓

Du-ston Vajra-sva-ra (Ngu-ston Vajreśvara)

↓

mKhan-chen bSod-nams-rgyal-mtshan

↓

mKhan-chen gZon-nu-śes-rab (Śes-rab)

↓

sLob-dpon gZon-nu-grags-pa

↓

mKhan-chen Sangs-rgyas-bzang-po

↓

bLa-ma brTson-'grus-dbang-phyug

↓

mTha'-bźi Grags-pa-rin-chen

↓

sLob-dpon Sākya-rgyal-pa (Sākya-rgyal-po-pa)

↓

'Gos Lo-tsā-ba gZon-nu-dpal[179]

↓

sPyan-sna Chos-kyi-grags-pa

↓

Sel-brag-pa Chos-kyi-blo-gros

↓

Khyung-chang-ba bLo-gros-dpal-ldan

↓

dPan-ston Karma-gu-ru-pa

↓

dPan-ston Chos-dbang-lhun-grub

|

Chos-dbang-kun-bzang
↓
dPan-ston Kun-bzang-chos-rgyal
↓
Rig-'dsin gTer-bdag-gling-pa

The last mentioned master was the teacher of the Fifth Dalai Lama and a great Discoverer of Concealed Treasures (*gTer-ston*). His hagiography is among those translated in part II. Thus this doctrine of the Section of Mind and Unending Dynamic of Being (*sems-sde* and *klong-sde*) ranges from Vairocana, the founder of this teaching tradition in Tibet, to gTer-bdag-gling-pa, the well-known Tantrayāna master of the 17th century.

'Gos Lo-tsā-ba calls this tradition by the name of one of the principal texts—"the history of the *rDo-rje-zam-pa*."[180]

2.6.2. THE TRANSMISSION OF THE SECTION OF INSTRUCTIONS (*man-ngag sde*)

For this section there are two parallel lines of transmission. In Tibet, the first line was founded by the *Ācārya* Padmasambhava, and the second by the *Ācārya* Vimalamitra. The first line of transmission has to be regarded as historical fiction, born from the Old School's later conception of history. The reliability of the DC as a source is augmented by the fact that its author (in addition to the generally repeated opinion of the first line) had recorded the second line of transmission with many old and substantially unknown traditions.

Besides the first line of transmission, which represents a characteristic example of the role of Padmasambhava in the Old School's present conception of history, is the second line, which is more credible historically. Through its founder Vimalamitra the second line is directly linked to the principal tradition of the *rDsogs-chen* doctrine.

2.6.2.1. THE LINE OF TRANSMISSION TRACED BACK TO PADMASAMBHAVA

Against the above background, Padmasambhava functions in

this line of transmission as the first teacher, because he is identical with the three aspects of Buddhahood, noetic (*chos-sku*) communicative (*longs-sku*), and authentic being (*sprul-sku*); his word is the pure Buddha word. In this line the emanation of noetic being, the *Guru*, is led back to noetic being, and thus is a representation of it. For the elucidation of this statement a quotation from Karma-phrin-las is added:[181] "Some think about *Nirvāṇa* as different from what is manifested by *Saṃsāra* (the epistemic referent of the situation); it is by thinking of Saṃsāra and Nirvāṇa as each being identical in the immediate psychic event that the logical constructions of *Saṃsāra* and *Nirvāṇa* are resolved in noetic being (*chos-sku*) as such and that expectations and fears which accompany all fictions come to an end by themselves." One only has to link the term *Nirvāṇa* with metaphysical ahistoricity and *Saṃsāra* with historicity and what seems mythical dissolves into metaphysical truth. Thus the question about the historical genesis of the person tainted by *Māyā* (an illusory power, much emphasized in *Vedānta*) is superfluous. Here the historical reality is retro-projected to the transcendental reality in a direct way which omits the descent by steps discussed in chapter 2.2.

The DC reports as follows:[182] Padmasambhava taught Śrīsiṃha and 'Jam-dpal-bśes-gnyen, so that both became masters in this doctrine (*bka'-bab-pa*). When one takes into account the principal transmission of the *rDsogs-chen* it is at once evident that this statement has no historical validity. The report in DC does not record the particulars of Padmasambhava's teaching; but only the useful lessons derived from the meditative exercises of this system. Padmasambhava demonstrated them at the Tibetan court with the help of necromantic practices. The queen 'Brom-bza' Byang-chub-sman, in other sources called 'Bro-bza' Byang-chub-gron,[183] who was one of the wives of King Khri-srong-lde-btsan, had a daughter called Lha-lcam Padma-gsal. She died at the age of eight. Since the king was inconsolable in his grief and mourning for his daughter, Padmasambhava performed the following ceremony: he wrote the letter NRI on the corpse of the girl, near the heart. Because of his meditative concentration (*ting-nge-'dsin*), which was won through the *rDsogs-chen*, he re-awakened the consciousness, whereupon the corpse opened her eyes and started to speak.

Then Padmasambhava gave an empowerment (*dbang-bskur*) for the 'instruction in the *sNying-thig* of the Spiritual Beings' (*man-ngag-mkha'-'gro'i snying-thig*)[184] to Lha-lcam Padma-gsal. However, he hid the *sNying-thig* text in a secret place; that is, he made it a Concealed Treasure (*gter-ma*).

Here the transmission stops in its temporal sphere, but continues in the sphere of the transcendental as the 'transmission in the symbols of the Spiritual Beings' (*mkha'-'gro brda'i-brgyud-pa*). The process of emanation in stages as described in chapter 2.2. takes here a retrograde path. The Spiritual Beings (*mKha'-'gro*), as wisdom-impulses of nothingness (*stong-pa-nyid*) absorb these teaching traditions, because both the Spiritual Beings and the wisdom impulses emanated from nothingness and are, in their being, indivisible from each other. Later this Concealed Treasure (*gter-ma*) was unearthed by the *gTer-ston* Padma-las-'brel; but since he was not ordained in the tradition of this Concealed Teaching, he was unable to revise it. kLong-chen-rab-byams-pa was able to do so only after a Spiritual Being (*mKha'-'gro-ma*), representing *rDo-rje-phag-mo*,[185] initiated him into this instruction. Thus kLong-chen-rab-byams-pa became a master and representative of this doctrine (*bka,-babs-pa*). He now transmitted the *sNying-thig* again in its worldly form.

It is to be noted that, with the Old School, the 'transmission in the symbols of the Spiritual Beings' (*mkha'-'gro brda'i brgyud-pa*) does not rank lower than the transmission which took place in the worldly sphere and is therefore equally legitimate. For the Old School the difference between the unhistorical transcendental world and the historical temporal one is dissolved in the zero point. One of the reasons for this is seen in the central position of the term 'Mind' (*sems*) in the philosophy of the *rNying-ma-pa*. The *dGe-lugs-pa*, in contrast, reject the legitimacy of the New or Direct Transmission (*nye-brgyud*), which is transmitted via the unhistorical sphere; they recognize only the historical transmission, that is, the Old or Temporal Transmission (*ring-brgyud*). In the area of the Section of Instructions (*man-ngag sde*) kLong-chen-rab-byams-pa composed the following famous works : *mDsod-chen-bdun*, *Ngal-gso-skor-gsum*, *Rang-grol-skor-gsum*, a commentary to the *sNying-thig* which is also called *Tika-mun-sel-skor-gsum*, *sNying-thig-rnam-*

pa-gsum, and *Yang-thig-skor-gsum*. Since these works are available today, I may end the discussion of this chain of transmission at this point. The tradition about Padmasambhava and his Concealed Books (*gter-ma*) thus continues into the present time.

2.6.2.2. THE LINE OF TRANSMISSION TRACED BACK TO VIMALAMITRA

Vimalamitra was already two hundred years old when King Khri-srong-lde-btsan established the Buddha Doctrine in Tibet. The age of Vimalamitra should not be surprising; as we have seen above (footnote 131) such longevity was commonly accepted belief among the *rDsogs-chen* masters as well as among the Taoists. In other sources the age of this master is not mentioned; however, it fits the milieu of this line of transmission. The great visionary and ascetic Nyang (also spelled Myang) Ting-nge-'dsin-bzang-po,[186] who was the ancestor of the famous Nyang-ral Nyi-ma-'od-zer, begged King Khri-srong-lde-btsan to invite Vimalamitra immediately to Tibet, because he was the keeper of the secret doctrines i.e. the *rDsogs-chen* doctrines. Thus the king sent to India a delegation of learned men who were led by the two translators (*Lo-tsā-ba*) sKa-ba-dpal-brtsegs of the 'Bro family, and kLu'i-rgyal-mtshan from Cog-ro. They were supposed to go to King Indrabhūti, at whose court Vimalamitra stayed. Against the king's wish, the famous master went to Tibet. Soon the Indians plotted against Vimalamitra[187] so that the Tibetans became full of doubt concerning the legitimacy of Vimalamitra's doctrines about the Section of Instructions (*man-ngag sde*). Due to his superior knowledge, Vimalamitra was able to solidify and deepen the Tibetans' trust, and thus he escaped Vairocana's fate of being banished. Vimalamitra taught the general philosophy, with emphasis on causality (*rgyu-'bras*); like Vairocana he especially taught to the king and Nyang Ting-nge-'dsin-bzang-po the 'central doctrines of the instruction in the *rDsogs-chen*' (*rdsogs-chen man-ngag snying-thig*). So that none, except those who had been empowered, was able to learn these secret doctrines, the manuscript written in the Tibetan language was hidden in the hermitage mChims-phu near bSam-yas. As in the case reported in the transmission of the 'instructions in the *sNying-thig* of the Spiritual Beings' (*man-ngag mkha'-'gro snying-thig*), the tradition of the Pronouncements (*bka'-ma*) merges here with that of the Concealed Books (*gter-ma*). The *Ācārya* Vimalamitra stayed for thirteen years in Tibet; then he finally retreated to the Wu-tai-shan in China,[188] where he died. Nyang Tingnge-'dsin died fifty-five years later. Before his death he founded the dBu-ru-źva'i Lha-khang, a temple that has been famous till today.[189] He had hidden the entire literature of the Vimalamitra transmission in the main temple (*ke'u-tshang*) (it is likely that this main temple is the one within the complex of dBu-ru-źva'i Lha-khang) at the third column of the third door. He taught the Oral Tradition (*snyan-brgyud*) to Rin-chen-'bar-ba of the 'Bro family.

At this point our discussion of the founding of the Tradition of the Pronouncements (*bka'-ma' i brgyud-pa*) terminates. The aim of the present treatise is to lay bare the beginnings of this tradition; its continuance in Tibet presents a separate problem. From the Section of Instructions (*man-ngag sde*) the following charts of transmission can be established.

CHARTS OF THE TRANSMISSION OF THE SECTION OF INSTRUCTIONS (*man-ngag sde*) (chapter 2.6.2.)

I. The Line Based on Padmasambhava - according to the DC

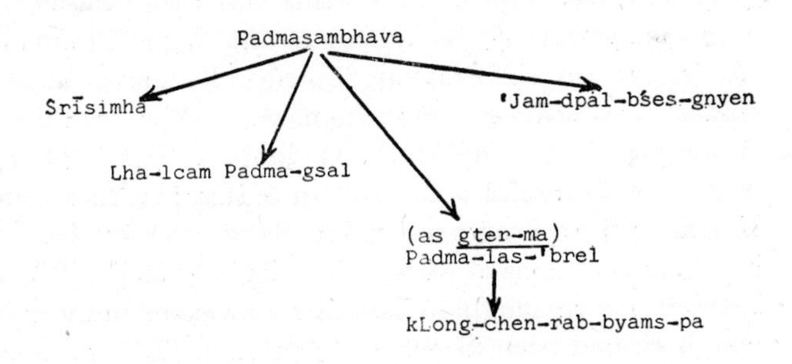

II. The Line Based on Vimalamitra - according to the DC

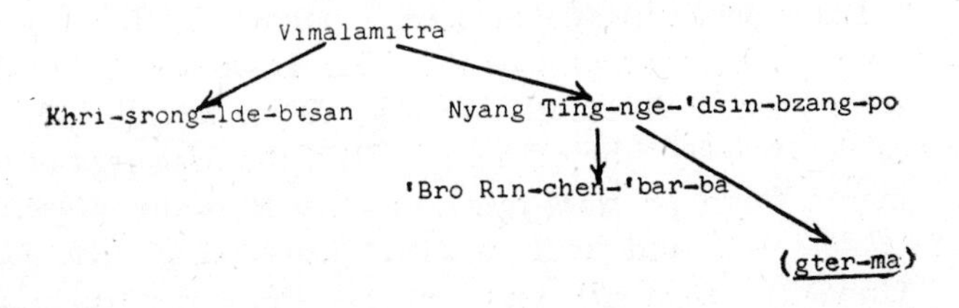

2.7. SUMMARY

If one views the entire tradition of the Old Transmission of the Pronouncements (*ring-brgyud bka'-ma*) in retrospect the following main points evolve:

1. The foundation of the *rDsogs-chen* philosophy:

The first transmitter, ever mentioned, is dGa'-rab-rdo-rje; he is, however, still a very hypothetical figure. With 'Jam-dpal-bśes-gnyen, the three main *rDsogs-chen* sections take form. The instructions took place in China (as all future ones will). 'Jam-dpal-bśes-gnyen had probably brought from India some memorial verses to China, and there taught them to Śrīsiṃha, whose birth-place also was within Chinese territory. Śrīsiṃha summarized these doctrines into books and hid them in the Byang-chub-śing and bKra-śis-khri-sgo temples; both of which were in China. There also he later on taught the two Indians Vimalamitra and Jñānasūtra.

2. The transmission of the *rDsogs-chen* doctrines in Tibet: In Tibet Vimalamitra founded the Mahāyoga of Development (*bskyed-pa mahā-yoga*); his student was rMa Rin-chen-mchog. The foundation of the system of the Eight Pronouncements (*bka'-brgyud*) is uniformly attributed to Padmasambhava, whose student was gNyags Jñānakumāra. The tradition of the Anuyoga of Accomplished Meditation (*rdsogs-pa anu-yoga*) originated in circles of the Indian *Siddhas*; its most important Tibetan representative was gNubs Sangs-rgyas-ye-śes. Atiyoga, in its three sections of Mind, Unending Dynamic of Being, and Instructions was taught in Tibet by Vairocana and Vimalamitra, who both had been disciples of Śrīsiṃha. The group of literature which became famous as *kLong-chen snying-thig* was supposedly hidden by Padmasambhava as a Concealed Treasure (*gter-ma*).

3. The spread of these doctrines in Tibet:
Later the entire system became known in Tibet under the name *mDo-sgyu-sems-gsum.*[190] 'Gos Lo-tsā-ba referred to this term when, in the translation of his DNg, he called the tradition of the *Anuyoga* "the school of *mDo*", the *Mahāyoga* of Development (*bskyed-pa mahā-yoga*) the "cycle of the *Māyā.*" (*sGyu-'phrul-rgyud*), and the *Atiyoga* the "mental class" (*sems-phyogs*).[191] Under the term *mDo-sgyu-sems-gsum* the entire teaching system of the *rDsogs-chen* is mentioned as the object of study of the Discoverers of Concealed Treasures (*gTer-ston*). The dissemination of this philosophy took place in successive stages by the masters: gNyags Jñānakumāra, gNubs-chen Sangs-rgyas-ye-śes, Zur Śākya-'byung-gnas, Zur Śes-rab-grags and above of all by Zur Śākya-seng-ge.

4. The transition of the tradition of the Pronouncements Literature (*bka'-ma*) to the Concealed Treasures (*gter-ma*):
Twice it has been stated explicitly that texts originaly belonging to the tradition of the *bka'-ma* were later handed down as Concealed Treasures (*gter-ma*) : the cycle of the Eight Pronouncements (*bka'-brgyad*) and the cycle of the *kLong-chen snying-thig.* Both cycles were brought to Tibet by Padmasambhava. It is the task of future research to investigate these cycles and show the extent (if any) to which they are related to Padmasambhava.

Because of kLong-chen-rab-byams-pa's brilliant commentary, the *sNying-thig* based on Padmasambhava has become far more famous than the *sNying-thig* of Vimalamitra, which is possibly the more authentic one.

5. Padmasambhava's importance in the *rDsogs-chen* tradition: Only once, in the transmission of the doctrine of the Eight Pronouncements (*bka'-brgyad*), is Padmasambhava a true transmitter of *rDsogs-chen* doctrines. These doctrines originated from the circle of the Eight Wisdom-Holders (*Rig-'dsin brgyad*) to which Padmasambhava belonged. He hid these texts and made them a Concealed Treasure (*gter-ma*). Only in this instance was he a true founder of a doctrinal system. Similarly, he is also supposed to have hidden the books known as *kLong-chen snying-thig*. Thus he became the master of the Concealed Treasures; i.e. the master of the *gter-ma* in general. Since during the course of Tibetan history texts and books were hidden again and again by different masters, Padmasambhava was later, at the time of the rediscovery of the Concealed Books, praised as the master and founder of all Concealed Literature. In this way he became more and more a central figure in the tradition of the Old School, in spite of the fact that the *rDsogs-chen* tradition mentions him only peripherically and that he is in no way connected with the principal tradition of the *rDsogs-chen*. This is supported by bDud-'joms Rin-po-che's[192] statement: "So after all, the followers of the Buddha Doctrine in the *Kaliyuga* (i.e. in contemporary times) are guided principally by the Concealed Treasures (*gter-ma*)."

3. THE NEW TRANSMISSION OF THE "CONCEALED TEACHINGS" AND THEIR DISCOVERERS (*nye-brgyud gter-ma*)

3.1. THE NATURE OF THE "CONCEALED TEACHINGS" (*gter-ma*)

The Tibetan word *gter* appears in many combinations, each of them having a specific meaning. The original meaning of *gter* seems to have been 'treasure', 'store'; consequently the word became associated with the idea of something 'worthy of preservation' or 'precious'. The objects termed *gter* may be jewels, gold or silver, indicating 'material' values, or they may be figurines, cult objects and reliquaries, representing 'religious' or 'spiritual' values. A *gter* object can also be precious in the sense that it embodies an aspiration for liberation; in which case its preciousness would be the doctrinal content laid down in written works or their oral teaching. Whether precious teachings or cult objects, common to all of them is that they have at least once been concealed and been rediscovered. Furthermore, they have a hidden meaning; the significance of these teachings, scriptures or cult objects is revealed only to the religious man who is qualified and predestined for such.

The term *gter-ma* designates a text of religious content which was concealed by a master of the Buddhist teachings during the first missionary period of Buddhism in Tibet and was later brought to light by a religiously predestined and qualified person.

The locality where it was hidden is called *gter-gnas* in Tibetan, literally 'treasure place'. This 'place' is not only a concrete locality on earth but also a reference point in the sphere of religious thinking. This is symbolically expressed by the term 'protector of the Concealed Treasure' (*gTer-srung* or *gTer-skyong*). For instance, in the hagiography of Sangs-rgyas-gling-pa (1340-1396) this term is applied to *bsTan-rgod-chen-po*, a great, vulture-like spirit who belongs to the category of the *bTsan-demons*.

The Discoverer of a Concealed Treasure is called *gTer-ston*. This term means Discoverer and Teacher of the Concealed Treasure or Teachings. In the realm of literature, the gTer-ston is the discoverer and, sometimes also, the editor of the Concealed Treasures, the fragments that have been unearthed. The appearance of such a Discoverer is announced in a prophecy (*lung-bstan* or *gter-lung*). In most cases these prophecies are taken from the ninety-second chapter of Padmasambhava's hagiography, the *Padma-bka'-thang*.[193] Most of the hagiographies, presented in part II, cite these prophecies at their beginning. Because of his religious charisma the Discoverer of Concealed Treasure (*gTer-ston*) gets a 'hint' or 'key' (*kha-byang* or *lde-mig*); these terms designate lists which catalogue the books which are hidden at various locations in a district. These lists give precise descriptions of places in order to facilitate the discovery of these texts.

In the essay "Einige Aspekte der *gter-ma* Literatur der *rNying-ma-pa* Schule" (some aspects of the *gter-ma* literature of the *rNying-ma-pa* School,[194] I have described the historical background against which, during the first missionary epoch (*snga-dar*) Padmasambhava, his disciples and other masters following his example, concealed not only books but also figures and other cult objects in temples and meditation grottos. In this essay I have examined the inner structure of this type of literature and indicated its three sub-divisions: 'the book concealed in the earth' (*sa-gter*) to be considered as an actual archaeological fragment; 'the book twice hidden' (*yang-gter*) which is a text that had once been found but then concealed again to be discovered a second time or a text whose transmission had been interrupted and newly founded by a master; and the 'concealed teachings perceived in meditation' (*dgongs-gter*). (in this case the translation of *gter-ma* as Concealed Book is not quite suitable; it should rather be translated as 'the doctrine or the teachings of a concealed book perceived in meditation'); this term designates texts which were composed after a meditational and visionary experience and which elaborate the single fragment of a 'book hidden in the earth' (*sa-gter*) into a system of a Tantric cycle (*chos-skor*). I have tried to make the historical reality of the 'books concealed in the earth' (*sa-gter*) probable by the analysis of the colophons. I have also dealt briefly with the theme of the entire type of their literature and maintained that it consisted almost exclusively of the great

Tantra cycles of the Old School. What I have said in my essay applies here, too.

The doctrinal content of the literature of the Concealed Books (*gter-ma*) is well elucidated in the introduction to the sixth chapter of the DC. There Dharma is described as a quality of an ever-changing world. It may manifest itself in trees, stones and all those other objects from which the Discoverers of Concealed Teachings (*gTer-ston*) hear the teachings of Buddha.[195] The starting point is the doctrine of the Buddha nature (*bde-gśegs-snying-po*) or, to be more explicit, the doctrine of potential Buddhahood inherent in all living beings in its totality. This doctrine is central to *rNying-ma-pa* thought. It may be related to philosophical Taoism which claims that the Tao is revealed in water, mountains, clouds, in brief, in the whole of nature.

Without disputing the legitimacy of these works, their concealment can be related to the belief in Spiritual Beings, representatives of the transcendent, so as to ensure their transmission. When these books are rediscovered the Spiritual Beings merely return them to the discoverer. This tradition and transmission taking place through the 'transcendent sphere' is called the 'new and direct transmission' (*nye-brgyud*) and is contrasted with the 'old and temporal transmission' which takes place in the human sphere and appears first of all in the 'transmission of the Pronouncements' (*ring-brgyud bka'-ma*).

The Concealed Books turn out to be the focal point of contact with the absolute reality (*chos-dbyings*), which is the openness of being (*stong-pa-nyid*), and the transmigratory world with its fleeting character. The Concealed Treasures have symbolical character; they only point to this openness of being, which is palpable in the transmigratory world. Therefore all activities connected with the Concealed Books have a symbolic character. In analogy with the term 'rites de passage' one could speak here of 'mots de passage', word signs which open the passageway to liberation.

3.2. THE DISCOVERER OF CONCEALED TEACHINGS (*gTer-ston*)

The Discoverer of Concealed Books (*gTer-ston*) is a person embodying in himself the poles of temporality and extra-temporality. The former is the discoverer's historical existence which we know from his name and the events in his life. There also is preserved an account of his ancestry. The Discoverer comes either from famous clans of the Tibetan nobles or from families of Tantrics; sometimes he has to bear the harsh fate of an orphan.

The human existence which follows the rules of temporality is pervaded by the absolute reality of extra-temporality. The Discoverer of Concealed Books sees this reality in a vision. Nyang-ral Nyi-ma-'od-zer (1124-1192) saw Padmasambhava riding on a white horse whose four hooves were supported by Spiritual Beings; Padmasambhava gave him an empowerment and the heavens opened, the earth trembled and the mountains shook. This is obviously a symbol for the psychic break-through which Nyi-ma-'od-zer experienced. Guru Chos-kyi-dbang-phyug (1212-1270) saw the inexhaustible reality as *Vajrasattva*; a spiritual force formulates religious instructions by which the historical person will be qualified to understand the Concealed Teachings.

The first vision which decides the future religious life is in most cases a dream experience in which the perception of the ordinary world is suspended for the time being.[196] In this vision the future Discoverer of Concealed Books (*gTer-ston*) receives a mystic empowerment (*dbang-bskur*) which qualifies and empowers him to study the Tantric cycles. After having participated in a Tantric ritual he is given instruction. Here the auditive element dominates.[197] The dream vision thus turns into an instructional vision. In spite of this strong visionary experience the Discoverer's relationship with the sensuous world remains unbroken.[198]

It is within the tension between the two poles of the *gTer-ston's* existence that the Tantric metamorphosis takes place. It begins with the psycho-somatic realities of a human individual. These realities are fully recognized and reappear on the highest levels of Buddhist mysticism, which Europeans would like to classify as phenomena of 'lower levels' and to reduce to bodily occurrences. This trend of European philosophy and psychology to reduce the higher and more developed to the lower, has been termed 'psychological reductionism' by C. F. von Weizsacker.[199] An understanding of Tantrayāna is completely prevented by this outlook which claims that a crystal is 'acutally' and 'nothing but' a mass of atoms arranged in an orderly fashion, and by analogy 'explains' the unprejudiced and unbiased awareness, termed *bodhicitta* in Tantric works, as 'merely' bodily secretions.[200] If one wishes to understand the Discoverer of Concealed Teachings (*gTer-ston*) then one has to abandon this position, which is founded in the Occidental and Christian way of thought.

The Tantric metamorphosis starts when the mental vehicle, the *prāṇa*, has been mastered. This is the 'all-saturating subtle substance of life'[201] or the vitality in general.[202] This vitality carries the intellect (*sems*), so the Buddhist texts say, "like an elephant its rider." If the vehicle (i.e. the vitality) is mastered, then the intellect is mastered too. The controlled vitality, which in its raw state serves the biological process of reproduction causes now the intensification of awareness. This is experienced as the rising of creativity in the central pathway; it starts in the genital zone and has its goal in the vertex of the brain. It would, however, be false to describe this creativity as something 'spiritual' that is enveloped in the shell of sexuality which it can leave at will; rather both aspects of primary creativity are interwoven. This is the only explanation for the fact that terms which are used to describe sexual facts and experiences also refer to facts and experiences of a spiritual character. Creativity is the common ground for both. Only in this way can we understand the empowerment which Guru Chos-kyi-dbang-phyug gave his disciple Bha-ro, to whom *Vairocana* and *Amoghasiddhi* appeared in the form of bodily functions. Through the Tantric metamorphosis the human body becomes a *Maṇḍala* which mirrors the extra-temporal reality.

The goal of this metamorphosis is a kind of *unio mystica*, not in the sense of being something absolutely different, but rather of a fusion with total Being. The Tibetan texts call this process *chos-dbying-su thim-pa*, the submergence or dissolution in the sphere of absolute reality. This statement is found at the end of the temporal existence of the Discoverer of Concealed Teachings (*gTer-ston*) when the metamorphosis has been accomplished.

3.3. THE REPORT OF THU'U-KVAN RIN-PO-CHE BLO-BZANG-CHOS-KYI-NYI-MA CONCERNING THE TRADITION OF THE CONCEALED TEACHINGS[203]

"The *Ācārya* Padmasambhava and a few other persons who were full of the holy truth concealed for the benefit of future disciples many instructions concerning the most excellent spiritual potency (*mchog-gi dngos-grub*) and the common spiritual potency (*thun-mong-gi dngos-grub*) in hiding places. They blessed these books that no harm would come to them and entrusted them to the Protectors of the Concealed Treasures (*gTer-srung*) for safekeeping. They said a prayer so that only capable persons might find the books. In answering the question when it would be suitable to remove these texts, they described in the Lists of Hiding Places (*kha-byang*) the signs that would appear and indicate that the time of removal had come, and they also stated the name of the Discoverer of Concealed Books (*gTer-ston*), who was to take out the Concealed Books *gter-ma*), the family from which he would come and which signs he would bear. When the right place, time and being (i.e. the *gTer-ston*) are present, this Concealed Book (*gter-ma*) will be removed and handed over to many capable persons. This is known as the Teachings of the Concealed Books (*gter-chos*).

It is the defect of not being well informed if one considers the entire Teachings of the Concealed Books (*gter-chos*) as a theory of the Old School (*rNying-ma-pa*), because the general Teachings of the Concealed Books (*gter-chos*) exist also in India, and because they are also inherent in other Tibetan Schools. Although some people styled themselves falsely as Discoverers of Concealed Books (*gTer-ston*), and although they themselves had composed, hidden and taken the books out again, these only are liars, and the Concealed Books as a whole should not be condemned, as there certainly are many genuine ones.

"The most authoritative Discoverers (*gTer-ston*) from Sangs-rgyas-bla-ma to bDe-chen-źig-po-gling-pa, are listed in the prophecies of the *Thang-yig*.[204] There also came many Discoverers who are not directly mentioned in the prophecies. Later on Chos-rgyal-dbang-po'i-sde collected everything about them and accordingly composed a prayer about the hundred

Discoverers of Concealed Treasures (*gTer-ston-brgya-rtsa'i gsol-'debs*). In reference to these two categories of teachers and teachings, great men have said that the Teachings of the Concealed Books are completely pure. Among all these (Discoverers of Concealed Books) mNga-'bdag Nyang-ral Nyi-ma-'od-zer and Guru Chos-kyi-dbang-phyug are the greatest; they are as well known as the sun and the moon, and are the kings of the Discoverers (*gTer-ston*). The gTer-ston Grva-pa mNgon-śes founded the great monastic college of Grva-thang and built one hundred and eight-Stūpas. He brought to light many Concealed Books (*gter-ma*)—first of all *sMan-gyi-rgyud-bzi*[205] and many others concerning medicine (*dpyad-skor*). Therefore his blessing and charisma spread wide and far."

The above statement briefly summarizes all the essentials of the tradition of the Concealed Books (*gter-ma*). In addition, the above statement occupies a somewhat exceptional position as its author did not belong to the Old School (*rNying-ma-pa*) but was a *dGe-lugs-pa*. This school itself has not such broad tradition of Concealed Books (*gter-ma*); it often turned against what it considered too large a component of irrationality in the religious life.

3.4. LITERARY WORKS OF THE TRADITION OF THE PRONOUNCEMENTS (*bka'-ma*) MERGE WITH THE TRADITION OF THE CONCEALED BOOKS (*gter-ma*)

At the end of the second chapter about the works of the Pronouncement Tradition (*bka'-ma*) it was pointed out that in Tibet texts which originally belonged to the transmission of the Pronouncements (*bka'-ma*) were soon hidden and were then counted as part of the Concealed Books (*gter-ma*). Because of this fusion of two streams of tradition, Padmasambhava who undoubtedly was the founder of the system of the Concealed Books in Tibet, became in course of time more and more the central figure in the Old School. To the extent that the Old School (*rNying-ma-pa*) increasingly concentrated on Padmasambhava the memory of all other great masters of their own school and of the early times of Tibet was suppressed. The DC quite correctly states that the Discoverers (*gTer-ston*) are the carriers of the tradition of the Concealed Books (*gter-ma*) and of the Pronouncements (*bka'-ma*).[206] The people of Tibet, to say nothing of the scholars who did not belong to the Old School, have largely forgotten the other early great masters whom we have met in the literature of the *rNying-ma-pa*. Even the learned well-read Thu'u-kvan Chos-kyi-nyi-ma names Padmasambhava alone as the founder of the system of the *rNying-ma-pa*.[207]

G. Tucci tried to solve the problem which the person of Padmasambhava presents, by separating the historical Padmasambhava from the Guru Rin-po-che, the venerable teacher, the distant mediator of the path to liberation. In the person of the historic Padmasambhava which appears real to him (Tucci), he sees the necromancer and sorcerer.[208] In the light of the available tradition, discussed so far, it is possible to specify the philosophical systems which Padmasambhava taught in Tibet, to define historical activities, to show his slow emergence as the central figure of the Old School, and to trace this process in its various stages. The Tibetan tradition itself unmistakably shows the interaction as well as the difference between the historic Padmasambhava and his existence as a religious phenomenon beyond all historicity but psychologically real.

In this area the transition from the system of the Pronouncements (*bka'-ma*) to the system of the Concealed Books (*gter-ma*) has to be taken into consideration. The picture of the *rNying-ma-pa*, as we see it today, is definitely dominated by the Concealed Books (*gter-ma*). However, we must realize that there are other contributory factors as well.

3.5. THE EARLIER AND LATER CONCEALED BOOKS (*gter-kha gong-'og*)

The term 'Earlier and Later Concealed Books' above all designates the Concealed Books (*gter-ma*) which were unearthed by Guru Chos-kyi-dbang-phyug (born 1212) and by Nyang-ral Nyi-ma-'od-zer (born 1124). This term, which the Tibetan sources themselves do not define, is subsequently applied to all Books Concealed in the Old Times (*gter-rnying*) contrasted with the Books Concealed in More Recent Times (*gter-gsar*).

The foundation of these Earlier and Later Concealed Books (*gter-kha gong-'og*) rests on Guru Padmasambhava, the *rDsogs-chen* system, and the meditation on *Avalokiteśvara*. In the Tibetan sources these three topics are called *bLa-rdsogs-thugs-*

gsum. In the same way as the three literature cycles *mDo-sgyu-sems-gsum*[209] describe the content of the Transmission of the Pronouncements (*bka'-ma'i brgyud-pa*) by mentioning the most important literary works in abbreviated form, so the term *bLa-rdsogs-thugs-gsum* contains the main cycles of the system of the Concealed Books (*gter-ma*):

1. The various instructions for the meditative realization of the *bLa-ma*, i.e. Guru Padmasambhava (*bLa-ma'i sgrub-pa chos-skor*).

2. The *rDsogs-chen* system, mainly in the summary of the Tree Sections of the *rDsogs-chen* (*rDsogs-chen-sde-gsum*).

3. The Tantric cycles for meditative realization of the various forms of the Bodhisattva *Avalokiteśvara* (*Thugs-rje-chen-po-skor*). In the hagiographies the future Discoverer of Concealed Treasures (*gTer-ston*), for instance Guru Chos-kyi-dbang-phyug, is advised to study these three subjects, otherwise he would not understand the Concealed Teachings (*gter-ma*) and would even promulgate heretical teachings. A comparison of the *mDo-sgyu-sems-gsum* with the *bLa-rdsogs-thugs-gsum* shows the difference between the method of the Transmission of the Pronouncements and the method of the Transmission of the Concealed Teachings. In the former the study of literature is cultivated; in the latter experience in meditation.

3.6. THE NEWLY CONCEALED BOOKS (*gter gsar*) AND THE REVIVAL OF THE OLD SCHOOL

The Discoverers of Concealed Books (*gTer-ston*) who are discussed in part II appear in an uninterrupted sequence from Sangs-rgyas-bla-ma (approximately 958-1006) to gTer-bdag-gling-pa, who was born in 1646. The next discoverer was 'Jigs-med-gling-pa, who was born in 1729. He, however, mostly represented the *rDsogs-chen* system and wrote commentaries and treatises about it, he compiled and catalogued the Hundred Thousand Tantras of the Old School (*rNying-ma rgyud-'bum*) and thus continued the work of Ratna-gling-pa (born 1403). Since Źig-po-gling-pa was born in 1892, there is a gap of almost two-hundred years in the sequence of the Discoverers of Concealed Books.

The new epoch, which begins with Źig-po-gling-pa, is introduced by a very promising prophecy written in the *rTen 'brel-mdo-chings* : "At this time nearly all translators (*Lo-tsā-ba*), scholars (*Paṇḍita*), and the King Khri-srong-lde-btsan with his entourage will meet." It is especially stressed that Źig-po-gling-pa is to be taken as the incarnation of the royal prince Mu-rub-btsan-po, and that his teacher mKhyen-brtse'i-dbang-po Padma-'od-gsal-mdo-sngags-gling-pa[210] is the incarnation of King Khri-srong-lde-btsan (754-797), so that this king and his son Mu-rub-btsan-po, also called Mu-rug-btsan-po,[211] after one thousand years are incarnated as teacher and disciple in order to revive the early times of Buddhism (*snga-dar*) with the flourishing of the *rNying-ma-pa*.

The greatest initiator and supporter of this renaissance was Źig-po-gling-pa, who is recognized as its founder and who is said to possess the Seven Currents of Pronouncements (*bka'-babs-bdun-ldan*). He dedicated himself to the discovery of *rDsogs-chen* texts, of which the *rDsogs-chen-sde-gsum* and the Concealed Book *Thugs-sgrub-bar-chad-kun-sel* are probably the most important ones. His teacher mKhyen-brtse'i-dbang-po dedicated himself to the *rDsogs-chen* tradition as such and tried to spread it and revitalize its philosophy by discovering lost texts and editing the rediscovered texts. mKhyen-brtse'i-dbang-po intentionally stood aloof from the wonder and magic surrounding the image of the Discoverers of Concealed Teachings in earlier times. He called all these miraculous aspects, especially the doubtful art of consulting oracles (*smos-pa*), a pack of lies, [212] and warned against prophecies in unmistakable terms.[213] His dedication to the *rDsogs-chen* system is shown not only in the texts which he found and edited but also in his visions. He saw 'Jam-dpal-bśes-gnyen, the *rDsogs-chen* master, and received instruction from him in a vision. The prediction that in his next life he (mKhyen-brtse'i-dbang-po) would be born at Wu-tai-shan, the center of the *rDsogs-chen* tradition, was like an affirmation of his activities in the field of *rDsogs-chen* teachings. His disciple was Padma-gar-dbang-yon-tan-rgya-mtsho, the famous sKong-sprul Rin-po-che[214] who continued the work of his teacher with surprising diligence, and has left many works.

The texts of the renaissance of the Old School, unearthed by the Discoverers of Concealed Teachings (*gTer-ston*), are rarely old original scriptures of the time of the Yar-klung dynasty; they are rather Twice Concealed Books (*yang-gter*). These books had been already found by a Discoverer; however, the tradition of their teachings had been lost, and the Discoverers of the nineteenth century founded it anew. Thus we find at the end of nearly all hagiographies of the Discoverers of Concealed Teachings (*gTerston*) who lived during the Tibetan middle ages (approximately from the tenth to the sixteenth century) that the lost traditions were re-established by mKhyen-brtse'i-dbang-po, and that his disciple sKong-sprul Yon-tan-rgya-mtsho, alias Padma-gar-dbang, had heard and transmitted them. G. Smith designates this period of the *rNying-ma-pa* as the epoch of the eclectics (*ris-med*).[215] At this time the *rNying-ma-pa* certainly were inspired by the *dGe-lugs-pa*; the fact that the reconciliation and adjustment of the various Buddhist schools of Tibet had not been very successful, is shown by Pha-bong-kha Rin-po-che's negative attitude towards the *rNying-ma-pa*. His disciples have partially retained this attitude.

Two flourishing periods of *rNying-ma-pa* thought are discernible during the second missionary period of Buddhism (*phyi-dar*). The first occurred in the twelfth and thirteenth century when old documents and manuscripts from the first missionary period (*snga-dar*) were found in quantities, with which the *rNying-ma-pa* solidified their own school tradition. This was the time of Nyang-ral Nyi-ma-'od-zer (1124-1192) and Guru Chos-kyi-dbang-phyug (1212-1270). The second period began in the nineteenth century and reached into the twentieth century. Between these two epochs gTer-bdag-gling-pa (1646 or 1634 to 1714) stands alone. The first golden age of *rNying-ma-pa* thought finds its literary expression in the *gter-kha gong-'og*, the Earlier and Later Concealed Books; the second in the Newly Concealed Books (*gter-gsar*). At the present time bDud-'joms Rin-po-che is the most important representative of this tradition.

3.7. COLLECTION OF THE CONCEALED BOOKS

Because of this newly revived religious zeal scholars have undertaken the preservation for posterity of the most important Concealed Books by collecting and compiling them into cohesive works. Żig-po-gling-pa had done this with the One Hundred Thousand Tantras, the *rNying-ma-rgyud-'bum*. mKhyen-brtse'i-dbang-po, together with his disciple sKong-sprul Yon-tan-rgya-mtsho, checked the legitimacy of the separate Discoverers of Concealed Books (*gTer-ston*). In this process the legitimacy of some Discoverers and some books was contested. However, only those works which were beyond doubt and in every respect reliable Concealed Teachings were included in the collection; this collection is the *Rin-chen-gter-mdsod*, 'The Great Treasure of Precious Concealed Books.' It is rumoured that several versions of this work exist.

The history of the *gter-ma* literature presents a problem in itself. Although it is indicated by the hagiographies of the Discoverers of Concealed Books, it cannot be solved by this material. The sources for such a history of literature are, first of all, the 'histories of origin of the Concealed Books' (*gter-'byung*) which were composed by many Discoverers and which are authentic reports of the discovery of the Concealed Books (*gter-ma*). In addition there are the following compilations of the history of the tradition of the Concealed Books and their Discoverers:[216] *Śa-gzugs-pa bkra-śis rnam-rgyal- gyigter-ma'i lo-rgyus dpag-bsam-rab-rgyas*, *Ẓab-lung gdan-sa-pa dbang-gi-rgyal-po'igter-ston-brgya-rtsa'i chos-'byung*, *gYag-sde 'dul-'dsin-mkhyen-rab-rgya mtsho'i chos-'byung nor-bu'i bang-mdsod*, *mKhas-mchog ngag-dbang-blo-gros-kyi snga-'gyur-chos-kyi 'byung-khungs mkhas-pa-dga'-byed*. The second bloom of the teachings of the Concealed Books resulted in the compilation of old manuscripts and their revised editions. The above named works constitute the literature of the *rNying-ma-pa* which is available to us today.

NOTES TO PART I

[1] Shakabpa, *Tibet-a political history*, p. 27 ff.

[2] This king is to be supposed to have lived during the third century A.D. (Haarh, *Yar-luṅ dynasty*, p. 132). According to Shakabpa, op.cit., (p.24) he was born, however, in the year 173 A.D.

[3] Haarh, *Yar-luṅ dynasty*, p. 81.

[4] op. cit., p. 85

[5] Zürcher, *Buddhist conquest of China*, vol. 1, p. 81.

[6] op. cit. p. 199.

[7] op.cit., p. 409. n. 88.

[8] Tte text shows the Chinese sign for Chiaṅg for the Chinese sign of loc. cit.

[9] ......

[10] op. cit. p. 279.

[11] op. cit. p. 240.

[12] op. cit. p. 212.

[13] op. cit. p. 226.

[14] Snellgrove-Richardson, *Cultural histoiy of Tibet*, p. 71.

[15] Tucci, *Religionen*, p. 276 : there is the year 620 (?) reported, in Shakabpa, *Tibet—a political history* (p. 25) the year 630, and in Snellgrove-Richardson *Cultural history of Tibet* (p. 275) the year 627 A.D.

[16] cf. MBT II, p. 12 ff.

[17] DM fol. 17a/b.

[18] cf. Chattopadhyaya, *Atīśa and Tibet*, p. 291 and Tucci, Rin-c'en-bzaṅ-po e la rinascita del Buddhismo nel Tibet intorno al mille, p. 12 ff.

[19] Tucci, *Religionen*, p. 13 ff.

[20] MBT II, p. 32.

[21] Tucci, Religionen, p. 25 ff.

[22] Bacot, *La vie de Mar-pa*; Guenther, *The life and teaching of Naropa*;—, *The royal songs of Saraha*.

[23] "The following year (781 A.D.) an envoy came from T'u-fan (Tibet) and begged the Throne to send to his country learned monks to discourse on Buddhism" (Jan, Yün-Hua, *Chronicle of Buddhism*, p. 71)

[24] PJ pt. II, p. 170.

[25] Liebenthal, *The book of Chao*, p. XVI.

[26] Chan, Wing-Tsit, *Source book on Chronicle philosophy*, p. 344.

[27] Liebenthal, *The book of Chao*, p. 8 f.

[28] op.cit., p. 8 .

[29] op. cit., p. 17.

[30] GR p. 181 "*dbu-ma'i lta-ba la/ston-min-pa bya-ba dang / tsen-min-pa bya-ba gnyis-su byung-nas/*" "Concerning the Madhyamaka theory, both, the *sTon-min-pa* (Hva-shang and his disciples) as well as the *Tsen-min-pa* (Śāntarakṣita and his adherents) originated from it."

[31] MBT II, p. 44 f.

32 op. cit., p. 68 ff.

33 Simonsson, *Indo-tibetische Studien*, p. 233 ff.

34 Snellgrove-Richardson, *Cultural history of Tibet*, p. 196.

35 Guenther, *Saraha*, p. 44.

36 *TM* vol. Kha, *dkar-chag* fol. 3/4 and PK fol. 61a. 7 ff.

37 *TM* vol. Pha, DD *nang-dbang* fol. 3b.1.

38 Neumaier, bKa'-brgyad raṅ-byuṅ-raṅ-śar, ein rJogs-c'en Tantra, in *ZDMG*, p. 154 ff (1970).

39 cf. Guenther, *Naropa*, p. 267: "......thus insists on the harmony between action, speech and thought, which are called *vajra* because in this realm of discourse there is unbiased perspective (*thugs*), not opinionatedness; authentic communication (*gsung*), not empty verbiage; and significant being-in-the world (*sku*), not the anonymity of the mass man."

40 Communication by H.V. Guenther.

41 Fol. 61a.

42 Dagyab, *Dictionary* p. 586: *bžed-pa*—'*dod-pa* or *dgongs-pa* .

43 Reported according to the *TM* vol. Pha, DD *nang-dbang* fol. 3b ff.

44 fol. 61b.

45 *TM*, loc.cit.

46 tib. bSil-ba'i-tshal, a famous cremation ground near Bodh Gaya. The Buddhist mystics preferred this place for meditating (Grünwedel, Edelsteinmine, p. 108, 112).

47 Guenther, *Saraha*, p. 4.

48 This way of distribution implies a hidden meaning because the *Stūpa* signifies Buddha's body; and in regard to this body the *Stūpa* used to be filled with sacred books. According to this scheme of filling the *Stūpa* with books they were unearthed in later days by the Discoverers of Concealed Teachings (*gTer-ston*).

49 The original text was first published and translated into German by Neumaier, *ZDMG* 1970, p. 131 ff.

50 *DNg*, p. 102, 164.

51 Schiefner had translated it fiʁst 1869 "Tāranātha's Geschichte des Buddhismus in Indien." (p. 275). cf. CHATTOPADHYAYA, Tāranātha's History p. 345 f.

52 *gsang-sngags* means literally 'the secret formulas'. But it is a fact, that *gsang-sngags-gyi theg-pa* and *rdo-rje theg-pa* are synonymous, both expressions are also combined: *gsang-sngags rdo-rje theg-pa*. If one would stick to a word by word translation, one would miss the implications of the Tibetan term.

53 Guenther, *Buddhist philosophy*, p. 187 ff.

54 DC chapter II, fol. 48a.

55 fol. 61a ff.

56 reported according to the *PK* fol. 61a ff.

57 *KD*, p. 103.

58 op.cit., p. 89 ff.

59 *MBT*, II, p. 21 f, 60ff.

60 Communication by H.V. Guenther.

61 cf. Richardson in *KhG* pt. I, p. X: There it is ensured that dPa.

bo-gtsug-lag-phreng-ba, the author of the *KhG*, wrote his essay on the political history of Tibet by relying on ancient documents and inscriptions. "It is reasonable to assume that he also drew carefully and extensively on the old records of that most ancient Tibetan monasteries and sometimes quoted from them verbatim." Therefore it will be reasonable to suppose that he had also been painstaking in writing the historical development of his own religion.

[62] DC fol. 60a-69a.

[63] *KhG*, pt.I, p. 202 reports the queen's name as 'Od-ldan-ma'. These events happened in the year 360 after Buddha Śākyamuni's *Nirvāṇa*, according to *KhG*.

[64] Heiler, *Erscheinungsformen und Wesen der Religionen*, p. 491; on the legend of Sophia vide Conze, *Buddhist studies*, p. 207f; becoming pregnant of 'light' vide Widengren, *Mani und der Manichaismus*, p. 53 and 62.

[65] The following informations are given according to the DC loc. cit., (n.62).

[66] Guenther, *Naropa*, p. 134

[67] Commonly there are four empowerments (cf. Lessing-Wayman, *Fundamentals of Buddhist Tantra*, p. 309-325). By these empowerments the disciple obtains the authority to study and practise the mystic cycles.

[68] *KhG* pt. I, p. 203: *glegs-bam-du bkod*—composed in the form of books.

[69] *KhG* pt. I, p. 203: He was born to the west of Bodh Gaya in a village of the second grade (*rim-pa gnyis-pa'i grong*), his family was of brahmanical origin.

[70] This took place at the fountain of the river Ngan-tig in the year 540 after the *Nirvāṇa* of Buddha Śākyamuni (*KhG*).

[71] *KhG* I, p. 204: 24,000 verses.

[72] Guenther, *Naropa*, p. 2n.1.

[73] KhG I, p. 204: *rnar-rgyud* "ear Tantra" and *bśad-rgyud* "declaring Tantra".

[74] *KhG* loc.cit. "129 years".

[75] *KhG* loc.cit: The account of the *KhG* about the events that took place after the death of Śrīsiṃha is based on the statements in the *DNg*.

[76] Tāranātha, *KD* p. 58.; *DNg*, p. 754, 803 .

[77] *KD*, p. 88, passim: the other masters are also mentioned.

[78] *DNg*, p. 158: the '*Dus-pa-mdo* might be identical with the '*Dus-pa'i rgyud*, as the *rNying-ma-pas* do not distinguish between *mDo* (sūtra) and *rGyud* (*tantra*) consistently.

[79] p. 89 ff.

[80] *KhG* I, p. 204: "At this time a son was born to a house-holder in China; he was called Śrīsiṃha."

[81] *KhG* I, p. 204: This happened in the year 830 after the *parinirvāṇa* of Buddha Śākyamuni.

[82] *KhG* I, p. 204: He was incarnated after 125 years as 'Jam-dpal-bśes-gnyen the Younger.

[83] sLob-dpon Āryadeva was a disciple of Nāgārjuna, vide KD, p. 102.

[84] This instruction is a part of the *gNad-gtso-bo-la man-ngag*, as divided by 'Jam-dpal-bśes-gnyen.

[85] *KhG* I, p. 205: Jñānasūtra remembered the prophecy.

[86] *KhG* I, p. 205: Vimalamitra and Jñānasūtra covered the distance -usually taking nine months in one day because of their psychical faculties. Then, a Spiritual Being (*mKha'-'gro-ma*) showed to them the way to bKra-śis-khri-sgo and further on to the cremation ground Sil-byin where they met their master Śrīsiṃha.

[87] *KhG*, pt. I, p. 205, adds to *snyan-brgyud*, 'the oral tradition', *phyi-, nang-, gsang gsum-skor*, the 'cycles of exoteric, esoteric and secret teachings'.

[88] *rtogs-pa*: ,'To understand the presential value of mind as an idea is an exclusive concentration on it (*rtse-gcig*) and nyams; to understand it directly as it happens when all judgements and subjective evaluations are about to be suspended (*spros-bral*) is *rtogs-pa*." (Guenther, *Saraha*, p. 116 n. 42; see also by the same author sGam-po-pa, p. 12).

[89] *spros-pa* refers to the habit of the awareness to divide the sensual perception into subject and object. The four empowerments must be considered as a steadily growing disappearance of these propositions. This development becomes manifest in the outer sphere as a declining interest in ritual elements. (Guenther, *Naropa*, p. 4n. 3;—, *Saraha*, p. 77 n.2, 117 n. 42).

[90] *KhG*, pt. I, p. 206: The King dPal-byin invited him.

[91] A book with the title *gZer-bu* is mentioned in the *DNg* (p. 145) together with other ones which also belong to the Old School.

[92] *KhG*, pt.I, p. 206: "in the forest of the cremation ground Ba-sing"; this happened in the year 984 after Buddha Śākyamuni's *Nirvāṇa*.

[93] *DNg*, p. 533.

[94] *KhG*, pt. I, p. 206: *sems-nyid zang-thal-du song*, which has the same meaning as the expression in the *DC*.

[95] *KhG*, pt. I, p. 206: in the year 994 after Śākyamuni's *Nirvāṇa*.

[96] The same event is reported in the *KhG*, pt. I, p. 206: *o-dya-na-gyi yul rgya-mtsho gser-gyi bye-ma brdal-ba'i gling*.

[97] *KhG*, pt.I, p. 206: "in a Kashmirian village, where Barbarians and other illbred peoples [lived], near a rock, called gSer-gling."

[98] According to the language of existence-philosophy: "the intimate existence" (Guenther, *Naropa*, p. 73).

[99] *KhG*, I, p. 207: Vimalamitra is contemporaneous with King Khri-srong-lde-btsan.

[100] Suzuki, *Die grosse Befreiung*, p. 123 ff.

[101] Due to the *DC* fol. 42a.4 and fol. 90a.4.

[102] For the terminology cf. Guenther, *Naropa*, p. 119 n.1 and p. 64 n.1.

[103] Vol. *Kha* DK fol. 9a.1 .

[104] Cf. *DNg*, p. 352. The book *rDo-rje-sems-dpa'-sgyu-'phrul-drva-pa* is included in the *rNying-ma-rgyud-'bum*, Rin-chen-bzang-po translated the Tantra from Sanskrit into Tibetan.

[105] *DNg*, p. 103 f. gives a detailed history of the transmission of the *gSang-snying* Cycle. This refutes the doubts of Sum-pa-mkhan-po about the

authenticity of the *gSang-snying* tradition (cf. *PJ* Sarnath ed. p. 321 f.).

[106] *DNg* (p. 158) speaks of the "Cycle of Māyā", instead of the *sGyu-'phrul* cycle.

[107] *DNg*, p. 153.

[108] mChims-phu is a famous place near bSam-yas. When the Chinese Buddhist masters were expelled, the Chinese books were hidden there.

[109] *DNg*, p. 103, 104, 108.

[110] *DNg*, p. 103.

[111] *DNg*, p. 102, 164.

[112] *KD*, p. 109: Kukurāja is identical with Indrabhūti, the Middle One.

[113] *KD*, p. 97 f: Hūṃkara should be the same as *Ācārya* sMan-pa-źabs—Vaidyapāda.

[114] The basic text is mentioned in *DNg*, p. 102, 164.

[115] Due to the *DNg* p. 103 Indrabhūti (brGya-byin-sdong-po) wrote a commentary about *Myam-sbyor* (*Śrīsarvabuddhadsamaya-yogaḍākinīmāyāśambaratantrārthodaraṭikā*).

[116] Guenther, *Saraha*, p. 155 n. 62.

[116a]. Report according to the DC fol. 55b-56a.

[117] Neumaier, Raṅ-byuṅ raṅ-śar, ein rJogs-c'en Tantra, *ZDMG* 1970 p. 131 ff.

[118] *MBT*, II, p. 49, 64 ff.

[119] *DC* chapter IV fol. 91a-93b.

[120] *PJ* II (ed. Das), p. 173, line 5 ff.

[121] *Lha* does not mean an ordinary deity, but a spiritual, psychical power, which must be brought to realization on the way to gain Buddhahood (Guenther, Tibetan Buddhism without mystification, p.25).

[122] Haarh, *Yar-luṅ dynasty*, p. 57.

[123] Neumaier, *Matarḥ und Ma-mo*, p. 14 ff.

[124] A group of harmful deities.

[125] This is a part of the *bKa'-thang-sde-lnga* (cf. Catalogue of the Toyo Bunko Collection of Tibetan Works on History nr. 351-2618).

[126] This term includes a part of Tibetan Buddhist literature, cf. Neumaier, *Einige Aspekte der gTer-ma Literatur*, p. 852.

[127] PK fol. 62a.

[128] The *KhG*, I, p. 243 f. reports the same events as the PK fol. 62a.

[129] cf. Pt. I n. 113.

[130] *KD*, p. 103=Mañjuśrīmitra.

[130a] Śāntigarbha propagated the *Jam-dpal-sku* Tantra in Tibet This is a famous treatise included in the eighteen main Tantras. He also took part in the inauguration of bSam-yas (DNg, p. 106).

[131] Zürcher, *Buddhist conquest of China* pt. I, p. 146.

[132] Neumaier, *ZDMG*, 1970 p. 144 ff.

[133] *DC* fol. 59a.

[134] Account due to the *DC* fol. 56a-60a.

[135] *DNg*, p. 359, 361 ff., 385, 390, 553, 856, 869; Tucci, *Religionen*, p.61

[136] Lva-ba-pa=Kambala; his whole hagiography is given in Tāranātha's *KD* p. 53 ff. In the *DNg* (p. 362) he is called the "sleeping bhikṣu", hearing the *Guhya-samāja* Tantra.

[137] *KD*, p. 53.

[138] *Sahaja-siddhi* might be translated somewhat like 'spontaneous all comprising awareness'.

[139] *DNg*, p. 552 speaks of a commentary of the basic text (*rtsa-'grel*).

[140] *KD*, p. 54-55.

[141] In *KD*, he is also called Lalitavajra (loc. cit.); it is also said that there does not exist an account of him.

[142] *KD*, p. 109.

[143] *DNg*, p. 159.

[144] *DNg*, p. 137.

[145] *DNg*, p. 353.

[146] Kosala=province of Oudh (Lamotte, Histoire du Bouddhism Indien, p. 12).

[147] cf. Pt. II, n. 246.

[148] Bru-śa is nowadays called the Land of the Hunzas (Snellgrove-Richardson, A cultural history, p. 31).

[149] *DNg*, p. 104, further p. 153, 158, 534.

[150] *DC* fol. 93b.

[151] *DNg* in the index is quoted p. 136, this is a mistake, p. 137 is right, cf. also p. 199.

[152] *DNg*, p. 159 f.

[153] Snellgrove-Richardson, *A cultural history*, p. 118 ff, 132 ff.

[154] *DC* fol. 60a ff. and fol. 93b ff.

[155] *DC*: *'phags-yul nub-phyogs o-rgyan-gyi yul dha-na-ko-sa'i-gling zes-bya-bar* (fol. 60a.6).

[156] Mitscherlich, *Auf dem Weg zur vaterlosen Gesellschaft*, p. 322 f.

[157] Thomas, *Tibetan literary texts and documents*, pt. I, p. 3 ff.

[158] *DNg*, p. 22 and 25.

[159] *DNg*, p. 168 and 191.

[160] For the person of gNubs Nam-mkha'-snying-po cf. *MBT*, II, p. 21.

[161] *DC*, fol. 80b.

[162] Identical with *Sems-sde-ma-bu-bco-brgyad* (*DNg*, p. 534).

[163] cf. Guenther, *Saraha*, p. 22: " 'Buddha' (*sangs-rgyas*) is used in the purely philosophical sense of 'felt knowledge' in which a subject as such and not as this or that specific (empirical) subject knows itself as subject in its act of being aware. It does not refer to the person known by the title 'Buddha'. A term coming closest to what is understood by 'Buddha' in Tibetan would be 'Buddhahood'."

[164] Pt. I, p. 24.

[165] For comprehending the meaning of *rtogs-pa*: Padma-dkar-po in his *Phyag-chen-gyi-zin-bris* fol. 7a explains as follows: "To understand it (the presential value of mind by hearing and thinking) directly as it happens when all judgments and subjective evaluations are about to be suspended (*spros-bral*) is *rtogs-pa*" (Guenther, *Saraha*, p. 117).

166 The same facts are reported by Tucci in *MBT*, II, p. 115 and in KhG, I, p. 208.

167 Haarh, *Yar-luṅ dynasty*, p. 57.

168 *DNg*,, p. 167.

169 *DNg*, p. 170.

170 Identical with the report in *DNg*, p. 170.

171 For his dates cf. *DNg*, p. 170 ff.

172 Cf. the short outlines in *DNg*, p. 167-172.

173 The same supposes *DNg*, p. 171.

174 *DNg*, p. 173 reports the same lineage (*brgyud-pa*) under the nam 'klong-sde'.

175 *DNg*, p. 173 calls the grotto Va-seng-ge-brag.

176 The full biography of Dseng Dharmabodhi is given in *DNg*, p. 175-186 together with the dates of his life (born 1052), for the content of the teachings discussed here see op.cit, p. 178.

177 *DNg*, p. 171.

178 *DC* is here in line with *DNg*, loc.cit.

179 Here the report on the lineage ends in *DNg* (p. 191) because its author is the last member in the line of transmission.

180 *DNg*, p. 191.

181 Guenther, *Saraha*, p. 32.

182 *DC* fol. 107a ff.

183 Tucci, *Validity*, p. 318; Haarh, *Yar-luṅ dynasty*, p. 57, there all variants of her name are given.

184 A *mKha'-'gro-snying-thig* is cited in *DNg* p. 497.

185 *rDo-rje-phag-mo* is in Sanskrit *Vajravārāhī*. She signifies pure wisdom (*prajñā*) visualized by the Yogi.

186 *DNg*, p. 107, 167 cites Ting-nge-'dsin-bzang-po as disciple of Vimlamitra; op.cit., p. 192 reports his long life; also see Tucci, *Religionen*, 28, 53.

187 *KhG*, I, p. 208.

188 *DNg*, p. 192.

189 Ferrari, *Guide*, p. 110 n. 114.

190 *GT* rNying-ma-pa chapter fol. 8a.1.

191 *DNg*, p. 167 f, 191 ff.

192 *DC* fol. 253b (introduction to chapter 6) see translation in pt. II, p.102.

193 Toussaint, *Le dict de Padma* p. 376.

194 *ZDMG*, Suppl. I, p. 849-862.

195 See translation of the introduction to chapter 6 of *DC* in pt. II; the same opinion is expressed by mKhas-grub-rje in *rGyud--sde-spyi'i rnam-bzag-pa* (ed. by Lessing-Wayman p. 54: *thugs bden-pa'i stobs-kyis byin-gyis-brlabs-pa'i bka' ni/ bcom-ldan-'das-kyis bden-pa'i stobs thugs-kyis brjod-pa'i mthus / ri dang/ śing dang/ rtsig-pa sogs-las chos-kyi-smra byung-ba lta-bu'o//*) "The Pronouncements endowed with the operative truth of Buddha's responsiveness: When the Bhagavat let become manifest the operative truth through his

responsiveness then the *Dharma* is caused to become apparent through mountains, trees and walls."

[196] Benz, *Visionen*, p. 104 ff.

[197] op.cit., p. 150.

[198] op.cit., p. 90.

[199] Weizsäcker, *Biologische Basis*, p. 28 f.

[200] Guenther, *Naropa*, p. 160 ff.

[201] Weizsäcker, *Biologische Basis*, p. 25.

[202] Guenther, *Naropa*, p. 271.

[203] *GT* rNying-ma-pa chapter fol. 10b.

[204] Toussaint, *Le dict de Padma*, chapter XCII.

[205] cf. Vostrikov, *Literature*, p. 125, 371.

[206] *DC* fol. 258a.

[207] *GT* rNing-ma-pa chapter fol. 7a.

[208] *TPS*, p. 87.

[209] Cf. pt. I chapter 2.7.

[210] Cf. pt. II, p. 229.

[211] Tucci, *Validity*, p. 312 f; Haarh, *Yar-luṅ dynasty*, p. 58.

[212] Tt fol. 185a.

[213] Cf. pt. II, p 204 f.

[214] G. Smith, Introduction in: *Kongtrul's Encyclopaedia of Indo-Tibetan culture*, p. 28 ff. (ed. by L. Chandra).

[215] loc. cit.

[216] Tt fol. 232 b.

PART II

THE TRANSMISSION OF THE CONCEALED TEACHINGS AND THEIR PROMULGATORS
(11th—19th century)

THE HISTORY OF THE PROFOUND NEW TRANSMISSION (*nye-brgyud*) OF THE CONCEALED TREASURES AND BOOKS (*gter-ma*) BASED ON THE TEACHING OF THE SŪTRAS ONLY

(A translation of the 6th chapter of bDud-'joms Rin-po-che's 'Rise of the Old School')

1. INTRODUCTION

STATEMENTS ON THE CONCEALED TREASURES AND BOOKS IN THE SŪTRAS (DC)

In the *kLu'i-rgyal-pos žus-pa'i mdo*[1] it is stated: "The important Concealed Treasures and Books (*gter-chen-po*) are inexhaustible in that uninterrupted continuation of the Lineage of the Three Precious Jewels (i.e. the Buddha, the Doctrine and the Community). The important Concealed Treasures and Books are inexhaustible in making immeasurable beings of the future really perceive the Teachings. The important Concealed Treasures and Books are as inexhaustible in offering delight to the beings. The important Concealed Treasures and Books are as inexhaustible as are the heavenly spaces. It is in view of these four statements that the important Concealed Treasures are inexhaustible." Thus the essential features of the Concealed Treasures and Books have been pointed out. —The same is stated in the *'Phags-pa bsod nams thams-cad sdud-pa'i ting-nge-'dsin-gyi mdo*;[2] "The great beings, the great Bodhisattvas longing for the immaculate, radiant enlightening Doctrine will seize the mystic formulas (*gzungs*)[3] and the countless approaches to the Doctrine which are hidden as Concealed Treasures in mountains, hills and in the midst of trees, and form them into books."—Thus the Doctrine of the Concealed Treasures (*gter-chos*), the places where the Treasures were hidden, and the persons bringing them forth were concisely formulated. If one's mind is really sublime, one will recognize the Doctrine, which is to be found in the heavenly spaces, on walls or trees, even when no Buddha lives on earth. The cosmic Doctrine (*gnam-chos*) is thus indicated. The essentials, the real meanings, the enumerations and the necessity of the Concealed Books and Treasures were delivered furthermore in Sūtras and Tantras which will be known everywhere again and again. They are likewise known in India and Tibet. It is not fitting to maintain that some persons have composed them recently in Tibet.[4]

NECESSITY OF HIDING THE PRONOUNCEMENTS (*bka'-ma*)

Now to the necessity of hiding (the Treasures and Books): It is stated in the *Chu-klung-rol-pa'i mdo*: "The main features of my Doctrine are flowing from heart to heart, which also is called the heart of the earth. Should thus a heretical, pig-headed fellow disturb the true significance (of the Doctrine) the flow of it will not be cut off."—Further on in the Prophecy on Concealed Treasures and Books (*gter-lung*) by Chos-rgyal Ratna-gling-pa[5] (1403-1479) it is stated: "The essentials are extremely profound and through them the goal of deliverance is attained. In general because the Tibetans love all new things, and in particular because the beings deserve pity in this evil age (*kaliyuga*) the Books and Treasures were hidden throughout the country, in the middle of it and abroad. Prayers were spoken that qualified disciples may discover them. It may be that in future times dialectical quibblers, Yogis and other narrow-minded, haughty and self-praising people will disparage the Concealed Books and Treasures, although in these evil times the followers of the Doctrine are mostly guided by these very teachings. These instructions are profound, satisfying and comprehensive, and do not deviate from reality. The beings will gain deliverance (by hearing) a single instruction. This is certain! When qualified disciples with matured fate (*las-sad-pa*) think of their own death, they will practise the Doctrine of Concealed Treasures (*gter-chos*). In a single lifetime they will gain the road to deliverance (*thar-lam*). Prayers are uttered for the qualified ones who will follow the Teachings of the Concealed Treasures in these evil times so that they may see the face of the Guru presently. They are suitable persons because of their previous deeds; therefore they meditate joyfully. This very saying of mine is more precious than a jewel of gold !"— The same is stated also by countless other Concealed Books.

In these evil times the Pronouncements (*bka'-ma*) are like milk which is being sold at the bazaar, because the religious empowerments (*dbang-bskur*) and instructions (*gdams-ngag*) are vulgarized. The operational basis of a great blessing is spoiled because in many cases the transmissions are interrupted and the pledges broken. On account of this the great Master of Uḍḍiyāna (i.e. Padmasambhava) adopted this or that actual being (*sPrul-sku*) as his follower and enabled it to be a Discoverer of Concealed Teachings [to bring forward] these Treasures. He bestowed on the Discoverer all the empowerments which bring spiritual maturity and deliverance (*smin-grol*), and instructed him thoroughly. Thus the profound Doctrine, the Discoverer brings forward, is like a Spiritual Being's (*mkha'-'gro-ma*) breath not yet vanished, it is the New and Direct Transmission (*nye-brgyud*) with radiant blessings and without any counterpart.

THE SIX LINEAGES OF TRANSMISSION

Now, with reference to these Concealed Teachings (*gter ma*): they are connected with the three special lineages of tradition in addition to three common lineages, i.e. the lineage of Buddha's Intentionality (cf. pt. I chapter 2.1.), the lineage of the Symbolical Transmission by Spiritual Beings (*mKha'-'gro-ma* and *Rig-'dsin*) (cf. pt. I, 2.2.), and the lineage of the Oral Transmission by Human Beings (cf. pt. I, 2.3-2.6). Therefore the Concealed Teachings are stated as being connected with six lineages. The three common ones have been pointed out above. [The three special ones are:]

1. The Empowerment by Prayer (*smon-lam dbang-bskur*): A (specified) person will be authorized to bring forward these Concealed Teachings. For this purpose a prayer of true statements was uttered.

2. The Prophecy that this Person is Endowed with the Pronouncements (*bka'-babs lung-bstan*): The person removing the Concealed Treasure is encouraged (by Padmasambhava who had directed) the whole intentionality of his primeval

awareness of Reality, which he had gained in his own psychic sphere (*mtshon-bya don-gyi ye-śes*), to this person. Thus, (this individual) is enabled to remove (the Concealed Treasures).

3. The Seal Given by Spiritual Beings (*mKha'-'gro gtad-rgya*): After the literal symbols have been formed into sentences they will be bestowed on the individual Protector of the Concealed Treasures, and hidden in diamond rocks, in mysterious lakes, and unchanging boxes. The Treasures were sealed so that they will be invisible. When later on the time has come for fulfilling the prophecy, and the power of the prayer has matured, and when the fruits of the former acts have ripened (*las sad-pa*), and when the Protector of the Concealed Treasures has uttered his admonitions, then the box with the Treasure inside, will be presented to this very Discoverer of Concealed Treasures; there may be a literal hint (*kha-byang*) or not.

DECLARING THE THEORY OF THE CONCEALED TREASURES

Now, concerning the profound teaching of the Concealed Treasures: They are delivered mostly by literal symbols in the manner of the Spiritual Beings' script (*mKha'-'gro brda'-yig*). None other than the qualified person will be able to bring forth the Concealed Treasure. To this purpose the Great Master of Uḍḍiyāna had actually impressed on (the Discoverer of Concealed Treasures) the lines of his word's seal. Therefore the lineage is not interrupted by ordinary men; the symbols [of the Concealed Teachings] are genuine, and the sentences are not disorderly, and the content is not erroneous. If the Spiritual Beings' mysterious symbols (*mKha'-'gro- gsang-ba'i brda'*) are translated into human language, and if the content is profound, then the blessing will be great. Persons who are not qualified, however sensible they may be otherwise, are like blind persons describing an elephant. What these people have to say does not withstand criticism. On account of this, the person who discovers the Concealed Treasure (*gTer-ston*) is only [to be comprehended] by great confidence, as this [matter] goes far beyond the common understanding.

PADMASAMBHAVA AND HIS CONSECRATED CONSORT YE-ŚES-MTSHO-RGYAL

Here in Tibet the mysterious Vajrayāna is the heart of the Doctrine in general; countless disciples, however, were guided by the efficacy (*phrin-las*) of the Concealed Teachings. The leader is the second Buddha, Padmasambhava. In the *Myang-'das das-kyi-mdo* is stated: "Twelve years after my *Nirvāṇa*, on an island in the lake of Dhanakośa, a person will be born who will be greater than I am." This great Guru is a man who has not only attained the five stages of the method of deliverance (*lam-gyi rim-lnga*), and who not only is an exalted one, having reached the stages of saintly perfection of a Bodhisattva (*sa*), but who has conducted by various methods men and other beings who are difficult to educate; it may be that he has become actually visible as Buddha *Amitābha* or as the King of the Śākya. For this reason not even sublime ones are able to recognize his course of life and deliverance (*rnam-thar*). I have said something about him above. The special greatness of his action is, that he has been hiding religious objects, treasures, medicines, things for astrological divination and for devotion, as countless Concealed Treasures in India, Nepal and Tibet, thinking always of the Doctrine and of the disciples of future times. As there are the three Yogas and the numberless appropriate Tantras, the traditional commentaries, instructions and rituals, he has, above all, been preaching the common and the special approaches to the Doctrine here in Tibet. Of whatever kind the disciples have been, [Padmasambhava] knew the actual right method [for educating him].

dByings-phyug Ye-śes-mtsho-rgyal, the mistress of all mysteries, had been gathering the Pronouncements (*bka'-ma*) by seizing them through the ability of not forgetting anything. In the symbols of the Spiritual Beings (*mKha'-'gro brda'i yi-ge*) she wrote down treatises on the Five Methods of Spiritual Maturing (*rigs-lnga*). She hid them in various receptacles and impressed on them an undiminishing seal. Guru [Padmasambhava] together with his elevated consort (*yum*) (Ye-śes-mtsho-rgyal) had been hiding [the Concealed Treasures) in appropriate places (*gter-gnas*), entrusting them to the Protector of the Treasure (*gter-srung*). When Guru [Padmasambhava] reached [the miraculous sphere] rNga-yab-gling, Ye-śes-mtsho-rgyal remained here for a further one hundred worldly years, hiding countless Concealed Treasures (*gter-kha*) in the upper and lower countries of Tibet and in her midland, and she prohibited the remove [of the Concealed Treasures].

ORIGIN OF CONCEALED TREASURES HIDDEN IN THE EARTH (*sa-gter*)

Later, the great scholar-saint Vimalamitra, the King Khri-srong-lde-btsan and his disciples, the great Translator Vairocana, gNubs Sangs-rgysas-ye-śes, gNam-mkha'-snying-po, gNyags Jñānakumāra, sNa-nam rDo-rje-bdud-'joms, Nyang-ban Ting-dsin-bzang-po and others also had been hiding mysterious, Concealed Treasures and Books. They gave a blessing for the benefit of all beings, so that also in the future the right might come to guide the beings and to practise the Concealed Teachings. When the prophecies and prayers had been uttered, then, one after the other, the Master with his followers had come into existence as actual beings (*sPrul-sku*) whose families and ways of life were not determined. They were propagandists of the Doctrine. This is the main way in which the Concealed Books and Treasures, hidden in the earth (*sa-gter*), have originated.

ORIGIN OF THE PROFOUND AND VISIONARY CONCEALED TEACHINGS (*dgongs-pa'i gter*)

The beings should hear the Doctrine's sound from birds, trees, from the light, and the heavenly space, and especially through the prayers of the Bodhisattvas.[6] As the power of their prayers is strong, and as there is no reason for them to be lacking in the Doctrine, they continuously hear the sounds of the Doctrine from the noise of the elements and the deer; this is effected by the might and power of their prayers. The Buddhas and Bodhisattvas show [the Discoverer of Concealed Treasures] their countenance and in this way they preach them the Doctrine.

THE DISCOVERERS OF CONCEALED TEACHINGS (*gTer-ston*)

It is stated in the *bSod-nams-thams-cad-sdud-pa-ting-nge- 'dsin-gyi mdo.*[7] "Listen Dri-med-pa'i-gzi-brjid, the great Bodhisattvas longing for the Doctrine have sublime thoughts and are full of reverence. Although the Elevated Buddha stays in another world, he shows his countenance to enable them to perceive the Doctrine."—Due to the fact that the mind is so elevated there is only a single pure vision, no impure one. [The Discoverers of Concealed Teachings] gain boundless and profound instructions because the three main roots of religious training[8] (i.e. the Guru, the Tutelary Deity, and the Spiritual Beings) as well as the superior gods continue to teach them (the Discoverers) the Doctrine in a marvellous way at any time. As these [Discoverers] are suitable to propagate [the Teachings] to qualified ones, they make visible every special part of the Doctrine as an operating field appropriate to the individual wishes of the beings. This is referred to in the hagiographies of the Discoverers of Concealed Treasures (*gTer-ston*), of the Mystics (*Grub-thob*), and in those of the scholars (*dGe-ba'i-bśes-gnyen*) who had an unprejudiced attitude (*ris-med*) and were [followers of] the Old or New Tantras in India or in Tibet. Accordingly [these Concealed Treasures] are renowned as Visionary Concealed Teachings (*dgongs-pa'i gter*). Thus in the Sūtras is stated: "Listen Mañjuśrī, just as the four elements come forth from the cosmic repository, so the whole of reality (*chos thams-cad*) arises from a Buddha's spiritual significance (*thugs*).[9] Therefore the meaning of the Concealed Treasures has to be perceived as a communicative one."—In accordance with that statement it is said, that the Concealed Teachings of the Doctrine pour out from the undulating movement of intentionality towards the elevated persons. It is stated in the *Chos-yang-dag-par-sdud-pa'i-mdo*: "On account, of the pure thoughts of the Bodhisattvas and their very wish, their own minds bring forth all Teachings according to the instructions (*gdams-ngag*)." In another Sūtra it is stated: "If one were to find the firm basis of truth, then a hundred thousand Concealed Teachings would pour out from one's mind." Thus it is stated, and accordingly great scholars and mystics came into being, endowed with countless profound instructions of thorough intentionality. In brief, these elevated Discoverers may open the approaches to the Doctrine, to jewels, and ritual objects as they like. At the end of these evil times they will grasp the revered Doctrine by means of a wonderful activity furnished with the four ways of liberation. Even if the Teachings of the Vinaya (i.e. the rules of monastic life) and the Sūtras will cease to exist, the Teachings of the mystic Vajrayāna will not come to an end. It is stated in the Guru's Sentences (*guru'i gsung*) : "In these evil times the Doctrine will be sheltered from coming to an end through the Concealed Treasures."—In other words, until the appearance of the fifth Leader's (i.e. Buddha *Maitreya's*) Teachings, the activity of the profound Concealed Treasures will not come to an end. This is said so in general.

Now to the performance of Wisdom-Holders and Mystics unearthing the Concealed Treasures. I was not able to discuss at full length the scanty prophecies about the Discoverers together with their coming in time and their omina as stated in the *Padma-bka'i-thang-yig*,[10] nor the hagiographies of those who are not obviously referred to in this book, but who are nevertheless regarded as determining and well-known persons. On these topics one may consult former and later editions of the *gTer-ston brgya-rtsa'i rnam-thar*. The stories and transmissions of some of the most famous Mystics (*Grub-thob*) endowed with the Pronouncements (*bka'-babs-pa*) are contained in these works. In the sequel I shall point out the essentials of some of the most important Mystics who prepared the way for the Teachings of the two divisions of the Old Translations (i.e. those of the Old School) that is the tradition of the Concealed Treasures (*gter-ma*) and the one of the Pronouncements (*bka'-ma*).

2. HAGIOGRAPHY OF SANGS-RGYAS-BLA-MA (ca. 1000-1080), THE FIRST DISCOVERER OF CONCEALED TREASURES

(Tt) THE PROPHECY

It[11] is stated in the *Padma-bka'-thang-yig* : "On mTse'o-bar-gyam-nag in La-stod[12] eight or ten generations after King Khri-srong-lde-btsan (755-797), a famine, pestilence and a great plague will break out. This Concealed Treasure is hidden in gLo-bo-dge-skar.[13] A sign will be shown that it will not remain longer there and should be taken away. The Discoverer Sangs-rgyas-bla-ma[14] will come." So states the prophecy.

(DC+Tt) FORMER INCARNATIONS AND BIRTH

Sangs-rgyas-bla-ma was the first of all the Discoverers of Concealed Treasures and Books. He was also the first of thirteen incarnations of rGyal-sras-lha-rje.[15] He was born in mTsho-bar in La-stod about the time of the second half of the lifetime of the great Translator Rin-chen-bzang-po (958-1055).[16] He lived like a follower of the Tantras (*sNgags-pa*) but had his head shaved like a venerable [monk].[17]

ACTIVITY AS DISCOVERER OF CONCEALED TEACHINGS

[Sangs-rgyas-bla-ma] got [a Concealed Book] on *bLa-rdsogs-thugs-gsum* from the rooftree of the temple at gLo-bo-dge-skar in mNga'-ris. He also took out the *rTsa-gsum-dril-sgrub-brtan-gzigs* from the shoulder of the nearby rock rTa-mgrin. From Khog-glang in Thang-ban he brought forth the *rTa-mgrin-dregs-pa-zil-gnon* together with many rituals of the Sūtra-system which were translated from the Chinese.[18] He got also lists of synonyms (*kha-sgyur*). Wandering to the provinces dBus and gTsang he accomplished his prosperous actions for the beings.

HIS DEATH AND THE FATE OF HIS FAMILY

[Sangs-rgyas-bla-ma] remained on earth for about eighty years. His ceremonial dagger (*gter-phur*) was at Tsā-ri mTsho-dkar,[19] and it is said that Chos-rje-gling-pa[20] had still seen it in later days. Sangs-rgyas-bla-ma's family stayed in the country of La-stod for many subsequent years. Obviously the Discoverer Sangs-rgyas-'bar[21] was also of this family. Afterwards only a few and small Sūtras were read constantly by the Tantrics [of this family] but not a single book of the religious empowerments (*dbang*) and of the commentaries of the oral tradition (*lung*) was preserved.

REVIVAL OF SANGS-RGYAS-BLA-MA'S TEACHINGS

The Master of Uḍḍiyāna, the sage of the three aspects of time (i.e. Padmasambhava) and his disciples had been perceiving through primeval wisdom, and had still retained an unchangeable pity, so they demonstrated a special feeling towards the Tibetan people at these evil times. For that reason the pity of Vimalamitra and of the three kings [Srong-btsan-sgam-po, Khri-srong-lde-btsan, and Ral-pa-can] (*mnga'-bdag mes gsum*[22]) made itself felt without any hindrance.

Padma-'od-gsal-mdo-sngags-gling-pa[23] (1820-1892), the great initiator of the ocean of profound Concealed Books took encouragement in the firm prophecy that he would master the Teachings of the Seven Currents of Pronouncements (*bka'-babs-bdun*), and that he would grasp by himself, or through transmission, all Concealed Teachings revealed by the hundreds of Discoverers. This prophecy has come true; again and again opportunities were offered him. This great Discoverer seized the essentials of these Concealed Teachings, i.e. the scroll (*śog-ser*) of the twenty-one questions and answers of the *rTsa-gsum-dril-sgrub*.[24] He thought fit to revise the basic text (*gter-gźung*), and in accordance with the intentions of the basic text he evolved rituals and empowerments in connection with the offering of sacrificial cakes (*gtor-dbang*).[25] He propagated these books; nowadays they are included in the *Rin-chen-gter-gyi-mdsod-chen-po* ('The Great Treasure of Precious Concealed Teachings').

(Tt) Mercifully I[26] partook of [these Teachings] and allowed them to be included in the *Rin-chen-gter-gyi-mdsod-chen-po*. These Concealed Teachings were handed down to the great Discoverer mChog-gyur-[bde-chen-źig-po]-gling-pa[27] (1829-1870)— and to other tolerant Bodhisattvas through Padma-'od-gsal-mdo-sngags-gling-pa. In this way the Concealed Teachings of the first Discoverer [Sangs-rgyas-bla-ma] were transmitted to the evil times we live in. This is a wonder and a lucky token to be hailed with gratitude.

3. HAGIOGRAPHY OF GRVA-PA-MNGON-ŚES (ca. 1012-1090), THE DISCOVERER OF THE FAMOUS MEDICAL WORK *RGYUD-BŹI*.

(Tt) PROPHECY

"The Dsing[28] and the Chinese will raid the Tibetan country

coming forth like ants from a broken ant-hill. This Concealed Book is hidden in the three chapels of Jo-mo-gling.[29] A sign will come that it shall not remain longer and shall be taken away. The discoverer of the Concealed Books and treasures will be Grva-pa-mgon-śes.[30] He will found one hundred and twenty-eight temples on earth, and he will lay the foundation of another temple (*gtsug-lag-khang*) in the lowlands of Grva. The king will appoint him proprietor of this newly founded temple."
—This is stated about the Discoverer Grva-pa-mgon-śes.

(DC+Tt) FORMER INCARNATIONS AND BIRTH

Grva-pa-mgon-śes was an incarnation of Śud-bu-dpal-gyi-seng-ge[31] and of the great Translator (*Lo-chen*) Vairocana. Before the first sexagesimal cycle had begun, he was born to rDo-rje-spre'u-chung of the mChims family[32] at gYo-ru-gra'i-skyid[33] in 1012 A.D.

HIS YOUTH

When he was still young, his knowledge of the elevated Doctrine awoke and he joined the religious college of bSam-yas. Yam-śud-rgyal-ba-'od who had been a disciple of kLu-mes[34] bestowed on him the monastic vows. He was called Grva-pa because his native country was Grva; further he was named mNgon-śes because he knew the Abhidharmakośa (*mngon*). After having taken the monastic vows he became famous by the name dBang-phyug-'bar.

HIS ACTIVITY IN DISCOVERING CONCEALED BOOKS

He fetched the cycles of *Dsam-dmar-gsang-sgrub* and *gNod-sbyin-rdo-rje-bdud-'dul* together with the Tantra and the guidance for meditative realization (*sgrub-thabs*) from above the door of the main temple of bSam-yas, which is called dBu-rtse. According to the prophecy of Źang-blon, it was from the pillar Bum-pa-can in the middle storey of the main temple dBu-rtse in bSam-yas that in particular he took the main book of the *rGyud-bźi*[35] which deals with medicine (*gso-ba-rig-pa*). This took place three hours after midnight on the fifteenth day of the seventh month in the year 1038. He copied the last book (i.e. the *rGyud-bži*), and replaced the original in its place. He concealed the copy he had made for one year.

TRANSMISSION OF THE RGYUD-BZI

Later on Grva-pa-mngon-śes presented this copy to *dGe-bśes* Khu-ston Dar-ma-grags from Yar-klung. After the second king of the Tibetan physicians, gYu-thog Yon-tan-mgon-po,[36] had mastered these teachings (*bka'-babs*), their effects spread widely. This fact itself is a miracle that surpasses imagination.

THE FOUNDING OF TEMPLES AND RELIGIOUS COLLEGES

Having practised a meditative realization (*sgrub-thabs*) of *Jambhala*,[37] the god of wealth, he obtained golden things through this spiritual potency. In the centre of the valley of Grva he founded a large religious college, called the venerable Grva-thang.[38] The golden things he had obtained were used for financing the college. This is only one example of his founding many monasteries. He looked like a great scholar (*dGe-ba'i-bśes-gnyen=Kalyāṇamitra*), because he was the master of these monasteries and of the religious college at bSam-yas.

TRANSMISSION OF HIS TEACHINGS

The transmission of the empowerments (*dbang*) and oral commentaries (*lung*) of the cycle *gNod-sbyin-rdo-rje-bdud-'dul*, and the transmission of the defining commentaries (*bśad-lung*) on the medical treatises *rGyud-bži* remained uninterrupted in its entirety.

(Tt) I (sKong-sprul) also partook in this transmission. The venerable bLa-ma mDo-sngags-gling-pa mastered a short, but basic and profound, treatise on the meditative realization (*sgrub-thabs*) of *Vajrapāṇi* in his red appearance (*Phyag-rdor-dmar-po'i-sgrub-thabs*).

4. HAGIOGRAPHY OF NYANG-RAL NYI-MA-'OD-ZER (1124-1192), THE FIRST OF THE FIVE DISCOVERER KINGS

(Tt) THE PROPHECY

"A troublesome time will come to a great country. The Tantrics will teach falsities by practising magic. Holy figures and religious books will be given as blood money for having killed a man. The Tantrics will lead the beings on the path of rebirth while roaming about in the upper and lower parts of the villages. A Concealed Treasure is hidden in Srin-mo-sbar-rjes-mkho-mthing.[39] A sign will be shown that it is not to remain there, but that it is to be taken away. There will come the actual being (*sPrul-sku*), a *mNga'-bdag* (i.e. a ruler) who will be called Nyang-ral. So it will happen."—Such a prophecy was given by the great *Ācārya* Padmasambhava, surrounded by the Five Kings of Discoverers of Concealed Treasures (*gTer-ston-rgyal-po lnga*) and a hundred servants.[40]

(DC+Tt) NYI-MA-'OD-ZER ONE OF THE FIVE DISCOVERER-KINGS

The prophecy on the Five Kings of Discoverers and the Three Most Important Actual Beings (*mChog-gi sprul-sku-rnam gsum*) is as follows: "The first of them is the well-known Nyi-ma-'od-zer;[41] having made up his mind, he entered his next existence as Tshangs-pa-lha'i-me-tog."

BIRTH AND CHILDHOOD

Nyi-ma-'od-zer was born at Jed-sa-ser-dgon[42] which belongs to the territory of Lho-brag gTam-śul in the year 1124. His father was Nyang-ston Chos- kyi-'khor-lo and his mother Padma-bde-ba-rtsal. At a tender age he abundantly demonstrated testimonies of wonder.

VISIONS

At the age of eight he had visions of the exalted Śākyamuni, *Avalokiteśvara* and Padmasambhava. He passed a whole month having such visions. Especially he envisaged Guru Rin-po-che (i.e. Padmasambhava) riding on a white horse whose legs were supported by four Spiritual Beings (*mKha'-'gro-ma*). He bestowed on Nyi-ma-'od- zer the four empowerments[43] (*dbang-bskur*), by using the nectar from the ritual flask (*bum-pa bdud-rtsi*). Simultaneously there came three portents: the sky opened, the earth quaked, and the mountains trembled. At this point [Nyi-ma-'od-zer] displayed many life-styles (*spyod-pa*). Everybody thought him to be insane. From his father he heard the ritual of the empowerment of *Hayagrīva* (*rTa-mgrin*). When he was practising this meditation (*sgrub-pa*) at 'Dsed-phu-gangs-ra[44] he saw the countenance of this divine power (*lha*). Nyi ma-'od-zer's ceremonial dagger re-sounded with the neighing of a horse. He marked the rocks with imprints of his hands and feet.—When [Nyi-ma-'od-zer] had arrived at the rock rMa-bo-cog-gi-brag,[45] in accordance with the Spiritual Beings' prophecy, Ye-śes-mkha'-gro confer-red on him the name Nyi-ma-'od-zer. Since that time he has been well-known by this name.

ACTIVITY AS DISCOVERER OF CONCEALED BOOKS AND TREASURES

The Yogi dBang-phyug-rdo-rje, an actual being (*sPrul-pa*) of the Precious Master [Padmasambhava], gave him a list of the places where the Concealed Books could be found (*kha-byang*), another list of Hidden Books (*yang-byang*) that had been hidden twice, and a paper on the essentials of these Concealed Books (*gnad-yig*). He urged him to work on this subject. In former days, at the hiding place (*gter-gnas*) of Brag-srin-mo-sbar-rje, Grva-pa-mnogn-śes (1012-1090)[46] and Ra-śag gTer-ston[47] had received the lists of the Concealed and Twice Con-cealed Books. Therefore Nyi-ma-'od-zer proceeded to this place. He stayed the night there. The next morning a woman came who was the actual being (*sPrul-pa*) of Ye-śes-mtsho-rgyal.[48] She led a white mule which was loaded with two closed trunks. She took a casket, covered with tiger-skin, out of one of the trunks and offered it to the venerable Nyi-ma-'od-zer. When he had discovered the door of the hiding place, he perceived a little box made of copper, an earthen vessel, holy figures, relics and many different jewels. He took from the copper-chest a figure of *Avalokiteśvara* (*Thugs-rje-chen-po*), the Great Merciful One, and a figure of Guru Padmasambhava in both his mild and fierce aspects (*zi-drag*). Out of the earthen vessel he obtained a figure of the Protector *Mahākāla*[49] and many evil spells (*ngan-sngags*). From the chest with the tiger-skin he took many books about the Spiritual Beings (*mKha'-'gro'i chos-skor*). Later on, the venerable Nyi-ma-'od-zer received from a trader a finger that previously had been broken off from a figure. Behind the figure of *Vairocana* in mKho-mthing[50] he discovered a dark brown chest and another whitish one. From the dark brown chest he took the Tantra, the oral commentary (*lung*), and the instructions (*man-ngag*) of the cycle *bKa'-brgyad-bde-gśegs-'dus-pa.*

(DC) Further he got one hundred and three treatises (*chos-tshan*); the manuscripts were written by Vairocana and Dan-ma-rtse,[51] and had been revised and arranged in book form by the religious King Khri-srong-lde-btsan.

(DC+Tt) Out of the whitish chest he took figures, books (*gsung*) and Stūpas (*thugs-rten*) of *Hayagrīva* (*rTa-mgrin*) and also many sacrificial objects (*dam-rdsas*). He also fetched many Hidden Treasures from the anchorage Brag-gi-lha-khang. The anchorage was near mChims-phu at bSam-yas, amidst the mountains of gNam-skas-can-gyi-srin-bya-brag.

NYI-MA-'OD-ZER'S TEACHERS

His teachers were his own father Nyang-ston chen-po, rGya-smyon-pa Don-ldan, Źig-po-nyi-ma-seng-ge, Mal Ka-ba-can-pa, and sTon-pa Kha-che[52] and many other *bLa-mas.* Nyi-ma-'od-zer studied philosophy and the theories of the Tantras.

HIS VISIONS

For three years he practised the meditative realization of the *bLa-ma* (i.e. Padmasambhava) who represented himself in a shape which embraced the three significances of his being[53] (*bla-ma sku-gsum 'dus-pa'i sgrub-thabs*). Practising these meditations he became concretely aware of *Ācārya* Padmasambhava who bestowed on Nyi-ma-'od-zer many instructions. When Nyi-ma-'od-zer was meditating on the spiritual significance of the *bLa-ma* (*bla-ma'i thugs-sgrub*) in Mu-tig-śel-gyi-spa-gong, Ye-śes-mtsho-rgyal appeared to him and gave him the book 'A Hundred Questions and Answers of a Spiritual Being' (*mKha'-'gro'i źus-lan brgya*). They both made their appearance at the cremation ground of Śītavana.[54] When they had arrived there they found the Precious Guru [Padmasambhava] staying with the Eight Wisdom-Holders (*Rig-'dsin brgyad*) who had mastered the Pronouncements Teachings (*bka'-babs*) and who had endowed [Nyi-ma-'od-zer] with a common empowerment (*dbang*) of the Eight Pronouncements (*bka'-brgyad*)[55] as well as with sections belonging to each of them. He fully taught Nyi-ma-'od-zer the Tantras (*rgyud*) and instructions (*man-ngag*).

NYI-MA-'OD-ZER'S MARRIAGE

The Discoverer of Concealed Books (*gTer-ston*) married Jo-'bum-ma,[56] an actual being (*sPrul-pa*) of Ye-śes-mtsho-rgyal. She bore him two sons : 'Gro-mgon Nam-mkha'-'od-zer and Nam-mkha'-dpal-ba, the latter was an actual being of *Avalokiteśvara.*

HIS MEETING WITH THE MYSTIC DNGOS-GRUB

Once when dNgos-grub, a Mystic (*Grub-thob*), visited this Discoverer of Concealed Books, he said : "I possess the Concealed Teaching of the Eight Pronouncements (*bka'-brgyad gter-kha*)." The Mystic replied: "And I got the corresponding Pronouncements (*bka'-ma*). This is the path belonging to them !" When the Discoverer of Concealed Books had heard these Pronouncements (*bka'-ma*), the Teachings of the Pronouncements and the Concealed Books met like two rivers. From Lha-sa the Mystic had brought a Concealed Book about *Avalokiteśvara*, The Great Merciful One (*Thugs-rje-chen-po*), consisting of five scrolls. The Mystic said to the Discoverer of Concealed Books: "You are its master ?" and offered him the scrolls.

HIS LAST YEARS

Once when the Discoverer was practising a meditation for

his health (*sman-sgrub*), a goddess of medicine (*sMan-gyi-lha-mo*)[57] appeared. She offered him a leafy branch from an A-ru-ra tree. Cross-legged he rose in the air and his feet did not touch the earth. Such and many other miraculous deeds were performed by him. Nyi-ma-'od-zer devoted himself to his own sanctification (*sgom-sgrub*) as well as to his teachership. His charismatic activity was as infinite as the sky. He disseminated the Doctrine to an extent that is simply inconceivable.

HIS DEPARTURE AND CREMATION CEREMONIES

When he was sixty-eight years old ((1192)[57a] many miraculous signs were visible. First of all, the letter HRĪ appeared on his heart.[58] He went to rest in *Sukhāvatī*, his body dying in the manner of this world. By himself it was prophesied that later on three actual beings of his existential, communicative and spiritual significance (*sku*, *gsung*, *thugs*) will become visible. When Chags Lo-tsā-ba[59] laid down the corpse, the fire would not scorch it. Later on the corpse burnt out by itself. Inside the cremation chamber (*gdung-khang*) a tender child was seen surrounded by Spiritual Beings (*mKha'-'gro*) shouting "Harinisa". This and many other miracles were perceived by the people, and many relics of different shapes had become visible.[60] Paṇ-chen Śākyaśrī[61] together with his attendants was invited to take part in the funeral ceremonies (*dgongs-rdsogs-dngos-gži*). Much gold was presented to him and he enjoyed it very much.

THE PROPHECY ON NYI-MA'OD-ZER AND HIS SON

One of the deceased's sons asked Paṇ-chen Śākyaśrī's permission to become a monk, but Sākyaśrī replied : "Both your father and you yourself are great Bodhisattvas. I must not interrupt the chain of generations of Bodhisattvas. The way of life you practise nowadays will be of benefit to the beings." Śākyaśrī refused him ordination of a monk, and pronounced many glorifications about the Teachings of the Concealed Books (*gter-chos*), and about these two persons (i.e. father and son): Indisputably they are going to be great Discoverers of Concealed Treasures, bearing evidence to the truth of these Teachings.

They are going to be famous all over the world, sweeping away the heretical interpretations of the New Tantras (*sngags gsar-ma*) which are cultivated today. In Tibet they will become as well-known as sun and moon.

NYI-MA-'OD-ZER'S DISCIPLES

Nyi-ma-'od-zer's pre-eminent disciple was his son 'Gro-mgon Nam-mkha'-dpal-ba. The Discoverer conferred upon him the Teachings of the Pronouncements by introducing him to all empowerments leading to spiritual maturity and liberation (*smin-grol*). Thus he became master of Nyi-ma-'od-zer's Teachings.

(DC) He was an actual being (*sPrul-pa*) of *Avalokiteśvara*, as had been prophesied. Endowed with magic abilities (*rdsu-'phrul*) he thought to drive stones up into the sky like a flock of sheep driven up the slopes of the Śam-po mountain.[62] People declared that it was not clear from which place the stones had been coming. These stones covered the banks of the sKyid-chu river at Lha-sa like a white and grey mass. At the sKid-chu an embankment was built with these stones to protect the Jo-khang temple. In former times it was said that these stones were distinguished ones. He also let become visible one hundred-and-eight painted scrolls (*thang-kha*). They were as tall as several storeys and looked like paintings produced in Nepal. On account of his unsurpassed magical power and strength the Protectors of the Buddha's Doctrine (*Chos-skyong*) served him like servants. He destroyed meteors, hailstorms and other enemies from sunrise to sunset, regardless of the (astrologically) right time and the phases of the moon. It was impossible to comprehend the extent of his pity.

From among the crowd of his disciples there emerged many actual beings (*sPrul-sku*) of Guru Chos-kyi-dbang-phyug (1212-1270)[63] and others. 'Gro-mgon Nam-mkha'-dpal-ba's son was an actual being of *Mañjuśrī*, mNga'-bdag bLo-ldan by name. The latter's son was an actual being of *Vajrapāṇi*, mNga'-bdag bDud-'dul by name.

(DC+Tt) These three men are exalted as the Actual Beings attached to the Three Action Patterns leading to Liberation (*rigs-gsum sprul-pa*).[64] This is the transmission of the sons (*sras-brgyud*) in succession.

gNyos Grags-rgyal,[65] Źi-po-bdud-rtsi and sMan-lung-pa Mibskyod-rdo-rje and the other two disciples were called the Five Main Disciples (*bu-lnga*) as they had mastered the Pronouncements (*bka'-babs*). This lineage of disciplse extended the range of their activity of propagating the Doctrine all over the Tibetan country. Thus, it exists still to this day.

(Tt) It would be appropriate to compose a hagiography of this great Discoverer of Concealed Books in full length, despite the fact that detailed hagiographies of the Discoverer himself and his sons are existing within the Accounts on the Origin of the Concealed Books (*gter-'byung*). There are also reports about them in the corresponding chapters of the catalogue (*dkar-chag*) of the *sNga-'gyur-rgyud-'bum*.[66] So I am hesitant of going into this matter in too lengthy a way. Therefore I only summarize the essential features.

TRANSMISSION OF NYI-MA-'OD-ZER'S TEACHINGS

From the ocean of his profound Concealed Teachings (*zab-gter rgya-mtsho*) the following treatises have been handed down to this very time : *rNam-thar-zangs-gling-ma*, *bLa-ma-źi-drag*, *Thugs-rje-chen-po-gro-'dul-dang-rgyal-po-lugs*, *rGyal-rgyam-lha-lnga*, *bKa'-brgyad-bde-'dus*. *mKha'-'gro-chen-mo-dang-khros-nag*, *gTer-mgon-phyag-bźi-pa-gyul-mdos*, *bsTan-srung-dur-khrod-ma-mo* and others.

I (sKong-sprul) also studied these treatises and have heard the empowerments (*dbang*) and oral commentaries (*lung*) at full length. The basic book of the Eight Pronouncements (*bka'-brgyad gźung*)[67] I had printed in nine volumes. I was well deserving of these teachings, practising meditation through mystic formulas (*bsnyen-pa*) and realization (*sgrub-pa*).

5. HAGIOGRAPHY OF GURU CHOS-KYI-DBANG-PHYUG (1212-1270), THE SECOND OF THE FIVE DISCOVERER-KINGS

(Tt) THE PROPHECY

Thus it is stated: "The country will be opened at sNa-thags and the Mongolian warriors will invade Tibet. The prophesied events will surpass even the bad ways of existence (*ngan-song*) in trouble and misery. The Tibetans will be chastised by the Mongolian government. There will be many myrmidons. Prisoners will be buried alive. At the same time a sign will rise: The Concealed Treasure hidden in gNam-skas-mkhar-chu[68] shall not remain there but shall be taken out. The Discoverer of Concealed Books, Chos-kyi-dbang-phyug, will come into extistence."[69]

(DC +Tt) GURU CHOS-KYI-DBANG-PHYUG'S FORMER EXISTENCES AND HIS FAMILY

The precious Guru Chos-kyi-dbang-phyug is well-known to have been the second in the line of the Five Discoverer-Kings (*gTer-ston rgyal-po lnga*) and of the Three Most Important Actual Beings (*mChog-gi sprul-sku-rnam gsum*). The religious King (*Chos-rgyal*) Khri-srong-lde-btsan (755-797) presented himself as the actual being Nyang-ral Nyi-ma'od-zer (1124-1192). The latter, having gained the ultimate goal of Buddhahood, indicated Guru Chos-dbang to be the actual manifesta--tion of Buddhahood in its communicative aspect (*sangs-rgyas-pa'i gsung-gi rnam-'phrul*) in the purified sphere which is called Ma-chags-padma-can.

(DC) Furthermore, in the time of the first dissemination of the Doctrine (*snga-dar*) there was a Bon-po called gNya'-rings. He asserted that he would kill King Khri-srong-lde-btsan by hurling meteors. But there was also a capable Tantric called sPang-rje bTsan-khram who had been a disciple of *Ācārya* Padmasambhava, Vimalamitra and Vairocana. When the Bon-po hurled the meteors like five arrows, sPang-rje bTsan-khram simultaneously made a threatening gesture by pointing with his forefinger (*sdigs-mdsub*). [sPang-rje bTsan-khram] caught and threw the meteors back at the Bon-po who died by this act. The King greatly rewarded sPang-rje bTsan-khram.

sPang-rje bTsan-khram had a son called sPang Rig-'dsin-snying-po. He was appointed temple-guard and he took care of the four temples which had been founded for the renewed educating [of the Tibetan people] (*yang-'dul-gyi lha-khang*).[70] Once a year Rig-'dsin-snying-po visited mKho-mthing to celeb-rate a religious ceremony (*mchod-pa*). Meeting the duke (*dPon-chen*) of La-yag-rdsa-bar[71] the latter offered many jewels to

Rig-'dsin-snying-po. With the words "In former times this was my country !" he took possession of them.

[sPang Rig-'dsin-snying-po's] son was Kun-mkhyen Śes-rab-rgyal-po. From his time up to sPang-ston Grub-pa'i-snying-po this lineage of knowledgeable and capable Tantrics remained without interruption. [sPang-ston Grub-pa'i-snying-po] asked bLa-ma Sangs-rgyas-nyi-sgam to bestow on him the pure way of a Brahman-like life (*tshang-par spyod-pa*). He said: "The Bodhisattva's way of life is of greater benefit to all beings than the eight ways of conduct of the celibate monk (*dGe-slong*).[72] For this reason, the lineage of the Bodhisattvas must not be interrupted." When Grub-pa'i-snying-po was still living with his parents he received the prophecy that he would get mKha'-'gro Gar-gyi-dbang-mo for his wife. But later on he became aware of dKar-bza' mGon-skyid who came from a good family of mystics able to walk about in the sky and he married her.

PROPHECIES ABOUT GURU CHOS-DBANG

When his father heard the basic Sūtra of *Vajrakīla* (*Phur-pa-rtsa-ba'i mdo*) from 'Bri-gung-skyobs-pa[73] (b. 1177) the latter said : "Teach your little son the Doctrine and he will accomplish his activity !"—When Źang Rin-po-che[74] was staying with the scholar (*dGe-bśes*) Lo-chung-pa he said: "I'm going to be re-born as your son ! Well, that's just for sport, but you will get a son like me !" Such and other prophecies were prevalent.

CHOS-DBANG'S BIRTH

When Guru Chos-dbang entered his mother's womb, the sun and the moon shaded off into one another above her vertex. Again and again the sound AH[75] (symbolizing unoriginatedness) was heard to come out of the mother's womb. When she was given a ceremonial arrow [the unborn Guru Chos-dbang] uttered a verse. Such unusual signs had become manifest. Guru Chos-dbang was born at sunrise on the fifteenth day of the first month in the year 1212 A.D. He was named [Chos-kyi-dbang-phyug] after an auspicious passage from the *Manjuśrī-nāma-saṃgīti*,[76] written in gold; *chos-kyi-dbang-phyug chos-kyi-rgyal.* Some eye-witnesses reported that gods and demons worshipped the child.

CHILDHOOD AND EDUCATION

At the age of four his father taught him to read and to write. He studied the following subjects: *sMra-sgo-mtshon-cha, Rig-klag-sde-lnga, Bi-brta-chen-mo,* altogether [he studied] thirteen grammar works (*sgra'i bstan-bcos*); *sKye-bo-gso-thig* and so on, together with ten treatises on proper conduct (*nīti-śāstra*); astrology and medicine; the Pronouncements (*bka'-ma*) and the Concealed Books (*gter-ma*); the seven divisions of dynastic history (*rGyal-rabs-sde-bdun*); the *sDe-brgyad-chen-po'i-sgrung-'bum* together with one-hundred and four tractates on ceremonial dances and songs; further he studied seventy-five tractates on the main teachings of the *Bon* religion; one-hundred tractates on the main teachings of thread-cross ceremonies (*mdos*),[77] and many other treatises on drawing *Maṇḍalas* of the exoteric and esoteric Tantrayāna (*gsang-sngags phyi-nang*). Later he composed four big volumes on the *Vajrakīla* cycle (*rDo-rje-phur-pa*). When he was ten years old, he heard six tractates on *Vajrapāṇi* (*Phyag-na-rdo-rje*) according to the system of the New School (*gSar-ma-pa*). Once when he practised the meditative realization the water in the ritual flask began boiling. He accomplished the meditation by mystic formulas (*mantras*) of the cycle of *Yamāntaka* (*gŚin-rje-gśed*) and *Vajrakīla* to the highest degree. When he was eleven years old he perfected the empowerments (*dbang*); the Tantras and instructions (*man-ngag*) of the *sGyu-'phrul* cycle. When he was twelve years old he studied *Ka-ka-ni-grva-lnga.* He knew one hundred texts of meditative realization and practised the mystic formulas of *Vajrasattva* (*yig-brgya*). At the age of thirteen he heard the cycles of the Merciful One (i.e. *Avalokiteśvara*) and of *Hayagrīva* according to the methods of the New School (*gSar-ma-pa*) and of the Old School (*rNying-ma-pa*). He also practised meditation on these subjects.

VISION OF VAJRASATTVA

At thirteen he had a vision of *Tārā* (*sGrol-ma*) guiding him to the top of a crystal castle. There he perceived *Vajrasattva.*

A Spiritual Being (*mKha'-'gro-ma*) with four faces talked to him; with her white face turned towards him she said : "Seize the Buddha's Doctrine !"; the right and yellow face said :" Disseminate the venerable Doctrine !" the red face in the back said: "Raise the noble Community !"; the blue face on the left said : "Guide the beings strictly in these evil times in order to educate them !" After these words the Spiritual Being offered him a ceremonial arrow (*mda'-dkar*) with five feathers.

FURTHER EDUCATION

At the age of fourteen he heard the *Pramāṇavārttika* (*Tshad-ma*) of Ti-se-gro-gyang-gsar-ba, and also the *Abhidharma-samuccaya* (*mNgon-pa-kun-btus*), the *Bodhisattvacarya-avatāra* (*sPyod-'jug*), the *Hevajratantra* (*dGyes-rdor*)[78] and other basic texts. Later he heard *Mahāmudrā* (*Phyag-rgya-chen-mo*)[79], *rDsogs- chen,*[80] the six teachings of the *Ẓi-byed-pa* School (*Ẓi-byed-chos-drug*)[81] together with the appropriate instructions mTha-skor-ba taught him the *dBu-ma-bden-chung*. mTshur-ston and his disciples[82] taught him the *Atiyoga* and many Sūtras and Tantras of both the transmission of the Old and the New School. He meditated on these subjects. From his father, he heard the *Ẓi-byed*, the *Phyag-rgya-chen-mo*, the *rDsogs-pa-chen-po*, and the *gCod-yul.*[83] He heard many texts on the Protectors of the Doctrine (*bsTan-srung*) and on the evil spells (*drag-sngags*) and implanted these teachings in his mind.

THE BEGINNINGS OF HIS ACTIVITY AS A DISCOVERER OF CONCEALED BOOKS

When he was seventeen years old he met mNga'-bdag 'Gro-mgon,[84] who appointed him master of many Concealed Books which previously had been discovered by Nyang Rin-po-che Nyi-ma-'od-zer.[85] When he was eighteen he heard the essentials on the Enlightened Mind (*sems-bskyed*, Skr. *bodhicitta*) from Sa-skya Paṇḍita[86] and from Ti-se-gro-gyang-gsar-ba further teachings connected with the Doctrine. He attended also the ceremony of the temple foundation (*rab-gnas*) at the Stūpa of Lha-lung.[87]

VISION OF *MANJUŚRĪ*, INITIATING HIM INTO THE FULL KNOWLEDGE OF BEING-IN-ITSELF

One night he dreamt that he was going to the Wu-tai-shan (*Ri-bo-rtse-lnga*)[88] in China in search of the *Udumbara* flower. Sitting on a throne of blue lotus flowers the sublime *Mañjuśrī* declared : "The pure existence of the significance of wisdom ! (*jñāna-kāya-dharmadhātu*) I am the Lord of the Doctrine. I am your spiritual understanding through which the impurity of intellection has been removed (*sems-rtog*).[89] The spiritual understanding is the approach to being-in-itself, difficult to conceive. The ultimate reality of this approach to being-in-itself is not to visualize (it as something), but is the primeval wisdom rising by itself (*rang-byung-gi ye-śes*). Realize for yourself the real truth of the eighty-four thousand approaches to being-in-itself which I pointed out to you !" At this very moment Guru Chos-dbang awoke and realized that he had gained a firm knowledge (*nge-śes*) of the reality as such (*chos-thams-cad*).

GURU CHOS-DBANG'S LEGITIMACY TO DISCOVER CONCEALED BOOKS AND HIS FATHER'S TALK ABOUT THIS MATTER

Grva-pa-mngon-śes had taken from bSam-yas a scroll (*śog-ser*) which contained a list of hiding places (*kha-byang*).[90] Through transmission Guru Chos-dbang got this list at the age of thirteen. In the meantime many thoughtless fools had started to unearth Concealed Treasures by relying on this list of hiding places. Some of them died, some had to abandon their scheme due to meteors and hailstorms. If one allows this list of hiding places to lie at home, it will cause trouble by means of black magic. If one throws this list on a bad road, a cross-road, into water, or if one digs it into the soil, the list will come to no harm. As it was not possible to grasp it the name 'lost scroll' was given to it.

Guru Chos-dbang's father said to his son: "What about this 'lost scroll' ? It has brought trouble on everybody. Do you want to die ?" The father took the list from him, and hid it somewhere else.

Later on when Chos-dbang was about twenty-two, a man who had known of this matter and who had practised *gCod*[91] took the scroll with him. On account of this Chos-dbang took the list of the Twice Hidden Books (*yang byang*) out from Layag-nyin-gyi-lung-pa.

(DC+Tt) The Protectors of the Concealed Treasures—*kLu-bdud-mgo-dgu* and *Ye-śes-mkha'-'gro*, appearing in the shape of an ordinary woman—gave him the keys. He opened the door of the pagoda (*ke'u-tshang*).[92] A vulture as big as the *Kyung-*Bird[93] came out which was the essence of the Concealed Treasure (*gter-bcud*). Chos-dbang mounted the bird and flew up to the thirteenth stage of the sky. There was a tent consisting of a rain-bow. Chos-dbang perceived the Buddha of Undiminished Being (*rDo-rje-sems-dpa'*) and received the empowerment of 'The Strength of Wisdom' (*rig-pa rsal-gyi dbang*) and a ritual flask filled with nectar (*bdud-rtsi'i bum-pa*). According to the list of Concealed Treasures (*gter-byang*) he opened the door and took out two copper chests and a bronze figure of *kLu-bdud-mgo-dgu*, about fifteen cubits (*khru-gang*) large. Inside the fignre there were four different instructions (*gdams-ngag*), and inside the chests there were one-hundred-and-eight advices (*man-ngag*).

After the discovery of this first Concealed Treasure Chos-dbang took out further eighteen Concealed Treasures and a Concealed Teaching (which he had visualized) in his unbiased mind (*thugs-gter*). They were summarized into nineteen works : 1. *gNam-skas-can-gter*, 2. *Brag-dmar-gter*,[94] 3. *rTa-mgrin-źabs-gter*[95] 4. *Mon-khasteng-gi-gter*,[96] 5. *rTa-mnrin-gter*, 6. *sBen-rtsa'i-sgo'i-gter*, 7. *mKho-yi-gśin-dmar-gter*, 8. *rTa-mgrin-gter*, 9. *sGrom-chos-kyi-gter*, 10. *Sras-mkhar-gter*,[97] 11. *sKya-bo-phug-ring*,[98] 12. *Phyag-mtheb-ma'i-gter*, 13. *bSam-yas-ārya'i-ātnr*,[99] 14. *lCags-phur-gter*,[100] 15. *Mon-bum-thang-gter*,[101] 16. *rTsis-kyi-lha-khang-gi-gter*,[102] 17. *Rong-brag-gter*,[103] 18. *Ha-bo-gnas-gyi-gter*,[104] and 19. *Rang-gab-don-gyi-gter*.

By means of his great merits Chos-dbang saw all these Concealed Treasures.

(DC) Intelligent men[105] took these Concealed Treasures out in public and great miracles used to accompanny these events. Often these masters of the Concealed Treasures were summoned to deliver the Concealed Treasures to Chos- dbang, otherwise clever messengers were sent to fetch the Concealed Treasures. Therefore there were no questions to their origin. Hearing about this the father said to his son: "People are saying you have taken out a Concealed Treasure. Bring along what you have unearthed?" Chos-dbang handed over the copper chests to his father who said: "Read the catalogue aloud?" The son read it. "Does there exist the *gCig-śes-kun-grol* Tantra on the subject of *Sangs-rgyas-mnyam-sbyor*? Then read it!'[106] The son read everything from the beginning. "It is absolutely accurate! It was not an insignificant matter that I had mentioned to you. But, today if we argue about this matter, it is nothing but idle words. Whether this Treasure will cause harm or misery is beyond us. This Concealed Book is doubtless the Pronouncement (*bka'*) of the Great Master of Uḍḍiyāna (i.e. Padmasambhava) who knows the three aspects of time. I, however, do not intend to use such profound Concealed Teachings (*gter-chos*), as I am now about forty years old and I have the wisdom of the *bLa-mas,* scholars and Mystics (*Grub-thob*) of the whole of the Tibetan country. All restrictions to a single meaning[107] I have renounced (*gcod*). Many times I have realized that mind-as-such (*sems-nyid*) is the only potential of both *Nirvāṇa* and *Saṃsāra.* If you want to be obedient to me try to master the *bLa-rdsogs-thugs-gsum* (i.e. the three main subjects of meditation according to the method of the Concealed Teachings). Failing this, one must not talk about magic, bad-spells, catapults, big weapons, bad signs or miracles. One must not speak about such theories which merely cause trouble if one lacks the accomplished practice of the *bLa-rdsogs-thugs-gsum.* Many people knowing this and that, when they have not reached the goal of Buddhahood. In general I do not oppose the Concealed Teachings. Buddha has prophesied [the existence] of the Concealed Treasures in all the Sūtras and Tantras. It is the system of the former Wisdom-Holders (*Rig-'dsin*). In former times Discoverers of Concealed Treasures were of weak mental strength, and had not attained a clear vision of the Doctrine. They had not accomplished the benefit of the beings because they were greedy of flattering praise and extolled themselves. rGya-źang-khrom destroyed the welfare of beings because he had propagated evil spells (*ngan-sngags*). Ku-tsha-sman-pa had practised medicine therefore he disturbed the beings' benefit from the Doctrine. As Ra-śag gTer-ston had only practised thread-cross-ceremonies (*mdos*) he was called 'Thread-cross-adherent' (*mDos-mkhan*). Because Bon-po Drag-rtsal had only practised the meditation on *Pe-har*[108] he turned into nothing but a magician. In this manner there existed many Discoverers. They had not handed down the essentials of the Doctrine the same way as before although the former Buddhas were always thinking of the benefit for the beings. Because these Discoverers had made frequent use of hollow rituals they had not attained mastership. If one practises the Doctrine, the Protectors of it will come by themselves. If one does not practise the meditative realization (*sgrub-thabs*) for the sake of gaining magic power, then one will get it easily. The Protectors of the Doctrine themselves have made such a promise. Therefore, study the practice of the *bLa-rdsogs-thugs-gsum* (i.e. the three main subjects of meditation according to the system of the Concealed Treasures), and do not be capricious! mNga'-bdag Nyi-ma'od-zer was in the people's confidence because he accomplished the meditation of the Great Merciful One (i.e. *Avalokiteśvara*). He is not a bad Discoverer ! In former days I said that I would die within six years. Now, this will happen in two months. I need not be afraid that the people will say that I was a deceitful Discoverer of Concealed Treasures. Thirteen generations of the family sPang have been before me and there is not a single person who has not attained the esoteric sign of accomplished meditation (*nang gi grub-rtags*). So I am not one of the worst." mNga'-bdag 'Gro-mgon declared: "I have a high opinion of myself on account of the Concealed Books !" After having seen Guru Chos-dbang's Concealed Book he found it to be satisfactory in every way.

CHOS-DBANG'S PROPHECY ON THE MONGOL INVASION

Chos-dbang prophesied that the Mongolian army would come and invade the Tibetan country. His adherents did not agree with this prophecy. With the words "Today there are no Mongols in our country !" they disparaged Chos-dbang. Thus he was dejected and inclined to hide his instructions.

VISION OF PADMASAMBHAVA

Two young women guided him on a white winged horse to the purified sphere of *rNga-yab-dpal-ri.*[109] The Great Master of Uḍḍiyāna (Padmasambhava) conferred upon him the whole empowerment of the Eight Pronouncements (*bka'-brgyad*) *gSangs-ba-yongs-rdsogs.* "The best of all ways is to be active for the benefit of other beings. The way to gain enlightment (*byang-chub*) will be long for the lazy." Chos-dbang felt consoled after being instructed and admonished in such manner. "Do not long for this place! If you yearn to be in this place you must fear dying." At that moment he was lifted by a radiant light which was like a shield and arrived at home.

THE MONGOL INVASION

In the year 1239[110] the Mongol army marched into Tibet. Thus Chos-dbang's prophecy was proven true.

EDUCATING HIS DISCIPLE BHA-RO-GTSUG-'DSIN

His most worthy disciple was Bha-ro-gtsug-'dsin, a native of Yam-bu-ba in Nepal. He had come to Tibet to prospect for gold. He received a prophecy by a Spiritual Being that he would see the Guru himself. For seven days Chos-dbang appeared to him as the real Master of Uḍḍiyāna. The direct understanding (*rtogs-pa*) emerged in him through the very hearing of Chos-dbang's voice. One night, performing the ritual of an empowerment, Chos-dbang asked his disciple: "What do I look like?"—"I look at you as the real Tutelary Deity (*Yi-dam*).[111]"—"There is no other place for offering the sacrificial objects of the *Gaṇacakra* (*tshogs-'khor*) or for offering sacrificial cakes (*gtor-ma*)." With these words Chos-dbang devoured one half of a slaughtered wild sheep and all the other things necessary for the celebration of a *Gaṇacakra*. "Well, what do you think about me?" —"You are really a Buddha?"—"Then let us perform the empowerment!" When the utensils for the ritual (*mchod-pa*) had been cleared away and the *Maṇḍala* been destroyed Chos-dbang performed a few steps of a ritual dance at this place. Chos-dbang's conduct was not confined to acting in accordance with the moral opinion of gaining virtues and renouncing defilements. He also knew the thoughts and the dispositions (*khams*)[112] of his qualified disciple who was not afraid of fulfilling the great vow of immutable being-in-itself.[113] Thus *Vairocana* emerged from the heavenly lower door of the *Maṇḍala* which was formed by [Chos-dbang's] own body and being the immutable itself Guru Chos-dbang bestowed the empowerments on Bha-ro-gtsug-'dsin. That was the reason that the disciple's mental capacity rose like a snake casting off its slough. Similarly the fragrant water of *Amoghasiddhi* flowed from the swift way of the mystic diamond (*rdo-rje-gsang-ba'i myur-lam*)[114] on to the tip of Bha-ro's tongue. Utmost Delight (*bde-ba-chen-po*) not defiled by distortions (*zag-med*), and primeval awareness (*ye-śes*) blazed in the meditative coemergence of nothingness and creative light (*thod-rgal*).[115] After Guru Chos-dbang had laid his finger on the heart of his disciple, he said : "Where will that which we call 'I' be truly grasped ? The comprehension of sensual objects is a mere bubble. My sight of the true nature of the 'I' is not lost in thought. Not by so much as a hair's breadth is meditation on such a topic to be performed." After Chos-dbang had made this pronouncement there arose in Bha-ro-gtsug-'dsin the pure understanding (*rtogs-pa*), the Great Accomplishment (*rdsogs-chen*) which is not one-sided (*ris-med*) and independent of activism (*bya-bral*). He had attained steadiness of his special wisdom. He thought : "Should the Buddhas of the three times appear I would not mind begging for an empowerment. I have also given up my own plan of returning to India." So he told his teacher. Chos-dbang answered : "If there should a Buddha appear and not roam in *Saṃsāra* he would not be a real Buddha ! When you return to India look for a *bLa-ma* in case you should need one ! Look for a disciple if you need one !" Bha-ro considered this to be a good advice. Since Bha-ro was actually a person whose *Karma* had matured (*las sad-pa*) and since he was a firm believer he saw the eyes of a fierceful deity (*khro-bo'i lha*) standing near his Guru whom he saw discussing the Doctrine with Spiritual Beings. Such pure visions had often come to him. Once Bha-ro asked Chos-dbang: "If one practises magic a sign will appear [to indicate success], isn't it so ?" (Chos-dbang replied :) "I have never had the time to practise (magic) earnestly, I rather spent my time reciting the prayer *Om-maṇi-padme-hūṃ*."

THE DISCUSSION ABOUT KILLING BY MAGIC POWER

The Nepalese (Bha-ro) asked him: "Please, demonstrate the power of killing !"[116] While a hare was running over the ground nearby Chos-dbang drew the shape of a hare on the soil. He spoke a spell (*mantra*) for seven times over a needle and affixed it to the drawing. At this moment the hare toppled over. "Now, we must expiate the defilement, bring me the corpse !" Chos-dbang fixed on it a diagram for the protection of the dead (*btags-grol*).[117] He guided the hare's mind upwards by offering oblations and sacrificial cakes (*tshog-gtor*), and by diverting his merits to the benefit of this being (*bsngo-ba*).[118] Bha-ro said : "If the same thing would happen with a man it would be tremendously helpful !"[119] Chos-dbang answered: "Men and marmots are the same !" and he performed the same ceremony as before on the drawing of a marmot. Thereupon the dead body of a marmot became visible in the burrow.

"If one practises magic power the effects are such that they bring harm to the beings. On this account I do not teach this method to anybody. Even my enemy I teach to become a Buddha. When these two animals died I conveyed them to another existence. Furthermore, as a human existence is hard to find unlimited evil would arise if a human life had been cut off. This act is not expiated by a single death. All the people around him will suffer pain. Even on one's enemies one must not practise magic. Above all, it is necessary to have compassion on them !" Thus Chos-dbang declared, and he devoted himself first and foremost to strive for the conduct of a Bodhisattva. Chos-dbang gave his solemn promise not to practise magic and miracle-work for his own welfare. It is said: "If all objects are treated with compassion the three evil ways of existence (*ngan-song*) are overcome !" The great Guru Chos-dbang had realized this truth. Chos-dbang had only killed the body which had come about by force of its *Karma* and the five poisons (*dug-lnga'i phung-po-can*),[120] and transferred the awareness component of the dead being to the dynamic centre of being-as-such (*chos-nyid-kyi klong*). Thus he had brought transmigration to an end. This was the most marvellous deed of 'killing and rescuing' (*gsad-gso*)[121] that had ever been done.

CHOS-DBANG DISABUSED BHA-RO OF HIS LONGING FOR GOLD

When the Nepalese Bha-ro intended to return he offered his teacher sixty *zo* of gold[122] and begged him to say a prayer so that no hindrance would arise on his way back to India and Nepal. [Chos-dbang] mixed the gold with flour and celebrated a burned offering (*sbyin-sreg*). Thus he effectively unravelled [Bha-ro's] knot of avarice. He showed his firm belief in the Three Precious Jewels (i.e. the Buddha, the Doctrine and the Community). [Chos-dbang taught Bha-ro :] "When people who are accustomed to give alms perceive that their offerings are not wholly consumed they do not feel disappointed because they are always thinking [of the meritorious act of making offerings to] the Three Precious Jewels. (Bha-ro should experience that there is no loss in offering gold which is not consumed by fire.) This virtuous attitude is joyful and satisfying for oneself."

[Chos-dbang] said to Bha-ro: "Throw the ashes of the burned offering into the water without hesitation ! When on your way back a person will offer you food accept it !" When a woman offered him a turnip he took it. Bha-ro presented it to [Guru Chos-dbang]. Chos-dbang told him to cover it with a cotton-cloth while he was eating it.

When Bha-ro later on returned to India Chos-dbang accompanied him. Once more he offered three *zo* of gold to Chos-dbang. Then Chos-dbang declared : "If one smelts [the gold] by fire the Spiritual Beings (*mKha'-'gro-ma*) will rejoice. But if one throws it into the water their joy will be boundless." That very moment [Chos-dbang] threw the gold into the water.

(DC—Tt) GURU CHOS-DBANG, AN ACCEPTED AUTHORITY

At some other time he had made visible at a single instant the six ways of bodily representations. He often went through the air and impressed the traces of his hands and feet on the rocks. In this manner he demonstrated many miracles. For this reason not only the Old School (*rNying-ma-pa*) extols him but also Kun-mkhyen 'Phags-pa-'od, Chos-'od of the Jo-nang-pa School[123] and Bu-ston (1290-1364)[124] (also an adherent of the Jo-nang-pa School). They all claim that Guru Chos-kyi-dbang-phyug was an incomparably great Mystic (*Grub-thob*). Chos-dbang remembered perfectly thirteen existences of himself, starting from the embodiment as 'Od-mtha'-yas, the heavenly son, who succeeded the Religious King Khri-srong-lde-btsan (755-797), up to that of mNga'-bdag Nyang-ral (Nyi-ma-'od-zer 1124-1192). Indra and many heavenly sons worshipped and praised him. He was the greatest of all Tibetan *bLa-mas*. His fame caused the earth to shake.

FOUNDING TEMPLES AND INSTALLING HOLY FIGURES

Chos-dbang built the temples of Tshong-dus-'gur-mo and bSam-'grub-bde-ba-chen. The great Discoverer of Concealed Teachings (Chos-dbang) discovered a figure of Śākyamuni that resembled the one in the Jo-khang (temple) in Lha-sa. Nāgārjuna had unearthed this figure at Ri-btang-bzung and it had been hidden once again by the Precious Guru [Padmasambhava] at Ha-bo-gnas. [Chos-dbang] installed this figure in the Guru-lha-khang in the village La-yag, which became its main residence.

HIS DEMISE

The great *bLa-mas* and the important people who at this time were living in Tibet sat at Chos-dbang's feet.

(DC) Through his immeasurable compassion and activity he turned everything to the beings' advantage. When his activity was coming to an end he pronounced : "The sentient beings will make different statements about me, Chos-dbang : If Chos-dbang is doing well some are pleased. Others are alarmed by Chos-dbang's happiness. Chos-dbang's spirituality (*sems-nyid*) is not concerned with either hope or fear. Chos-dbang's mind (*sems*) is without suffering, therefore those who are glad about my happiness will be glad. But Chos-dbang has not renounced suffering, therefore those who are glad about my suffering may be glad. Chos-dbang's mind is not attached to birth or death, therefore those who feel sorry about my death may be glad. But Chos-dbang's spirituality (*sems-nyid*) will come to an end in the absoluteness of Being (*chos-dbyings*), therefore those who feel sorry about my not-dying may be glad too. Chos-dbang's spirituality is unchanging, therefore those who want me to be alive for ever may be glad too. But Chos-dbang's mind is without any essence, therefore those who feel sorry about my everlasting [life] may be glad." He remained a Yogi of great power, having completely overcome hopes and wants. He ordered that the temples he himself had founded should be taken care of, since his own efforts had been effective [in their construction]. Even his own son should be cast out if he were to cause damage to one of the temples; and a beggar should be honoured if he were to render a good service to a temple. These were Chos-dbang's instructions.

HIS DEATH

When the educating capacities of his present existence had ended Chos-dbang's apparitional individuality (*sgyu-ma'i skyes-bu*)[125] was reduced to the sphere of genuine and delightful absolute Being (*kun-bzang bde-chen chos-dbyings*).[126] On his body a mark became visible when the evil *Karma* had been exhausted. Chos-dbang dissolved like a human shape in a dream. He dreamt of finding jewels while as a teacher he was with his disciples. "This is a sign that I and my adherents are going to attain the Great Delight (*bde-ba-chen-po*)." He also said: "Should anyone taste my relics, be they as small as peas or grains of mustard-seed, he will acquire the right method and savour the Great Delight!" These reflections brought him relief. At the age of fifty-eight he demonstrated the inconceivable miracle of going away to the Great Palace of Padmasambhava's Radiant Light (*Padma-'od-kyi-pho-brang-chen-po*).

HIS DISCIPLES

At this time two Tantrics met on the way and asked each other whether their individual methods consist in the 'Earlier and Later Concealed Books (*gter-kha gong-'og*). This event indicated how well-known [Guru Chos-dbang's] Concealed Teachings had become.

(DC+Tt) Out of his uninterrupted lineage eight spiritual sons (*thugs-sras*) emerged : Among others were Padma-dbang-chen, who was an incarnation of Lang-gro, and Nyi-ma-'od-zer of the gNyal family. The main branch of the transmission among his disciples is represented by Mi-bskyod-rdo-rje of the sMan-lung-pa family[127] who knew very well all Pronouncements (*bka'*) and Concealed Books (*gter-ma*), by the Nepalese Bha-ro-gtsug-'dsin as well as others, nine disciples in all. Maṇi-rin-chen, a member of the Kaḥ-thog monastery, attained the purified sphere (*dag-pa'i źing-khams*) without leaving his body. He and others accomplished a sublime stage of spiritual potency (*siddhi*). Through the particular blessing of the Great Merciful One (*Avalokiteśvara*) the activity of the transmission by his disciples spread all over India, Nepal, and Tibet's midland and borderland. This transmission has existed without interruption to our present time.

SOURCES FOR THE DATA OF HIS HAGIOGRAPHY

(Tt) The venerable [Chos-dbang] was a king of all Mystics (*Grub-thob*) and a Discoverer of Concealed Teachings. His hagiographies dealing with the aspects of his being-in-the-world (*sku*), his authentic communication (*gsung*), his unbiased perspective in noetic being (*thugs*), his value (*yon-tan*), and his charismatic activity (*phrin-las*) are still fully existing together with his teachings and instructions. I (sKong-sprul) gathered the content [of his hagiography] mainly from the catalogue of the One-Hundred-Thousand Tantras of the Old School (*rNying-ma-rgyud-'bum*). Out of the eighteen important Concealed Books (*gter-kha-chen-po*) which [Chos-dbang] had discovered, I have found and extracted the following works after a long time of inquiry; also I have meditated on these subjects by uttering mystic formulas and by having visual realization (*bsnyen-sgrub*) :

The *bLa-ma-gsang-'dus* and five treatises on the realization of the *bLa-ma* (*bla-sgrub*) along with its appendices; the *Thugs-rje-chen-po-yang-snying-'dus-pa*; the *'Khor-ba-dong-sprugs*; the *rDsogs-chen-sangs-rgyas-mnyam-sbyor*; the *bKa'-brgyad-gsang-rdsogs*; the

'*Char-kha-skas-ma*; the *rTa-mgrin-nag-po*; the *Yang-dag-bde-chen-snying-po*; the *gTum-po-seng-sgrob*; the *Phur-pa-spu-gri*; the *sNgags-rgod-lo-ktri-dpal-mgon-ma-ning*; in addition the minor Concealed Books and most of his Collected Works (*gsung-'bum*). Since these Earlier Concealed Books (*gter-kha gong-ma*) form the main basis of all Concealed Books I asked the propagators of the teachings of the Old School (*rNying-ma-pa*) to disseminate these Earlier Concealed Teachings by means of interpretation and discourse, and to train the mind by means of meditative realization, and thus to kindle the small flame of the Doctrine.

6. HAGIOGRAPHY OF THE FEMALE DISCOVERER JO-MO-SMAN-MO (1248-1283), THE CONSECRATED CONSORT OF GURU CHOS-DBANG

(DC+Tt) THE PROPHECY

Two Spiritual Beings with miraculous signs emerged from Ye-śes-mtsho-rgyal[128] who had collected the mysterious and important sayings of the venerable king of the Doctrine i.e. the Master of Uḍḍiyāna (Padmasambhava). The first of these beings was well-known as the great Discoverer of Concealed Teachings, Jo-mo-sman-mo by name. The prophecy in the Concealed Book *mKha'-'gro-gsang-ba-kun-'dus* discovered by her said : "A girl of a good family will be born within an ape year.[129] She will be blessed by the Spiritual Beings. In secret she will be called 'nun' (i.e. *Jo-mo*). The Spiritual Beings will bestow this vision on her. By recognizing this blessing she will be delivered almost instantaneously. At this time she will not be efficient in the other beings' advantage, but, if one continues to adhere to her one will reach the Stage of Utmost Delight (*bde-chen sa*). One will gain the enlightment (*byang-chub*) without no traces of the five psycho-physical constituents (*phung-po lhag-med*) left."

BIRTH AND CHILDHOOD

According to the clear prophecy abridged from her true hagiography she was born within a grotto at the country E[130] near gZar-mo-lung. In this grotto Padmasambhava had practised meditation. The girl bloomed forth like a lotus flower.

Her father was a Tantric rDo-rje-rgyal-po by name who belonged to a family of Dvags-po[131] and her mother was Padma-dpal-rdsom whose ancestry was with the Spiritual Beings (*mKha'-'gro-ma*). Her parents gave her the name Padma-mtsho-skyid. Because of the family's prosperous economic situation the parents brought her up painstakingly and with loving care in her early childhood. But when she was four years old her mother died. Her father married again, and in the meantime she was sent off to tend the cattle. She was charged with the hard work of peasants. At this time she looked slightly depressed.

VISION OF THE SPIRITUAL BEINGS

When she was twelve years old she happened to tend the cattle near a meditation-place (*sgrub-gnas*) of Guru Padmasambhava, called the 'Mysterious Grotto of Utmost Bliss' (*bDe-chen-gsang-phug*). This rock looked like a great *Khyung*-bird and was situated in the country E near the place gZar-mo-lung. There she fell asleep. When she heard a lovely voice come out of the rock she awoke. She looked at the entrance of the mysterious grotto which has been opened wide. At this instance her mind became changed and she went inside without any hindrance. Inside, in the midst of a terrifying cremation ground, a crowd of Spiritual Beings (*mKha'-'gro-ma*) had gathered. The girl joined them. She perceived the leader to be *rDo-rje-phag-mo*,[132] who greeted her by saying : "Welcome to you, girl of a good family !" She gave the girl a booklet, just as if she had fetched it from behind the rock and laid it on the girl's head. Thus, literally and completely, she bestowed empowerments and instructions on her. She handed the booklet to the girl and said : "This is an instruction that includes all the mysteries of the Spiritual Beings (*mKha'-'gro-ma*).[133] If you practise it very secretly you will truly attain the utmost spiritual potency (*dngos-grub mchog*) !" Receiving this prophecy the girl recognized the whole Doctrine. In this way she turned to a Yoginī who had reached the Developing Stage (*bskyed-rim*).[134] After she had partaken in the *Gaṇacakra* (*tshogs-'khor*), *rDo-rje-phag-mo* made the *Maṇḍala* disappear which they formerly had enjoyed. Thereafter Jo-mo-sman-mo went home.

HER CHANGED SPIRITUAL ATTITUDE

[Jo-mo-sman-mo's] mind matured by the nectar-like blessing of the venerable *rDo-rje-phag-mo*. Therefore many sentences of the Doctrine came to her mind at all times although she had never heard them before.

DISCORD WITH HER SURROUNDINGS

Some had confidence in her because she knew unchangeable songs and unchangeable dances and because she perceived the innermost being of other persons. But most people said that she had been blessed by a she-demon *sMan-mo*[135] while she had been sleeping in the mountains. At this time she became well-known by the name Jo-mo-sman-mo. Discontented she no longer thought of her native country. She determined to remain a homeless person and went to La-yag sPang-gron in the west of Lho-brag.[136]

MEETING WITH GURU CHOS-DBANG

By merely glancing at Guru Chos-kyi-dbang-phyug[137] (1212-1270) the primary awareness of spontaneity[138] (*lhan-skyes-ye-śes*) rose in her mind. Chos-dbang thought her to be one of the women who had the five auspicious signs that were prophesied by the Precious Guru (Padmasambhava). Therefore he took her as a consecrated woman. Because the knot of the focal point of the central pathway (*rtsa dbu-ma*)[139] had been unravelled by her he comprehended the real meaning of all signs of the Tantra *gSang-ba-yongs-rdsogs-man-ngag-gi rgyud-chen-po* included in the Eight Pronouncements (*bka'-brgyad*). Previously Chos-dbang had not been able to revise this Tantra, now he was able to translate it into Tibetan. In this way their union was to their profit and advantage. She remained with him for some time. When she had understood the essentials of all empowerments and instructions Guru Chos-dbang said at last : "Your profound book that was delivered by the Spiritual Beings contains the main feature of your daily religious exercises (*thugs-dam*) on Ye-śes-mtsho-rgyal which [you had practised] during your last existence. Still, the time has not yet come to disseminate these teachings to the benefit of the beings. Practise it by yourself in secret! When you will be wandering through the central provinces of dBus and gTsang your adherents will reach the Stage of Utmost Bliss (*bde-chen sa*). You will be of benefit to others without this being noticed publicly. At last you will get the spiritual potency to walk in the sky without leaving your body." Thus he strongly admonished her.

TRAVELS IN THE WESTERN AND CENTRAL PROVINCES OF TIBET

Accompanied by two capable Yoginīs she roamed all over the small and large villages up to Ding-ri[140] in the uplands (*sTod*).

(DC) Once she visited gLing-rje-ras-pa;[141] she opened in him the approach to the pathway of discrimination-appreciation (*śes-rab-kyi rtsa*) as she knew the methods of symbols. There arose in him the integral understanding (*rtogs-pa*) of the coemergence of nothingness and creative light (*thod-rgal*). Because of this he became famous as far as the banks of the river Gaṅgā.

(DC+Tt) HER DEATH

Her secret way helping all beings was accomplished when she was thirty-five years of age. At this time she went on the top of the mountain sPrags-lha-ri in the province of dBus. It was the tenth day of the seventh month (according to the Tibetan calendar). She celebrated a *Gaṇacakra* together with two of her maidens. Then they flew up to the sky higher and higher like birds without leaving their bodies. At the Copper-coloured Marvellous Mountain of Uḍḍiyāna (*O-rgyan-zangs-mdog-dpal-ri*) they forthwith joined the crowd of the Spiritual Beings (*mKha'-'gro-ma*).

EFFECT OF HER ACTIVITY

When the herdsmen who had remained behind perceived that [the three Yoginīs] had gone [to a purified sphere] they consumed the small crumbs of the *Gaṇacakra* by which they spontaneously gained the meditation (*bsam-gtan*) stage. This is well-known as the miraculous and important mystery of the cycle *mKha'-'gro gsang-ba kun-'dus*. Originally these teachings had been transmitted to the Spiritual Beings. The common people did not perceive them.

TRANSMISSION OF HER TEACHINGS

At the end of this troubled time of ours an occasion will arise to educate disciples. Because of his compassion and his prayers the great Discoverer of Concealed Teachings (*gTter-chen*) and the Wisdom-Holder (*Rig-'dsin*) Padma-'od-gsal-mdo-sngags-gling-pa (1820-1892)[142] mastered these teachings. The cause [of his mastering] was that in former times [Jo-mo-sman-mo] had been the secret lady friend of Chos-dbang Rin-po-che and that she had been blessed by *Ye-śes-mkha'-'gro*. For these reasons [Padma-'od-gsal-mdo-sngags-gling-pa] revised her miraculous book and added it to the *Rin-chen-gter-gyi-mdsod-chen-po*.

(Tt adds that Padma-gar-dbang—alias sKong-sprul—partook in this method and practised meditation on it; but Tt does not give any further information)

7. HAGIOGRAPHY OF ORGYAN-GLING-PA (1323—ca 1360), THE FAMOUS DISCOVERER OF PADMA-SAMBHAVA'S HAGIOGRAPHY AND THE *BKA'-THANG-SDE-LNGA*

(Tt) THE PROPHECY

"A king of completely honest conduct will originate in Yar-lung-mthil.[143] Phag-mo-gru-pa will subdue the whole country.[144] The provinces of dBus and Khams will be ravaged by the Mongols. In all directions strong castles will be erected, numbering one-hundred-and-eight. A sign will be shown that the Treasure hidden at Śel-gyi-brag-phug[145] shall not remain longer there but shall be taken out. A Discoverer of Concealed Treasures, O-rgyan-gling-pa by name, will come."[146]

(DC+Tt) This Discoverer O-rgyan-gling-pa was the seventh incarnation of Lha-sras mChog-grub-rgyal-po.

BIRTH AND CHILDHOOD

He was born in a highly respected family of Tantrics in the year 1323. His birth-place was Yar-rje at gYo-ru-gra-nang.[147] O-rgyan-gling-pa himself was a Tantric but behaved like a monk (i.e. he did not marry and drink alcohol). He was experienced in magic, medicine and astrology.

HIS ACTIVITIES AS DISCOVERER OF CONCEALED TEACHINGS

When he was twenty-three he took a list of Concealed Books (*kha-byang*) from the red Stūpa at bSam-yas.[148] There was a place where the Great Master of Uḍḍiyāna (Padma-sambhava) had celebrated a medical ritual in which nectar was employed (*bdud-rtsi sman-sgrub*). This was the miraculous crystal-grotto in the mountain-range of Padma-brtsegs behind Yar-lung-śel-brag.[149] As door-keeper [a figure of] *Rāhu* had been appointed to protect the gentle and fierce deities who had come into existence by themselves. [O-rgyan-gling-pa] extracted from the uppermost head [of this *Rāhu* figure] three treatises about the gentle and fierce deities (*źi-drag*) related to the Developing Stage (*bskyed-rim*); these treatises correspond to the *bLa-ma-bstan-gnyis* cycle. He further discovered the *Thugs-rje-chen-po-padma-snying-thig*, the *rDsogs-chen tshe-sgrub*, treatises about the *Atiyoga-*, *sPyi-ti-* and *Yang-ti* parts of the *rDsogs-pa-chen-po* system, forming the *bLa-rdsogs-thugs-gsum* (i.e. the three main training subjects of the method of Concealed Teachings). Out of the lower three heads [of this figure] he took the *Yi-dam-bka'-'dus* a representative work of some other one-hundred-and thirty-two tractates; from the neck [he took] the *Źi-khro-bka'-'dus*, the *mKha'-'gro-gros-nag*, and treatises about *mGon-po ma-ning*; from the heart the *Padma-bka'-yi thang-yig chen-mo*;[150] in the lower part of the snake-like tail [he found] the Tantra and meditations instructions of the *Ye-śes mgon-po-lha-mang* cycle, medical treatises, profound instructions about the Protectors of the Doctrine (*bsTan-pa-srung-ba*); in the hands and the end of the snake-tail [he discovered] some methodical instructions about injuring or helping others. Thus, this Treasure of Concealed Books (*gter-ma*) emerged by degrees. Furthermore, out of the rock-range Gra'i-gyu-gong-brag[151] O-rgyan-gling-pa took the books *gSang-sngags-lam-rim-chen-mo*, *Padma'i-rnam-thar-chung-ba*, *Ži-byed bKa'-chem-don-gsal*, and the *rTen-'brel-yang-snying-'dus-pa*, He also found the *bKa'-thang-sde-lnga* in various hiding places (*gter-gnas*) near bSam-yas, the *Thugs-rje-chen-po-ye-śes-'od-mchog* and the *dPal-mgon-stag-gžon* at the Stūpa in *Žur-mkhar-rdo*;[152] he discovered a text about the fierce aspect of the Guru and other texts about the Protectors of the Doctrine at On-phug-stag-tshang,[153] a treatise on *gŚin-rje-tshe-bdag* at Gra'i-phyi-brag-po-che.[154] In all he unearthed roughly a hundred books which are counted as Concealed Teachings. The *bKa'-'dus* alone comes to more than thirty volumes. But it is stated that he was able to revise the basic scroll (*śog-ser*) [of the *bKa'-'dus*] only with difficulties and therefore hid it again. In conclusion, O-rgyan-gling-pa discovered many holy figures, ritual objects (*dam-rdsas*) and precious jewels (*nor-gter*). He unearthed twenty-eight great Concealed Books along with their corresponding supplements.

TROUBLE WITH BYANG-CHUB-RGYAL-MTSHAN (1302-1373), THE FOUNDER OF THE PHAG-MO-GRU-PA DYNASTY

At last O-rgyan-gling-pa had the meditative realization to perform the great empowerment (*dbang*) of the *bKa'-'dus* cycle, after having opened the approach to the Doctrine at Khra-'brug-kyams-stod.[155] At this point the Tā-si Byang chub-rgyal-mtshan, Lord of sNe'u-gdong-rtse,[156] disgraced the Discoverer of Concealed Teachings by citing a derogatory marginal note of the hagiography on O-rgyan-gling-pa]. In this way the auspicious signs were obstructed (i.e. the meditation and the ritual were broken off). The great Discoverer of Concealed Teachings fled to the country E and to Dvags-po.[157]

HIS DEATH

Not much later he died at bLo-chung,[158] a village near the borderland of the country E. The body was brought back to the country of Dvags-po and it was buried as a whole within a sepulchral urn at the monastery of Źabs-rjes-dgon-pa.

O-RGYAN-GLING-PA'S BODY HAS BEEN TURNED INTO RELICS

Later on one of his descendants, an eager district-officer, had heard that the body should have turned into precious relics which would set a person who tasted them free within the next seven lives (*skye-bdun-myang-grol*).[159] [The district-officer] asked for a small piece of flesh of the corpse. After he had tasted it his religious zeal blazed up and he rose in the air one *khru* [i.e. about fifteen inches] above the ground.

(DC) He travelled to various countries through the air. On this account the corpse was highly esteemed.

In the meantime, 'Jam-dbyangs-mkhyen-brtse'i-dbang-po (1820-1892)[160] had sent mKhan-bla-ma bKra-śis-'od-zer from mDo-Khams to ask for some pieces of the relic. [mKhyen-brtse'i-dbang-po] mixed it with other sacrificial objects (*dam-rdsas*) and he dispensed [these relics] continuously and widely. Therefore Demo Rin-po-che,[161] the regent of Tibet, ordered the corpse to be transferred to the monastery Ban-gtsang-dgon-pa at sNe'u-gdong and to have it buried within a funeral Stūpa (*gdung-rten*) made of wood. From the relic he had demanded he had about thirty pounds (one *khal*) of sacrificial pills (*ril-bu*) made. These pills he ordered to be brought to the palace of Nor-bu-gling-ka (the Dalai Lama's summer residence.)

Later on, the Thirteenth Dalai Lama considered the theft of the relics to be a great offence which would not be to the advantage and welfare of Tibet. Therefore he ordered the corpse to be escorted to the precious *rTse-pho-brang* i.e. the Potala Palace. For this purpose Gung-thang-pa of mGron[162] was sent [and ordered] to bring the corpse back. But the great Protector of the Doctrine (*Chos-skyong*) at bSam-yas (i.e. the god *Pe-har*) hurled meteors. As it was the god's command not to allow the corpse to be conveyed from the southern country to some other place, it was left at its former place. When the Dalai Lama had travelled to the southern part of the country to settle this matter, he went to the monastery of Ban-gtsang-dgon-pa and there donated about eight pints (i.e. four *bre*) of sacrifiicial pills (*ril-bu*) that had been made from the relics for the advantage and benefit of the beings. The remaining relics were mixed with medical herbs. The Dalai Lama and his teacher (*Yong-'dsin*) Phur-lcog-byams-mgon. Rin-po-che[163] personally and with great diligence made [sacrifiicial pills] from these materials. The Dalai Lama decreed the construction of a Stūpa-like reliquary which was to be made of the best wood and placed on top of the crown (*bre*) of guilded copper. He had the corpse exhibited within [the Stūpa] behind a latticed window (*'phrul-mig-can*), which was between the crown (*bre*) and the dome (*bum-pa*). This window was sealed by the Dalai Lama himself. Later on he sent a letter to the village community of sNe'u-gdong and to the monastery-college of Bangtsang. It contained an enumeration of all the duties that were to be performed by the laity and clergy on behalf of the corpse; [these duties] were to be shared equally by both parties. The letter showed the personal seal of the Dalai Lama and it is reported that [the letter] was like a folding book (*deb bltab-og-ma*), it consisted of seventeen sheets of paper, each surrounded by a seal-band (*mgul-tham*). This booklet was filed by the managing board (*rtsis-khongs*) of the college of the Ban-gtsang monastery. Later on [Padma-'od-gsal-mdo-sngags-gling-pa] was happy to look at this document.—When the reliquary containing the relic pills (*ril-bu*) was opened the pills had multiplied by four.

Because Tā-si Bang-chub-rgyal-mtshan had reversed the auspicious signs, the rule of the Phag-mo-gru-pa [dynasty] and of its adherents passed away like rivulets at the end of autumn. This is a well-known fact.

THE DISCOVERER'S DESCENDANTS

(DC+Tt) The descendants of this Discoverer of Concealed Teachings lived in Grab-gtsang-kha and in other places. Although what they did to the advantage of the Doctrine is not clear, they all demonstrated varied signs of spiritual accomplishment. Thus, they are a miraculous family of Wisdom-Holders (*Rig-'dsin*).

TRANSMISSION OF HIS TEACHINGS

From the Teachings of the Concealed Books discovered by

him, the empowerments (*dbang*) and oral commentaries (*lung*) of the cycles *Ye-śes-'od-mchog*, *Guru-drag-po*, *Tshe-sgrub*, *sTag-gźon* had been well preserved up to the time of Rig-'dsin gTer-bdag-gling-pa (1646-1714).[164] These books do not exist anymore.

The *Padma-bka'-thang śel-brag-ma*, the *bKa'-thang-sde-lnga* and the *rTen-'brel-yang-snying-'dus-pa* still exist also their means of empowerments (*dbang*) and oral commentaries (*lung*). It is especially stated in O-rgyan-gling-pa's prophecy concerning Concealed Teachings (*gter-lung*) that the venerable Padma-'od-gsal-mdo-sngags-gling-pa (1820-1892) will get hold of an old booklet which summarizes the *bKa'-'dus-chen-mo'i-snying-po*. [Padma-'od-gsal] also revised some booklets which still exist as symbols of Spiritual Beings (*mKha'-'gro-brda'i-yi-ge*).

(DC) As these books include lasting empowerments and oral commentaries and as they are used as manuals (*yig-cha*) they are incorporated in the *Rin-chen-gter-mdsod-chen-po*.

(DC+Tt) It is not incorrect to use the term '*bKa'-'dus*' only for the cycles of *bLa-sgrub* and *bKa'-brgyad*. The whole *bKa'-'dus* as such has twenty-one parts, as is stated by the full-length hagiography (*rnam-thar chen-mo*) [of O-rgyan-gling-pa]. Because [all parts of the *bKa'-'dus*] are trustworthy, they marvellously kindled the flame of the Doctrine.

(Tt) The venerable *bLa-ma* [Padma-'od-gsal-mdo-sngags-gling-pa]revised the three cycles *bLa-ma-bstan-gnyis* by rGya Lo-tsā-ba.[165] He did it in the manner of an Once-more Hidden Book (*yang-gter*). Thus in spite of different stylistic peculiarities the meaning [of the three cycles] tallies with that of the profound Concealed Books (*zab-gter*) by O-rgyan-gling-pa. Therefore it is correct to merge both transmissions in one stream. There are also parts of the *bKa'-'dus* which belong to the section of manuals for daily prayers (*nyin-mtshan-rgyun-gyi rnal-'byor*). These treatises form the content of the three main training subjects according to the theory of the Concealed Teachings (*bLa-rdsogs-thugs-gsum*).

8. HAGIOGRAPHY OF RIG-'DSIN-CHEN-PO DNGOS-GRUB-RGYAL-MTSHAN ALIAS RIG-'DSIN RGOD-LDEM-CAN (1337-1409), THE DISCOVERER OF THE 'NORTHERN TEACHINGS' (*byang-gter*)

(DC+Tt) HIS PREVIOUS EXISTENCE

The Discoverer Rig-'dsin-chen-po dNgos-grub-rgyal-mtshan was one of the actual beings (*yang-srid*) that emerged from sNa-nam-rdo-rje-bdud-'joms[166] and from the three most important actual beings (*mchog-gi sprul-sku-rnam gsum*).

BIRTH AND CHILDHOOD

The family sNa-mo-lung[167] lived in the north-east of the village Ri-bo-bkra-bzang[168] in the country of Tho-gyor-nag-po. With many extraordinary miracles happening [the Discoverer of Concealed Treasures] was born on the tenth day of the first month of the year 1337. His father was sLob-dpon bDud-'dul, a mystic and an advocate of the *Vajrakīla* cycle (*phur-pa*). He was a descendant of the dynasty of the Mongolian King Gur-ser. According to the prophecy three feathers of a vulture became visible upon his head when he was eleven years old and five feathers when he was twenty-three. Therefore he is well known as Rig-'dsin rGod-ldem-can.[169] From early childhood he studied all subjects that were included into the Doctrine of the Old School (*rNying-ma-pa*), which had also been his father's religion. He reflected on these subjects and meditated upon them. Thus, he became accomplished.

RGOD-LDEM-CAN OBTAINS THE LIST OF HIDING PLACES

Mang-lam-bzang-po-grags-pa unearthed an important list of Hiding Places (*snying-byang*) with the title *Man-ngag-gnad-kyi don-bdun-ma* at rGyang-yon-po-lung.[170] Altogether he discovered about eight religious treatises. [Mang-lam-bzang-po-grags-pa] recognized this list to be useful for the unearthing of the Concealed Treasure of [Zang-zang]-lha-brag.[171] Therefore he handed this list to sTon-pa bSod-nams-dbang-phyug,[172] with the order to pass it on to Rig-'dsin-chen-po [rGod-ldem-can]. On the eighth day of the first half of the second month in the year 1366 rGod-ldem-can obtained a key-list for [discovering] three important Concealed Treasures (*gter-ma*) and about one-hundred minor Concealed Treasures. [This key-list was discovered] near the three obelisks (*rdo-ring*) at the rock 'Dseng-brag-dkar-po beneath the summit of the mountain Ri-bo-bkra-bzang. To compensate for the removal of the list he buried a Treasure (*gter*) there. He left the hiding place, and it is reported that up to this day there exists a cavity there. The next year during the New-Year Celebration a young plant grew, still existing today.

RGOD-LDEM-CAN'S ACTIVITY AS DISCOVERER OF CONCEALED TEACHINGS

The same year on the fourth day of the fourth month, rGod-ldem-can took out a blue rectangular chest with many partitions from the cave Zang-zang-lha-brag, situated in the midst of a mountain-range that looks like a heap of poisonous snakes. In the chest he found the profound Concealed Books of the *mDsod-lnga* : From the dark-brown, central hiding-place [within the chest] he removed three scrolls and three [treatises on] the *Vajrakīla* cycle, which were wrapped in a ceremonial silk scarf (*kha-btags*). From the eastern hiding-place which is white like a sea-shell he obtained some tractates on the cause-effect-situation (*las-rgyu-'bras*), the content of these works is as vast as heavenly spaces. From the southern gold-like hiding place he obtained for treatises on a meditation practice by uttering mystic formulas and by visual realization (*bsnyen-sgrub*), radiant like sun and moon. In the western red and copper-like hiding place he took out a sandal-tree resembling treatise on auspicious signs (*rten-'brel*). In the northern iron-like hiding place he found a treatise as pernicious as a poisonous tree with the title *bGegs-thal-bar-rlog-pa'i-chos*. From the central hiding place there emerged the important treatise *Kun-bzang-dgongs-pa-zang-thal* together with many sacrificial pills (*dam-rdsas*). rGod-ldem-can divided each of these Five Treasures (*mdsod lnga*) into one-hundred parts. He revised the basic scrolls (*śog-ser*) and transmitted the theory to qualified individuals. Thus it was disseminated all over Tibet. Generally speaking, it was only during this year and the next that welfare and happiness spread throughout Tibet due to his profound Concealed Teachings (*zab-gter*).

Especially he propagated the theory of the Northern Treasure (*byang-gter*). [Through his benevolent activity] final wars[172a] (*mtha'-dmag*) were averted, pestilences cut off, interior riots ceased, the bewitched ones were exiled, the varied branches of trade and farming were promoted, diseases and illness caused by the gNyan-demons[173] were cured. The necessities for sustenance were abundant. All over Tibet from gNgul-mkhar in the highlands of Khyung-lung [in the west][174] to kLong-thang-sgrol-ma in the low-lands of sMad-khams [in the east] extraordinarily happy ways of living were propagated. He obtained the key [to open the approach] to the seven most important Hidden Countries (*sbas-yul*)[175] and also the key to many lists of hiding places (*thems-byang = kha-byang*). This single Discoverer of Concealed Teachings became famous all over Tibet like *Ācārya* Padmasambhava.

When he was past his middle age he went to 'Bras-mo-gśongs,[176] and opened the door of a hiding place (*gter*). The King of Gung-thang[177] mChog-sgrub-sde appointed him as his teacher. Thereupon the happiness and welfare of Tibet was maintained.

HIS DEATH

When he had accomplished his achievements he showed many miracles and his intentionality (*dgongs-pa*) dissolved in the sphere of absolute being (*chos-dbyings*). This occurred when he was seventy-one.

(DC) TRANSMISSION OF HIS TEACHINGS

The transmission of his teachings has continued unceasingly to this day. It has been handed down by the lineages of his son, his consecrated consort (*yum*), and his disciples.

(DC+Tt) From these lineages came forth many mystics and persons who had realized the radiant light (*'ja-lus-pa*).[178]

(Tt) His most important teachings are : *bLa-ma-źi-drag*, *Thugs-rje-chen-po*, *'Gro-'dul-rdsogs-chen-dgongs-pa-zang-thal*, *bKa'-brgyad-rang-śar*,[179] *rTen-'brel-chos* and *bsTan-srung-gi-skor*. They still exist today. I (sKong-sprul Padma-gar-dbang) also used them.

(DC) HIS SUCCESSORS

The deceased regent sDe-srid gTsang-pa[180] caused some trouble in the days of the second rGod-ldem Rig-'dsin-legs-ldan-rje and the actual being (*sPrul-sku*) of mNga'-ris Paṇ-chen Byang-bdag (i.e. Protector of the Northern Treasure) called bKra-śis-stobs-rgyal-dbang-po. Because of this the whole religious community (*dge-'dun*, skr. *sangha*) of the monastic college became divided amongst themselves. A camp called E-vam-lcog-sgar was set up. During the time of Byang-bdag's son, the third [rGod-ldem] Rig-'dsin Ngag-gi-dbang-po, the residence was shifted to the central province of dBus. Since this time the monastery went by the name Thub-bstan-rdo-rje-brag.[181] The fourth Rig-'dsin Źabs-drung Padma-phrin-las disseminated this vision by way of three aspects (teaching, uttering mystic formulas, and meditation).[182] He thus reduced the teachings of the ancient translations (*snga-'gyur-bstan-pa*) i.e. the *rNying-ma-pa*, to a single teaching. The residence of the later incarnations of Rig-'dsin [rGod-ldem] remained here [in Thub-bstan-rdo-rje-brag]. On this account, the Doctrine was sufficiently supported so that many religious peoples appeared who maintained this transmission from the highland of mNga'-ris and La-dvags[183] (Ladakh) down to the lowlands of sMad-rgya Dar-rtse-mdo.[184]

9. HAGIOGRAPHY OF SANGS-RGYAS-GLING-PA, ALIAS RIN-CHEN-GLING-PA, ALIAS SANGS-RGYAS-BZANG-PO (1340-1396), THE DISCOVERER OF THE *BLA-MA-DGONGS-'DUS* CYCLE

(Tt) THE PROPHECY

"The fallacious ones and the right ones from gTsang-gi-dgyer-phu will fight against each other and a herd of pigs will become visible at Ru-lag Tshud-phud.[185] Then an auspicious sign will arise that the Concealed Treasure (*gter-kha*) of Kong-po mChims-yul[186] shall not remain any longer there, but shall be taken out. A man by the name of O-rgyan-rin-chen-gling-pa[187] will come." Later on, the Discoverer of Concealed Treasures (*gTer-ston*) went by the name of Rin-chen-gling-pa. This is not only evident from the prophecy of the hiding places (*gter-gnas*) but also from his full-length hagiography (*rnam-thar chen-mo*).

(DC+Tt) The great Discoverer of Concealed Teachings (*gTer-chen*) Sangs-rgyas-gling-pa was an incarnation (*sPrul'pa*) of Lha-sras Dam-'dsin-rol-pa-ye-śes.

BIRTH AND CHILDHOOD

At Brag-gsumrDo-rje-brag[188] near the meditation-cave O-rgyn-gying-phu-gyu-lung-gi-mda'-gdab, in the district of Nyang—a part of the province Kong-po, Sangs-rgyas-gling-pa was born to his father Khams-źig-stag-lung-smyon-pa who was an actual being (*sPrul-pa*) of *Hayagrīva* and to his mother A-hūṃ-rgyan who was blessed by auspicious signs and by *rDo-rje-phag-mo*. This happened in the year 1340 while many miraculous signs appeared. The parents gave him the name Rig-'dsin. In his fifth year he took the vows of a novice (*dge-bsnyen-gyi sdom-pa*) in the presence of *mKhan-po* gŹon-nu-dpal.[189] He had a vision of the Great Merciful One (*Avalokiteśvara*). He thoroughly mastered the art of writing and reading and became a well-educated person. At this time his father died. He himself became a nuisance to his step-father whom his mother had married. So the child suffered much.

PROPHECY AND RELIGIOUS TRAINING BY VARIOUS *BLA-MAS*

During this time a young woman with a red complexion gave him a prophecy that he ought to go to the Hierarch (*rGyal-dbang*) Rol-pa'i-rdo-rje (1340-1383)[190] in the valley of Long po Grong-gsar. Near the [holy mountain] Tsā-ri[191] was the monastery Byang-chub-gling. There he received the monk-name (*rab-tu-byung-ba'i mtshan*) Sangs-rgyas-bzang-po from *mKhan-po* Byang-chub-rdo-rje and *Ācārya* Śākya-ye-śes. When he had taken out the profound Concealed Treasure (*zab-gter*) he became famous by the name Sangs-rgyas-gling-pa. He heard many instructions from both the *mKhan-po* and the *Ācārya*.

When the venerable Rol-pa'i-rdo-rje had returned from the central province of dBus he asked the *bLa-ma* Byang-chub-rdo-rje : "Give me your nephew (*dBon-po*)!"[192] When Byang-chub-rdo-rje did so, he was very happy and prophesied that his nephew would become a leader of many beings.

When Sangs-rgyas-gling-pa had arrived at Lha-sa he gazed at the countenances of *Avalokiteśvara* and, in particular, of *Ācārya* Rin-po-che (i.e. Padmasambhava). Since this time he looked at many appearances and promised to exercise meditative realization (*sgrub-pa*) for three years. When *bLa-ma* Byang-chub-rdo-rje had died [Sangs-rgyas-gling-pa] went to *mKhas-grub bLa-ma* Chos-kyi-blo-gros at Tsā-ri and became his intimate disciple (*thugs-sras*). After the return of *bLa-ma* [Chos-kyi-blo-gros] to the central province of dBus he stayed behind at Lhun-grub-steng-gi-phur-bcad-rgya.[193]

HIS ACTIVITY AS DISCOVERER OF CONCEALED TEACHINGS

One night the Protector of Concealed Treasures (*gter-srung*) *bsTan-rgod-chen-po* (i.e. The Wild Great Vulture) appeared and handed him three little scrolls (*śog-dril*). From these scrolls he learned the list of hiding places (*kha-byang*), the prophecy, directions for meditative realization (*sgrub-pa*), and instructions. The *bLa-ma* also assisted him.

When he celebrated a meditative realization of the [discovery of] the Concealed Treasure (*gter-sgrub*) the Precious [Master of] Uḍḍiyāna (i.e. Padmasambhava) together with a group of Spiritual Beings conferred an empowerment (*dbang-bskur*) on him and gave him prophecies. Accordingly on the twentieth day of the seventh month in the year 1364 he discovered the basic text and the instructions of the *bLa-ma-dgongs-'dus-pa*, the medium *bKa'-'dus* which is renowned to be the single [real] Concealed Book under Tibetan earth, and the *Thugs-rje-chen-po'i chos-skor*. He showed these Concealed Books to his *bLa-ma* who enjoyed them very much. By meditating on the content of these works he became their first master. From this year onwards Sangs-rgyas-gling-pa unearthed the books *Phur-sgrub-thugs-kyi-nying-khu*, *gTod-khram-ru-sbal-nag-po*, *rTa-mgrin-nag-po*, and also *Thugs-rje-chen-po yang-gsang-bla-med*, and further hidden precious objects (*rdsas-gter*), sacrificial objects (*dam-rdsas*), sacrificial pills (*ril-bu*), a mask of Padmasambhava, a copper vase full of gold, an iron ceremonial dagger (*phur-bu*), and twenty-one relics of deceased persons ; [all this he found in the areas of] dKar-zug-'phrang, rJe-bo-rong,[194] Long-po Byang-sde-'bum-pa, Long-po Ka-mda'-'phrang,[195] and rKyen-gyi dKar-steng-'phrang.

When he took out the Concealed Treasure from Kong-po mChims-yul he met the Discoverer of Concealed Treasures Dri-med-lhun-po.[196] This happened also in accordance with the Spiritual Beings' (*mKha'- 'gro-ma*) prophecy. Together they unearthed the *Phyag-rdor-gos-sngon*, the *Ngan-sngags-mon-pa-dgu-rgyug*, and the *O-rgyan-yab-yum-gyi-byang-sems*. The *'Phags-pa-spyan-ras-gzigs* emerged from sPu-ri-rin-chen-'bar-ba, the *Thugs-chen*, the *bCud-len-skor*, and the *dBang-phyug-rlung-źags* from Bya-rgod-gśong.[197] Also the prophecy about *Byang-chub gling-pa-dpal-gyi-rgyal-mtshan* is derived from the last mentioned text. [A man] who had been ordered to go and look around in La-stod[198] gave firm credence to these Concealed Teachings after he had met the Discoverer himself. Sangs-rgyas-gling-pa took out the *kLu-rgyal-mgrin-bzang-sgrubs-thabs* from [the holy mountain) Tsā-ri and the *Tshe-sgrub-nyi-zla-kha-sbyor* from dGy-erbye-ma-dkar-po. In cooperation with the Discoverer Dri-med-lhung-po he found the *gŚin-rje-tshe-bdag*, the *Thun-phog-'gyel*, and the *O-rgyan-gyi-las-phur-gdengs-chog* in gŚin-rje'i-rba-dong.[199] Further on he unearthed a summary of the essentials of the *rDsogs-chen* system (*rDsogs-chen-snying-po-bsdus-pa*) in a meditation grotto of O-rgyan (i.e. Padmasambhava), and the *dGongs-'dus-rtsa-ba'i-rgyud-drug* in Kong-po Dam-rul,[200] and some most venerable figures of the Precious [Master] of Uḍḍiyāna (i.e. Padmasambhava) in bSam-yas mChims-phu, the jewel 'Lucky Tiger Flesh' (*sTag-śa-bde-da*) and the ornament of a Spiritual Being (*mKha'-'gro-ma*) in 'Od-śod-rlung-sgrom.

In between his twenty-fifth and thirty-second years he obtained eighteen great Concealed Treasures (*gter-kha chen-po*). His small Treasures were countless and it is not possible to list all those he had discovered.

It often happened that flowers came down like rain, that a rainbow appeared like a tent, that one heard music, and that the shapes of Spiritual Beings became visible. According to the prophecy of *rDo-rje-phag-mo* (*Vajravārāhī*) and of thirteen other Spiritual Beings (*mKha'-'gro*) he divided the *dGong'dus* cycle into thirteen books, cut the sheets of paper to size and painted the fore-edge with red colour. This very manner is still used up to this day.

PROPHECY ABOUT HIS ADHERENTS

It is stated in the prophecy : "A hundred-thousand times ten-million persons will surely attain the Developing Stage (*bskyed-rim*). Eight-hundred-thousand persons will evidently attain the distinguishing attributes of a Mystic (*Grub-thob*). Ninety-thousand people will become free of the filthy body (*mi-dag-pa'i lus*) and attain the body of apparition (*sgyu-lus*).[201] A hundred times one-hundred-million people [will reach] a single spiritual potency (*siddhi*). The number of those who will reach the foundations of liberation will be countless. This will not happen all at the same time but step by step." Thus, it is stated in particular. Therefore, there are about twenty main lineages of transmission of the *dGongs-'dus*.

DISCIPLES OF SANGS-RGYAS-GLING-PA

The number of other Concealed Teachings (*gter-chos*) and of other masters of these Teachings (*gTer-bdag*) [who are in this lineage] is beyond calculation. The most famous [of these masters) are : the Fourth *Karma-pa* Hierarch (*rGyal-dbang*) Rol-pa'i-rdo-rje (1340-1383), mKha'-spyod-dbang-po (1350-1405)[202] of the *Źva-dmar-pa* School, sNe'u-gdong *Gong-ma-chen-po* (i.e. Byang-chub-rgyal-mtshan, 1302-1373),[203] the noble *bLa-ma* bSod-nams-rgyal-mtshan of the *Sa-skya-pa* School,[204] gYag-sde Paṇ-chen,[205] Jo-bstan mKhan-chen bSod-nams-bzang-po,[206] the Religious King (*Chos-rgyal*) of 'Bri-gung and many other great men, *bLa-mas* and similarly important persons.

THE ESTEEM IN WHICH THE CONCEALED BOOK *DGONGS-PA-'DUS-PA* IS HELD

It has been reported that the Chinese sovereign (*rGyal-po*) Ta-ming had sent an invitation to De-bźin-gśegs-pa (1384-

1415)[207] the Hierarch of the *Karma-pa* School. In this letter he wrote that the *Karma-pa* Hierarch should take along a pure and original sample of the Concealed Teachings (*gter-chos*) of the Mystic of Uḍḍiyāna (Padmasambhava), *Chos-rje* De-bźin-gśegs-pa brought along the profound treatise *dGongs-pa-'dus-pa,* a miraculous bluish water flask, and a golden *Vajra.* Thus, he went to the [Chinese] sovereign and offered him [the presents]. Thereupon the ruler was very pleased and rewarded him excellent clothes and a privy seal (*sgal-tshing-gi dam*).[208]

DEATH OF SANGS-RGYAS-GLING-PA

[Sangs-rgyas-gling-pa] founded the monastery sNyi-phu-bde-chen-bsam-sgrub and made it his main residence. While he was performing a medical ceremony by using nectar (*bdud-rtsi-sman-sgrub*),[209] exceptional auspicious signs emerged, these were more miraculous than other ones. Having benefited the beings his intentionality (*dgongs-pa*) dissolved in the being-itself (*chos- kyi-dbyings*). This happened on the thirtieth day of the third month in the year 1396 when he was fifty-six years old.

THE NEXT FOLLOWING INCARNATIONS

At Nel-pa-sme-'ur the next (i.e.'the second') incarnation [of Sangs-rgyas-gling-pa] was born to Don-grub-rgyal-po but the [incarnated child] died at tender age. The third incarnation was born at Long-po-gyin. This *sPrul-sku* Sangs-rgyas-dpal-ldan went to his proper residence, and it is reported that he was of benefit to others. The lineage of the later incarnations was not noted particularly.

HIS DESCENDANTS AND THE TRANSMISSION OF HIS TEACHINGS

[The Discoverer's] descendants existed into later times. The transmission lineages of his sons and disciples involve his own son Ye-śes-rdo-rje and his most eminent disciple dPal-ldan-seng-ge[210] who had become master of these teachings and who was a member of the Bya-khyung-bśad-gling monastery. By and by many scholar-saints (*mKhas-pa*) and Mystics (*Grub-thob*) originated in [these lineages]. All over Tibet, but especially in the province of mDo-Khams, these profound

Concealed Teachings [of Sang-rgyas-gling-pa] particularly the [*bLa-ma*]*dgongs-'dus* were disseminated through transmission of the *bLa-ma* of the rTse-le monastery, his successor, and by the elder and younger Ta-bla-ma.

(DC) Later on, mThu-chen-ngag-dbang-rnam-rgyal, the sovereign of Bhutan (*'Brug źabs-drung*) situated in the south, received the complete empowerments (*dbang*) and the oral commentaries (*lung*) of the *bLa-ma-dgongs-'dus* cycle from Kong Rig-'dsin-snying-po, the seventh successor [of Sangs-rgyas-gling-pa] ; thus, the sovereign became a master of these teachings (*Chos-bdag*). He celebrated the Great Representation (*sgrub-chen*) of the *bLa-ma-dgongs-'dus* cycle[211] and the Ritual of the Tenth Day (*tshe-bcu'i mchod-pa*)[212] by materially demonstrating (*spros-bcas*) them. This great ceremony which took place at sPungs-thang bDe-ba-chen-po, the residence (i.e. Punakha of the maps), was attended by the nobles and the religious people who have their own monasteries and castles. This system has survived up to this time. Even today the ritual formulas for expiatory sacrifices (*skang-ba*) are well known in the countries of the south and of the Mon people.

THE MOST FAMOUS BOOKS OF SANGS-RGYAS-GLING-PA

(Tt) I (sKong-sprul Padma-gar-dbang) have heard the following empowerments and all the other important and still existing instructions from the ocean-like teaching of this great Discoverer of Concealed Teachings : The *sPu-ri'i-bka'-thang*, the *bLa-ma-dgongs-'dus*, the *Thugs-rje-chen-po-nor-bu-skor-gsum*, the *rTse-chen-phur-ba*, the *'Jam-dpal-dkar-dmar-nag-gsum*, the *Khyung-gsang-ba-yang-khol*, the *Dri-med-bśags-rgyud*, and the *Tshe-sgrub-nyi-zla-kha-sbyor*. Many times I practised meditation by uttering mystic formulas and by visual realization of the *bLa-ma-dgongs-'dus* cycle.

I have published all the prayers of the [*bLa-ma-*] *dgongs-'dus* cycle because other people asked me and because I myself wanted to do so. Also I composed a practical book [with supplements]. From among the divine representations (*lha*)[213] of the *bLa-ma-dgongs-'dus* cycle I have three times painted the ninth, eleventh, and fifteenth Tanka. [I also have painted] the Protectors of the Buddha's Word (*bKa'-srung*). I have published all books [which belong to the *bLa-ma-dgongs-'dus*].

(Now a small sentence for blessing follows).

10. HAGIOGRAPHY OF RDO-RJE-GLING-PA (1346-1405), ALIAS PADMA-GLING-PA, KUN-SKYONG GLING-PA, GYUNG-DRUNG GLINGA-PA, 'JAM-DPAL-CHOS-KYI-BŚES- GNYEN, THE THIRD DISCOVERER KING

(Tt) THE PROPHECY

"There will appear a herd of pigs in the country sTod- khu. The fortified country will have small castles on each hill. Narrow passes and impassable paths will be guarded by dogs. A sign will be shown that the Treasure Concealed at Kong-po Bu-chu shall not remain there but be taken out. A man by the name of O-rgyan-rdo-rje-gling-pa[214] will appear."

(DC+Tt) According to this prophecy rDo-rje-gling-pa is the third of the Discoverer Kings (*gTer-ston rgyal-po*) and he is as venerable as Vairocana.

BIRTH AND EDUCATION

He was born to his father Khu-ston bSod-nams-rgyal-mtshan[215] a descendant of a family of Tantrics (*rDo-rje-'dsin-pa*) and to his mother dKar-mo-rgyan at the place Gra-nang dBen-rtsa[216] in the province of dBus. This happened during the sixth month in the year 1346. He received the name O-rgyan-bzang-po. He showed unimaginable signs and miracles of his achievement in the noble method of spiritual maturity (*dam-pa'i rigs sad-pa*). When he was seven years old he received the pledges of a novice from Kun-mkhyen-khrab-pa-śākya at sPang-gśod-lha-ri-khar. From this and other *bLa-mas* he heard all the Sūtras and Mantras of the New and Old Schools (*gSar-ma-pa* and *rNying-ma-pa*). When he was thirteen years old he envisaged the countenance of the Precious Master of Uḍḍiyāna (i.e. Padmasambhava).

ACTIVITY AS DISCOVERER OF CONCEALED BOOKS

From behind the figure Khra-brug Jo-mo,[217] according to

the list of hiding places (*kha-byang*) included in the Concealed Treasure of Guru Chos-dbang (1212-1270),[218] rDo-rje-gling-pa's first Concealed Book on the meditation about the three main roots of religious practice (*rtsa-gsum sgrub-thabs*) became visible together with small treatises on meditation (*sgrub*), lists of hiding places (*kha-byang*), and lists of Treasures that had been concealed once again (*yang-byang*), evil spells (*drag-sngags*) and instructions for special dietetics (*bcud-len*); [219] each book consisted of one hundred and eight treatises. He obtained these together with special oral commentaries (*sgos-lung*). When [rDo-rje-gling-pa] was about fifteen years old he opened the door of the hiding place (*gter*) at Bying-mda'-'od-dkar-brag.[220] After he had entered the spacious meditation-grotto (*sgrub-phug*) and had built a *Maṇḍala* (*dkyil-'khor*) the Precious Guru (i.e. Padmasambhava) conferred upon him an empowerment (*dbang-bskur*). He also taught him the oral commentaries which dealt with the central problem of each scroll. He gave to rDo-rje-gling-pa some hidden objects (*gter-rdsas*) and a figure of the Precious Guru, four books, one-hundred scrolls (*śog-dril*), four ritual water flasks (*bum-pa*)filled with the elixir of life (*tshe-chu*),[221] and a box with relics (*dam-rdsas*). rDo-rje-gling-pa unearthed all the following things : The eighth chapter of the *rNam-thar-thang-yig*,[222] which belongs to the Buddhist literature (because he also unearthed some *Bon* scriptures), the *rDsogs-chen* treatise *lTa-ba-klong-yangs* which belongs to the *pha-rgyud* division,[223] the *kLong-gsal-nyi-ma* which belongs to the *ma-rgyud* division, the *Nyi-zla-kha-sbyor* which belongs to the *mKha'-'gro-yang-tig*, ten treatises on the *Bu-rgyud-snying-thig*, four on the '*Dus-pa* and eight other texts. Then he removed ten tractates on 'The Commentary of the Practice' (*Nyams-len khrid*) from Mu-tig-śel-gyi-bsam-gong. Thereupon Ye-śes-mtsho-rgyal herself entered the life-bestowing grotto (*tshe-phug*) of Bum-thang Byams-pa-lha-khang. She gave him the elixir of life (*tshe-chu*) and holy medicines (*chos-sman*), whereupon he performed a ritual at Yang-le-śod; further he obtained the Spirit-Upholding Turquois (*bla-gyu*) '*Nor-bu-bsam-'phel*[224] [which had belonged to] the Religious King [Khri-srong-lde-btsan] and Ye-śes-mtsho-rgyal; in addition he received religious things and many evil spells.

In the meantime [rDo-rje-gling-pa] discovered fortythree

great Concealed Treasures (*gter-kha*) at several hiding places and one-hundred and eight small Concealed Treasures at some special places. When he was taking out the Treasure hidden at mChims-phu he envisaged [the Master of] Uḍḍiyāna (Padmasambhava) thirteen times. While [rDo-rjegling-pa] let two authentic beings come into existence whom he ordered to walk towards Chu-bo-ri,[225] starting from two different directions, he took out a Concealed Treasure in public (*khrom-gter*). Also he impressed on this place his foot-mark one *khru* in size (about 15 inches) while he stayed in the [meditation-grotto] of gNyan (*gNyan-gyi phug-pa*) called Zab-lungme-chor,[226]. [*gNyam-chen*] *Thang-lha*[227] and *Gangs-dkar-ṣa-med*[228] had proved themselves dispensers of gifts (*sbyin-bdag*). All important gods and demons of the Snowland (i.e. Tibet) had assembled and celebrated a great ritual performance of the Eight Pronouncements (*bka'-brgyad-kyi sgrub-chen*). In his *sPrul-pa* form [rDo-rje-gling-pa] hurried to the eight great cremation grounds. There he perceived the Eight Wisdom-Holders (*Rig-'dsin brgyad*) and heard the eight explanations (*gding*).[229] At the time when he took out the Concealed Treasure (*gter-kha*) he envisaged the Precious Guru (Padmasambhava), Ye-śes-mtsho-rgyal, and Vairocana. He received empowerments and instructions. He worked many miracles and demonstrated miraculous appearances in order to free all those who had attained a firm belief, from the chains of doubts. He left a variety of marks of his body, hands and feet. He discovered empowerments (*dbang*), foundation-ceremonies (*rabgnas*), expiatory rituals (*skang-bśags*), [rituals] of burnt sacrifice (*sbyin-sreg*) destructive charms (*mnan-pa*); forming one-hundred and eight tractates at Zab-lung,[230] mKhar-chu[231] and gŽostod-ti-sgro.[232] He disseminated these efficient methods all over Tibet. He discovered countless mysterious treatises which were included in the Buddhist Concealed Teachings. The main treatise refers to the *bLa-rdsogs-thugs-gsum* (i.e. the three basic subjects of religious training according to the method of the Concealed Teachings). He unearthed a figure of *rDo-rje-semsdpa'* from (the mountain) Phung-po-ri-bo-che.[233] From the column Bum-pa-can in the Lha-sa [Jo-khang][234] he took out a miracle-performing figure of the Eleven-Headed One (i.e. *Avalokiteśvara*) and, a sandal-wood figure of *Tārā*. Holy medicines (*chos-sman*) formed part of his Treasure of sacrificial things (*dam-rdsas gter*). The Treasure of Jewels (*nor-gter*) consisted of the 'Wish-Bestowing Gem' (*yid-bžin-nor-bu*). The *Bon* division of the Concealed Treasures discovered by him consisted of the *gSer-thur*, and the oral transmission (*snyan-brgyid*) of the *Tabi-hri-tsa*,[235] of medium and smaller instructions. He also unearthed many texts on astronomy (*rtsis-sker*) and medicine (*gso-rig*). Thereupon his activity spread far and wide.

DESCENDANTS

His own son was Chos-dbyings-pa, an incarnation of gNubs-chen and others. Thus his family still exists in the Mon country. It is reported that he taught the cycles of *gŚin-rje-gśed* (*Yamāntaka*) and of *Jambhala*, the god of wealth (*Dsam-bha-lha-rigs-lnga*), together with the five *Dhyāni-Buddhas* to the Fourth Hierarch of the *Karma-pa* School, *rGyal-dbang* Rol-pa'i-rdo-rje. The Discoverer built his residence at gLing-mo-mkhar. He stayed here and at other monasteries in Lho-brag,[236] Monspa-gro[237] and gZad-'ug-rnyed (or Zad-'ug-rkod). He disseminated the Doctrine for the benefit of all sentient beings.

HIS VARIOUS NAMES

Especially he went by the names of rDo-rje-gling-pa, Padma-gling-pa, Kun-skyong-gling-pa, gYung-drung-gling-pa, 'Jam-dpal-chos-kyi-bśes-gñyen.

HIS DEATH AND CREMATION

When he had completed his activity for the benefit of the beings and of the Doctrine he made his will at the age of fifty-nine years and delivered a prophecy (*Žal-chems-lung-bstan*). He performed many miracles, and in Brag-long (in the year 1405) he demonstrated his departure from the world. For three years his corpse did not decay. Sometimes it was heard to murmur prayer verses diverting all his merits to the benefit of the sentient beings (*bsngo-ba tshig*). Finally the corpse was cremated. Many holy figures and relics (*ring-bsrel*) appeared. The right leg was given to his spiritual son (*Thugs-sras*) braś̱is-'byung-gnas,[238] the left one to Thogs-med-rgya-gar-ba. This was their appropriate share of the relics. Both these legs were hurled out from the flames in the crematory (*pur-khang*)[239] while a cracking noise was heard. Many relics were scattered about, they existed till later times.

(DC) THE TRADITION OF HIS FAMILY AND HIS DOCTRINE

For a long time the descendants of his family lived at his residence O-rgyan-chos-gling in the town Mon-bum-thang. The Old Transmission (*ring-brgyud*) of his profound doctrines exists to this day and has never been interrupted. Some treatises state that the venerable mKhyen-brtse'i-dbang-po obtained the New Transmission (*nye-brgyud*) and mastered their teachings.

(Tt) Formerly his teachings were largely known in Lho-brag and the Mon country, but nowadays they have become scarce. Now there exist these tractates: Some treatises on *rDsogs-chen* belonging to the cycle of the *pha-rgyud* ('Father Tantra') *lTa-ba-klong-yangs*, some to the cycle of the *ma-rgyud* ('Mother Tantra') *kLong-gsal-nyi-ma*, and some to the cycle of the 'Non-dual' (*gnyis-med rgyud*) *Hūṃ-skor-snying-thig*. (Also there still exist :) The *bLa-ma-*, *Yi-dam-*, and *mKha'-'gro-'dus* belonging to the '*Dus-pa-skor-bži*, the *Thugs-rje-chen--po-ngan-song-kun-skyobs-rgyal-ba-rgya-mtsho* and the *sNyan-brgyud-gur-drag-rnams*. The Old Transmission (*ring-brgyud*) and the New Transmission (*nye-brgyud*) of these teachings were bestowed on me (i.e. sKong-sprul) by my venerable teacher [mKhyen-brtse'i-dbang-po].I have gained proficiency in these teachings. Earnestly I searched after these books and by prosperous circumstances I found them and became a talented one (*skal-ba bzang-po*). Although there remains the question whether the signs of the time the incarnated great Discoverer of Concealed Teachings appeared and whether the hiding place [*gter-gnas*] of the Concealed Treasures tally with the prophecy of the [*Padma-*] *bka'-thang*, he nevertheless is the third of the Five Discoverer Kings (*gTer-ston-rgyal-po lnga*) and belongs to the twelve [persons whose names end with] *-gling-chen-po*.[240] Only fools can say otherwise.

11. HAGIOGRAPHY OF RATNA-GLING-PA (1403-1479), THE COLLECTOR OF THE *RNYING-MA-RGYUD-'BUM*

(DC+Tt) PARENTS AND BIRTH

Ratna-gling-pa, the great incarnated Discoverer of Concealed Teachings (*sprul-pa'i gTer-ston*) is an authentic being of Lang-gro dKon-mchog-'byung-gnas. At Gru-śul[241] in the country Lho-brag he was born as the son of Phyug-po mDo-sde-dar, his father, and Sri-thar-sman, his mother, on the fifteenth day of the seventh month in the year 1403.

HIS YOUTH

In earliest youth he easily learned reading and writing. From his tenth year onwards he had many visions. By his former wisdom he thoroughly understood the ten arts without ever tiring of them. He studied the Doctrine and practised it in various manners.

VISION OF PADMASAMBHAVA

When he was twenty-seven the Precious Guru (Padmasambhava) appeared to him in the shape of an ascetic of Khams with yellowish cap and clothes. He personally gave Ratna-gling-pa many lists of hiding places (*gter-gyi kha-byang*) and admonished him many times.

HIS ACTIVITY AS DISCOVERER OF CONCEALED TEACHINGS

Thus when he was thirty he unearthed his first Concealed Treasure (*gter-kha*) on *rTsa-gsum sgrub* (i.e. the realization of the three main roots of religious practice) at Khyung-chen-brag.[242] Step by step he took out from 'Bri-thang Ko-ro-brag a guide book for meditative realization (*sgrub-thabs*) on *Haya-grīva* and *Vajravārāhī* in union (*rta-phag yab-yum zung-'jug*), from gNam-skas-can in Lho-brag he took out books on *'Dus-pa-skor-bźi, bLa-ma-źi-drag, Thugs-rje-gsang-'dus, rDsogs-chen-klong-gsal-*

nyi-ma. These are the main books from among twenty-five books. When he opened the Concealed Treasure of mKhar-chu dPal-gyi-phug-ring[243] he demonstrated amazing miracles such as clairvoyance (*mngon-śes*). For twenty-five times he gazed at the appearance of the Precious Master of Uḍḍiyāna (Padmasambhava). During such a vision he went to [the purified sphere] *Zangs-mdog-dpal-ri* and to other thirteen treasure houses, as is stated in his hagiography. Often he performed meditative realizations of his Guru's spirituality (*bla-ma'i thugs-sgrub*),[244] medical ceremonies (*sman-sgrub*) and ceremonies by using relic-pills which liberate within the next seven lives (*skye-bdun ril-sgrub*). When he was celebrating an empowerment (*dbang*), reading commentaries (*khrid*) or giving instructions, rainbows appeared, flowers were showered, and the smell of incense spread widely. Thus innumerable miracles happened and never was there any trouble.

HIS VARIOUS NAMES

He took out the three divisions of Concealed Treasures belonging to this very existence of his, and to the two subsequent incarnations because the auspicious signs (*rten-'brel*) grew better and better. On account of this he went by three names: Źig-po-gling-pa, 'Gro-'dul-gling-pa and Ratna-gling-pa. He put all the innumerable beings living in the countries between Mount Kailas (Gangs Ti-se),[245] Khams, and rGyal-mo-rong,[246] into the frame of spiritual maturity and liberation.

(DC) COLLECTING THE OLD TANTRAS AND COMPILING THE *RNYING-MA-RGYUD-'BUM*

The lDan-dkar-ma Catalogue[247] of the Kanjur states that the esoteric Tantras of the Vajrayāna (*gsang-sngags nang-rgyud*) were not included because they were dangerous [if studied by non-qualified persons]. The transmission of these books (*dpe*) and their oral tradition (*lung*) had become very scarce and precious because the Old Tantras of the First Period of Translations (*snga-'gyur rnying-ma'i rgyud*) were not taken into the collection of the Kanjur (*bKa'-'gyur*). With great enthusiasm Ratna-gling-pa earnestly searched for these books and the oral traditions in all directions of the compass. Finally he found the main bulk of the One-Hundred-Thousand Tantras (*rGyud-'bum*) at Zur-'ug-pa-lung.[248] He knew that in Khams, dBus, or gTsang the complete oral tradition was not handed down to anybody with the exception of Mes-sgom-gtan-bzang-po in gTsang. He could not imagine that this oral tradition was to be interrupted so soon. The master Mes-sgom, in spite of his old age, taught and gave him the instructions, showing great zeal in doing so for a long time.

Later on, Ratna-gling-pa compiled the One-Hundred-Thousand Tantras (*rGyud-'bum*) in a single collection at the Lhun-grub-pho-brang [palace] in Gru-śul. At first he wrote it in Indian ink but later on in golden tincture. Thereupon he did much for the dissemination of this oral tradition. Thanks to Ratna-gling-pa, the gracious and great Discoverer of Concealed Treasures, even today the Tantras of the Vajrayāna (*gsang-sngags rgyud*) are available for the use of everybody like a wish-bestowing jewel (*cintāmaṇi*). He was exceedingly useful to the whole *rNying-ma-pa* Doctrine.

(DC+Tt) HIS DEATH AND SUCCESSORS

When he had finished his useful doings at the age of seventy-six he departed to Padmasambhava's palace of Clear Light (*Padma-'od-kyi pho-brang*) by showing highly miraculous signs. (DC) His spiritual sons (*Thugs-sras*) were the 'four sons near to his heart' (*sNying-gi bu*). The tradition of his numerous and talented sons and disciples lasts till today. The charismatic qualities of his profound teachings did not diminish and they still continue.

(Tt) OTHER LITERARY SOURCES FOR HIS HAGIOGRAPHY

It might be suitable to explain this hagiography in full length but there exist Ratna-gling-pa's own works *gTer-'byung-chen-mo* and *Dag-snang-mdsod-khang-ma* up to this time. Also, Yar-'brog-pa Śes-rab-bzang-po and Nyang Don-grub-rgyal-po wrote a full hagiography [of Ratna-gling-pa].

WORKS DISCOVERED BY RATNA-GLING-PA

His famous Concealed Teachings are *rTsa-gsum*, *Phyag-chen*, *bLa-ma-zi-drag*, *Zab-lam* and besides these the *'Dus-pa-bskor-bzi*, *rDsogs-pa-chen-po-klong-gsal*, *Tshe-sgrub-rdor-phreng*, *Phur-pa-yang-gsang-bla-med*, *Ma-ning*, and other cycles of the Doctrine-Protectors (*Chos-skyong*) some smaller Concealed books, the Collected Pronouncements (*bKa'-'bum*) gathered in one volume. All these exist everywhere without discontinuity.

PADMA-GAR-DBANG'S ACTIVITY ABOUT RATNA-GLING-PA'S TEACHINGS

I (sKong-sprul Padma-gar-dbang) have thoroughly studied [these teachings] and practised meditative realizations (*sgrub-pa*) and meditations by uttering mystic formulas (*bsnyen-pa*) on the Life-Bestowing Dagger (*tshe-phur*) and other Tantric cycles. Thus, I have disseminated these teachings. I joined *dBon-sprul* Thugs-rje'i-gter-chen who was prophesied to be an authentic being of Lang-ro. Together we performed the ceremony of *Thugs-gsang-gi-bum-sgrub* in the temple of the great residence dPal-spungs,[249] and an Ever-Lasting-Great Performance (*sgrub-chen-rgyun-'jug-bcas*) in the crematory (*pur-khang*), both performed according to the pure method. These directories (*lag-len yig-cha*) were spread once more in this country and thus the promise was fulfilled.

12. HAGIOGRAPHY OF O-RGYAN-PADMA-GLING-PA (1450—unknown), THE FOURTH DISCOVERER KING

(Tt) THE PROPHECY

"'When the village 'Gos-kyi-phag-ri[250] will be overshadowed by castles (*rdsong*) and when at sTag-ru[251] in La-stod poison will be sold then the time will have come: this Treasure, hidden in [the lake] Me-'bar-mtsho shall not remain any longer there but shall be taken out. A man by the name of O-rgyan-padma-gling-pa will come."

(DC+Tt) O-rgyan-padma-gling-pa, the fifth incarnation of Lha-lcam Padma-gsal who, in turn, was a daughter of King [Khri-srong-lde-btsan][252] was the fourth of the Five Discoverer Kings (*gTer-ston rgyal-po lnga*).

HIS BIRTH

In the year 1450 while many miracles were appearing he was born as a son to his father Don-grub-bzang-po, who belonged to the family Myos at Mon-bum-thang, and to his mother Gron-med-dpal-'jom. This birth took place immediately after his former existence as Kun-mkhyen Dri-med-'od-zer.

YOUTH AND EDUCATION

He had a clear saint-like intellect (*dam-pa'i rigs-sad*) and knew the various arts (*yig-rigs*) and handicrafts although he had never been taught.

VISION OF PADMASAMBHAVA

Especially during the seventh month of the year 1465 at the village Yi-ge-drug-ma he actually envisaged the Precious Master of Uḍḍiyāna (Padmasambhava) and the latter blessed him.

HIS DISCOVERING ACTIVITY

O-rgyan-padma-gling-pa obtained the list of hiding places (*kha-byang*) of one-hundred-and-eight great Concealed Treasures when he was twenty-seven. The first of his profound Concealed Teachings (*zab-gter*) deals with *rDsogs-chen-klong gsal-snying-po*. He took it out of Me-'bar-mtsho, a meandering river, near the sNa-ring-brag[253] mountains. A large number of people had observed him when he had gone straight into the river holding a burning lamp. Later on when he reappeared from the river the lamp in his hand was still burning. He fetched a treasure-chest (*gter-sgrom*) which was shaped like a clay jug and which he had put into his bosom. Thereupon he put all people in a state of faithful attitude towards this miracle. His unquestionable renown spread all over the earth like sun and moon.

From bSam-yas mChims-phu he took out the book *rDsogs-chen-kun-bzang-dgongs-'dus*. From several other hiding-places (*gter-gnas*) he obtained the books listed below : *rDsogs-chen-*

gnyis-med-rgyud-bu-chung-gi-skor, *bLa-ma-nor-bu-rgya-mtsho*, *Thugs-rje-chen-po-mun-sel-sgron-me*, *bKa'-brgyad-thugs-kyi-me-long*, *Phur-pa yang- srog-gi-spu-gri*, *bDud-rtsi-sman-sgrub-kyi-skor*. The last three ones are comprised under the name *bKa'-phur-sman-gsum*. Further [he found :] The *Phyag-rdor-dregs-'dul*, the *gTum-chung* and three treatises on the fierce appearance of the Guru (*Guru-drag-po*), a full-length one, a medium-length one, and a short one; the *Tshe-khrid-rdo-rje-phreng-ba*, the *Tshe-sgrub-nor-bu-lam-khyer*, and the *Nag-po-skor-gsum*; further, there were many smaller and supplementary texts. Also he discovered relic pills which liberate when tasted (*myang-grol*), relic pills which liberate within the next seven lives (*skye-bdun ril-bu*) and figures of the Master Padmasambhava. He received many such relic objects (*dam-rdsas*), figures, and ritual objects (*rten*).

EXCAVATION OF AN ANCIENT TEMPLE

This Discoverer of Concealed Treasures has excavated the temple (*lha-khang*) of Lho-skyer-chu which had become invisible in former times. It was shaped like the temple of dPal-tshab-gsum-pa. [The excavation and restoration] was accomplished by removing earth and stones from a narrow rocky ravine. Today, everybody may visit this temple.

DISCOVERED TREASURES

He discovered the following precious objects (*nor-gter*): The Spiritual Turquois (*bla-gyu*), a jewel belonging to the religious King [Khri-srong-lde-btsan], named 'Radiant Light' ('*od-bar*); the Spiritual Turquois (*bla-gyu*) 'Thousand Mountains Radiating by Light' (*stong-ri-'od-bar*); the Spiritual Turquois (*bla-gyu*) 'The Red Mansion of the Glaciers' (*gangs-ri-khang-dmar*) and Maṇḍāravā's[254] seamless cloth. From the hiding place he took the mirror 'Clear From Afar' (*rgyang-gsal*) and other numerous precious jewels of the royal dynasty.

TESTIMONY ON DISCOVERING CONCEALED TREASURES

Although he had received the list of hiding places (*kha-byang*) of one-hundred-and-eight Concealed Treasures (*gter-*

kha) he could only procure half of them. When the Discoverer was at the point of departure, he asked his son to acquire other Concealed Treasures : "Even if it is annoying to you, as you must meticulously preserve your monastic vows, you must attempt to take out the Concealed Teachings. If you will say a prayer for me then you will be able to get some [Concealed Teachings]." Thus, his spiritual son Zla-ba became famous for having acquired some Concealed Teachings.

PROPHECY ABOUT THE ADHERENTS AND DISCIPLES OF THIS DISCOVERER

This Discoverer showed miracles passing one's imagination. He prophesied that in future times he would be reborn as Buddha *rDo-rje-snying-po* in the purified sphere of *Padma-bkod* that his adherents also would be born there, and that his disciples will become Buddhas. He delivered this Prophecy of Concealed Teachings (*gter-lung*) in reference to his spiritual sons and disciples : "Those who are connected with my activity (*las-kyi 'brel-ba*) will count ten-thousands, those who are connected with my prayers (*smon-lam 'brel-ba*) will count one-thousand-and-two, those who are connected with my profound essential teachings (*zab-mo'i gnad-kyis 'brel-ba*) will count eleven, my sons near to my heart will be four."

HIS DISCIPLES

Thus many [disciples] came : There came into existence six most important Discoverers of Concealed Teachings (*gTer-ston*), six great Mystics (*Grub-thob-chen-po*), and six important sons with evident signs of accomplished meditation (*sgrub-rtags*). Tshul-khrims-dpal-'byor, who had been a great abbot (*mKhan-chen*) at the Jo-nang-pa residence, Nang-so rGyal-ba-don-grub[255] and the incarnation mChog-ldan-mgon-po were equal to the Discoverer's spiritual meditative development. The above are his three spiritual sons.

HIS SONS

The Discoverer himself had four own sons; they were incarnations of the Three Protectors (i.e. *Avalokiteśvara*, *Vajra-*

dhara, *Mañjuśrī*. The actual being of *Avalokiteśvara* was the spiritual son Zla-ba. He was praised and exalted by *Sa-skya* bDag-chen, *'Bri-gung* Ring-chen-phun-tshogs, *Żva-dmar-pa* dKon-mchog-yan-lag and *dPa'-bo* Chos-rgyal-don-grub, for he was an important and venerable individual who was endowed with an unimaginable power of blessing and filled with his father's wisdom; his beneficient activity spread wide. Thus he was the teacher of the important persons listed above. All distinguished people of dBus, gTsang, Lho-kha, and the Mon country supported him. Although his own activity became great and others were benefited unimaginably he preferred a retired life (*sbas-pa'i rnal-'byor*).

TRANSMISSION OF HIS TEACHINGS

sPrul-sku sNa-tshogs-rang-grol and the choirmaster (*dBu-mdsad*) Don-grub-dpal-'bar, both known to be uncomparable masters of the Doctrine, passed on these profound teachings. Later they were disseminated by the incarnation of the communicative ability (*gSung-sprul*) and the spiritual son of Padma-gling-pa himself and his incarnation lineage. These incarnations lived at their residence Lha-lung[256] in Lho-brag. Thus the teachings spread far through Lho, Mon, dBus, gTsang, and mDo-Khams. The Discoverer's empowerments (*dbang*), oral traditions (*lung*), and commentaries (*khrid*) have been handed down to this day.

(Tt) I (sKong-sprul) Padma-gar-dbang heard the three main subjects of religious training according to the theory of the Concealed Teachings (*bLa-rdsogs-thugs-gsum*), the Eight Pronouncements (*bKa'-brgyad*) in their general and special aspects; the *Phyag-rdor-gtum-po* in its abbreviated as well as full-length edition; the *Tshe-sgrub* and the *Drag-dmar* cycles as well as the *Nag-po-skor gsum*, and all the other short rituals connected with them. I was useful to their dissemination according to my abilities.

13. HAGIOGRAPHY OF KARMA-GLING-PA (14th century), THE AUTHOR OF THE BAR-DO-THOS-GROL

(DC+Tt) HIS BIRTH

The Discoverer (*gTer-ston*) Karma-gling-pa[257] was an incarnation (*sPrul-pa*) of Cog-ro Lo-tsā-ba kLu'i-rgyal-mtshan.[258] He was born as the eldest son of Grub-chen Nyi-zla-sangs-rgyas at Khyer-grub in the uplands of Dvags-po during the sixth sexagesimal cycle (1326-1386).

CHARACTER AND ABILITIES

He preferred the Tantric way of life and had countless spiritual and intellectual abilities such as clairvoyance (*mngon-śes*)[259] without any obstacle.

ACTIVITY IN THE DISCOVERY OF CONCEALED TEACHINGS

At the age of fifteen the prophecy and the auspicious signs joined and he took out the treatises *Źi-khro-dgongs-pa-rang-grol* and *Thugs-rje-chen-po-padma-zi-khro* from the mountain sGam-po-gdar which looks like a dancing deity (*lha-bran*).

TRANSMISSION OF HIS TEACHINGS

He entrusted his fourteen main disciples with the whole cycle of *Padma-źi-khro'i chos-skor* and installed them as masters of his teachings (*Chos-bdag*). He passed the cycle *dGongs-pa-rang-grol* on to his son Nyi-zla-chos-rje only. He admonished him to deliver this cycle only to a single person until the third generation.

HIS DEATH

Because he did not get the prophesied wife (*gŹungs-ma*) and did not attain the auspicious signs, he did not remain alive for a long time but passed on to another world.

HIS SUCCESSORS AND THE SPREADING OF HIS TEACHINGS

Nam-mkha'-chos-kyi-rgya-mtsho of the third generation mainly spread the theory of the *Źi-khro-dgongs-pa-rang-grol* in the provinces dBus, gTsang, and Khams, but especially in mDo-

Khams and in the north and south. The appropriate empowerments (*dbang*), oral traditions (*lung*), and commentaries (*khrid*) still exist intact.

(DC) The great effect of the *Bar-do-thos-grol* spread far and wide.

(Tt) By a thousandfold *pūjā* (*stong-mchod*)[260] his teachings continued to spread till today. I (sKong-sprul Padma-gar-dbang) also heard and practised it by uttering mystic formulas (*bsnyen-pa*) and by visual realization (*sgrub-pa*).

14. HAGIOGRAPHY OF THANG-STONG-RGYAL-PO (1385-1510), THE GREAT ENGINEER

(DC+Tt) HIS BIRTH

Thang-stong-rgyal-po,[261] the master of spiritual potency was an authentic being (*sPrul-pa*) of *Avalokiteśvara* and *Hayagrīva*. He appeared like a [new] Padmasambhava, however, born by a woman. He was born at Ol-ba-lha-rtse in the upper gTsang[262] in the year 1385.

EDUCATION AND TRAINING

He had more than a hundred teachers from whom he heard and under whose guidance he practised the Doctrine. Although he was a great Mystic in his own way[263] he listened to the Northern Treasure (*Byang-gter*)[264] from Kun-spangs-don-yod-rgyal-mtshan and to the *Śangs-pa* theory[265] from rDo-rje-gźon-nu because of pedagogical reasons. He let become evident the spiritual potency attained by the practice of these two methods. As he was a great Mystic (*Grub-thob*) he roamed abroad all over the small World Continents (*gling-phran*), but above all, he went to the purified sphere *rNga-yab-padma-'od*.[266] There he heard the Doctrine from the Precious Master (Padmasambhava) and countless other Mystics. The Spiritual Beings (*mKha'-'gro*) and the Protectors of the Doctrine (*chos-skyong*) worshipped him on their knees.

ACTIVITY OF DISCOVERING CONCEALED BOOKS

At the focal points (*me-btsa*)[267] of the earth center Thang-stong-rgyal-po erected many temples in order to prevent the final wars (*mtha'-dmag*)[268] in Tibet. He tamed the evil gods and demons by vows. From mChims-phu near bSam-yas he took the book *Tshe-sgrub-'chi-med-dpal-ster* and others, altogether about five scrolls. He took the *Thugs-sgrub-yang-gsang-bla-med* from Gram-pa-rgyangs,[269] the *Man-ngag-rin-chen-gter-spungs* from the lake Padma-gling.[270] A scroll measuring ten fathoms in length and combining the profound content of all Sūtras and Tantras he took from Mon-spa-gro-stag-tshang.[271] He obtained the *Zab-chos-thugs-gter-skor* from Tsā-ri gSang-sngags-pho-brang, the prophecy *gSal-ba'i-sgron-me*, referring to himself, and the *Zing-skyong-gi sgrub-thabs* in Tsā-ri Zil-chen-phug. Many of these treatises he hid there once more.

CONVERSION OF A HERETICAL KING

The king of the heretics who was polluted by his way of life lived at Kamata, an Indian town. Thang-stong-rgyal-po educated him together with the barbarian tribes (*kLa-klo*) who settled along the Tibetan boundaries. He converted them to the Buddha-Doctrine and performed innumerable miracles.

BUILDING CONSTRUCTIONS

Thang-stong-rgyal-po erected countless monuments symbolizing being, communication and cognition (*sku*, *gsung*, *thugs-rten*), that is fifty-eight iron bridges and one-hundred-and-eighteen boats. He accomplished unimaginable things. All this is well known.

(DC) THEATRICAL PERFORMANCE FOR RELIGIOUS EDUCATION

He taught the hagiographies of former Bodhisattvas and religious kings (*Chos-rgyal*) by theatrical performances (*zlos-gar*) to admonish the people to be virtuous. There still exists the book which contains the text to the play called *A-ce-lha-mo* today. His charismatic activity became already effective by merely watching [the play].

(DC+Tt) DEPARTURE

When he was one-hundred-and-twenty-five he departed with his very body to the pure fields (*mkha-spyod*). When his spiritual son broke out into lamentations Thang-ston-rgyal-po appeared and declared his last will. At last he went to [the purified sphere] dPal-ri-bo-che.[272]

SUCCESSORS

The great Mystic Tshul-khrims-bzang-po, a native of mNga'-ris, was one-hundred-and-thirty years old when he dissolved in a mass of light. He and the Mystic Phyar-thul-can, a native of mDo-Khams, are renowned to be emanations of the great Mystic [Thang-stong-rgyal-po]. Up to this day there are many [Mystics] who had become his disciples through his existence as primary awareness (*ye-śes-kyi sku*).[273] At a large gathering of his disciples the Mystic himself attained the knowledge of deathless life (*'chi-med tshe'i rig-'dsin*). By joint auspicious signs many successors gained the spiritual potency of essential life (*sku-tshe'i dngos-grub*).

TRANSMISSION OF HIS TEACHINGS

The profound teachings of Thang-stong-rgyal-po's 'great oral tradition' (*snyan-brgyud chen-mo*) continue. The teachings of *Tshe-sgrub-'chi-med-dpal-ster* are known everywhere in the New School (*dGe-lugs-pa*) and the Old School (*rNying-ma-pa*). Later on [mKhyen-brtse'i-dbang-po] Padma-'od-gsal-mdo-sngags-gling-pa (1820-1892) was made Thang-stong-rgyal-po's disciple through the latter's primary-awareness-being (*ye-śes-kyi sku*). Based on this blessing he perceived by his dynamic meditative mind (*dgongs-pa'i klong*) the teachings of *Thugs-gter; grub-thob-snying-thig*.[274] The main book deals with the meditative realization of one's own Guru (*bla-sgrub*) and profoundly and completely explains the Development Stage (*bskyed rim*) and the Fulfilment Stage (*rdsogs-rim*). Five guides for meditative realization form the appendix. These agree with the Tantra section *sGyu-'phrul-gyi lam*. [mKhyen-brtse'i-dbang-po] composed a valuable treatise by summarizing the Tantric, oral, and instructional traditions (*rgyud, lung, man-ngag*). He gathered these tractates in the *Rin-chen-gter-mdsod*.

(Tt) (sKong-sprul states that he also participated in these teachings).

15. HAGIOGRAPHY OF MNGA'—RIS PAṆ-CHEN PADMA-DBANG-RGYAL-RDO-RJE (1487-1543) A SCHOLAR-SAINT AND REVIVOR OF BUDDHISM IN TIBET

(DC—Tt) HIS BIRTH

mNga'-ris Paṇ-chen Padma-dbang-rgyal-rdo-rje was the ninth incarnation of rGyal-sras Lha-rje, who, in turn, was an incarnation of the unbiased mind (*Thugs-sprul*) of the religious King Khri-srong-lde-btsan (742-797).[275] Padma-dbang-rgyal's father was the great scholar 'Jam-dbyangs-rin-chen-rgyal-mtshan,[276] who was of divine origin and the last incarnation of mNga'-bdag Mar-pa (1012-1096),[277] and his mother was 'Bro-lcam Khrom-pa-rgyan. He was born in the year 1487 at gLo-bo-ma-thang.[278] He received the name Padma-dbang-rgyal.

EDUCATION

He became a Buddhist devotee when he was only eight years old. His father bestowed on him the Bodhisattva vows. Padma-dbang-rgyal studied 'the three main objects of spiritual training according to the system of the Pronouncements' (*mDo-sgyu-sems-gsum*), and the Pronouncements (*bKa'-ma*) that had been translated previously. Thus he gained perfection. He practised meditation by uttering mystic formulas and by visual realization (*bsnyen-sgrub*) until he gained the signs of completed meditation. sLob-dpon Nor-bstan-bzang-po taught him the *Vinaya*, the Sūtras and the theories of the *bKa'-gdams-pa* School. When he was twenty he studied the *Mādhyamika* philosophy, logic, and the *Prajñāpāramitā* and a hundred other central systems of Buddhist philosophy. Thus he became a famous scholar (*dGe-bśes*) in name and in reality. When he was twenty-one he heard from 'Jam-dbyangs-chos-skyong and Tshul-khrims-dpal the empowerment rituals of the cycle of *gŚin-rje-gśed-dmar*

('The Red *Yamāntaka*'). When he practised meditation by mystic formulas and by visual realization he had a direct vision of the fierce appearance of *Mañjuśrī* (*'Jam-dpal drag-po*). When he was twenty-two his father instructed him in the Pronouncements, that had been previously translated (*bka'-ma*) and in the Concealed Teachings (*gter-ma*). Thus Padma-dbang-rgyal gained true understanding. While Padma-dbang-rgyal exercised the visual realization of The Eight Pronouncements (*bKa'-brgyad sgrub-thabs*), his father was greatly consoled by having a vision. Thereupon he praised his son loudly. This became evident later on. At the age of twenty-three he heard twice 'The Way and Goal Situation' (*lam-'bras*)[279] by gLo-bo Lo-tsā-ba.[280] At the monastic college of bSam-grub-gling, Padma-dbang-rgyal at twenty-five received the complete monastic vows from the master gLo-bo *mKhan-chen* bSod-nams-lhun-grub,[281] who was an incarnation of 'Jam-dbyangs Sa-skya Paṇḍita[282] and from the bestower of the monastic vows (*Las-slob*).[283] Then he practised the austere ascetic way of one who is content with just a place where he may sit.

PADMA-DBANG-RGYAL-DRO-RJE, A WELL-REPUTED SCHOLAR-SAINT

Because he observed the *Vinaya* in due form he was taken to be the leader of all keepers of the *Vinaya*. Furthermore, this highly esteemed scholar and Guge Paṇ-chen rNam-rgyal-dpal-bzang heard grammar and logic from 'Jam-dbyangs-blo-gros-dpal. Padma-dbang-rgyal studied much of the Tantrayāna of the New School (*gSar-ma-pa*), of Tantras and empowerments. He also practised these teachings. Thus he was styled a *Mahāpaṇḍita*. This title fitted him like an ear-drop (*cod-pan*).[284] He heard much about the 'Northern Treasure' (*Byang-gter*) from Drang-po gTer-ston Śākya-bzang-po,[285] he earnestly studied all traditions of empowerments (*dbang*), Tantras (*rgyud*), and instructions (*man-ngag*) of the New School Tantrayāna and the Old School which are still existing. He practised meditation on these subjects. Padma-dbang-rgyal even came to Nepal and there listened to many Tibetan and Nepalese *bLa-mas*. By making a pilgrimage to the holy places and fulfilling his pledges, he had many spiritual visions.

REVIVAL OF THE DOCTRINE IN DBUS AND GTSANG

Since his thirty-eighth year he had been teaching the doctrinal systems of the New School (*gSar-ma-pa*) and of the Old School (*rNying-ma-pa*) without any prejudice, thus the Doctrine poured like a heavy rain. He made up his mind to re-establish the doctrinal traditions of the New School (*gSar-ma -pa*)and of the Old School (*rNying-ma-pa*), as they had suffered in dBus and gTsang. He asked his father and the nobles of gLo-bo for their consent. Via Zang-zang-lha-brag[286] he arrived together with his younger brother Legs-ldan-rdo-rje in dBus. While looking at the wonderful temple (i.e. the Jo-khang) in Lha-sa, he received a prophecy.

SOJOURN IN CENTRAL TIBET

He heard the theory on *Maṇḍalas* according to the system of rNgog-ston [-rngog-dkyil] and on '*Yamāntaka* in his red appearance' (*gśed-dmar*) from rNgog-ston bSod-nams-bstan-'dsin, a native from gŹung-spre-źing,[287] and from the great Źva-lu Lo-tsā-ba, a resident of the monastery Gra-thang.[288] When he arrived at bSam-yas latent inclinations (*bag-chags*) arose; these resulted from his former existence during the lifetime of the religious King Khri-srong-lde-btsan (755-797). On the middle storey [of the temple] he celebrated the ritual of the extensive realization (*sgrub-thabs chen-po*) of the cycle *bka'-brgyad bde-gśegs-'dus-pa.* Thus Lho-brag Guru-pa made him his disciple. He heard *bLa-ma-dgongs-'dus* from Phreng-so O-rgyan-chos-bzang and Kong-chen Nam-mkha'-dpal-ldan. While he was performing his religious obligations (*thugs-dam mdsad*) at sGrags Yang-rdsong[289] and at mChims-phu he had direct visions of the countenances of many divine powers (*lha*).

SOJOURN IN SOUTH TIBET

The eighth incarnation of Guru Chos-dbang (1212-1270)[290] invited him to visit Lho-brag.[291] There he restored the damaged tradition. He performed excellent deeds through his kindness. The venerable Discoverer of Concealed Teachings had heard the *bKa'-brgyad bde-[gśegs]'dus-[pa]* at last twenty-five times. Only the last time he received an original and trustworthy instruction. He had it from the incomparable great Mystic (*Grub-thob-chen-po*) Nam-mkha'i-rnal-'byor, a member of the rJe'u family at the monastery Lho-brag dGon-dkar. Thereupon he was very much pleased.

DISCOVERING CONCEALED TREASURES

Now, the manner in which he received the profound Concealed Teachings: When he was forty-six he obtained a mysterious box from a figure of four *Vairocana* sitting back to back; [the figure] was found in the upper storey of bSam-yas.[292] In this box he found the last *bKa'-'dus'* i.e. the meditation advice from the seventh chapter of the prayer *Rig-'dsin-yongs-'dus*.[293] This text is still existing. With the help of Rig-'dsin-legs-ldan he invited 'Bri-gung Rin-chen-phun-tshogs. The master himself (i.e. Padma-dbang-rgyal) and his two disciples repeated the consecration (*rab-gnas*) of bSam-yas. This became a firm basis for the benefit of the whole of Tibet. This is only one example [of his meritorious deeds].

HIS DEPARTURE

In central Tibet he performed immeasurable benenvolent actions in favour of the Doctrine and of the beings. Finally in On-sme-thang[294] when he was fifty-six he departed to (the purified sphere) *Zangs-mdog-dpal-gyi-ri-bo-chen-po*.

FURTHER SOURCES FOR HIS HAGIOGRAPHY

However, an explicit hagiography of this venerable scholar (*mKhas-pa*), monk (*bTsun-pa*), and Mystic (*Grub-thob*) would be too voluminous. Thus the venerable one himself composed his own hagiography in verses.

OWN WORKS

Further, he composed the *sDom-gsum-rnam-par-nges-pa'i-bstan-bcos* explaining the full meaning in a few verses. By his merciful mind this treatise is like a necklace for those who preserve the Teachings of the 'Older Translations' (*sNga-'gyur-bstan-pa*).

DISSEMINATION OF HIS TEACHING AND HIS SUCCESSORS

He became famous as the great promulgator of the teachings of the Pronouncements and of the Concealed Texts of the Old School in view of [the fact of] his erudition and that of his successors. His next incarnation was Byang-bdag bKra-śis-stobs-rgyal alias Chos-rgyal-dbang-po'i-sde. He appeared as a Discoverer of Concealed Books (*gTer-ston*) and a Mystic (*Grub-thob*) whose biography surpasses imagination. Thus the tradition of his teachings still exists without decline.

16. SUMMARY OF THE HAGIOGRAPHY OF THE DISCOVERER LAS-'PHRO-GLING-PA (1585-1656) ALIAS RIG-'DSIN 'JA'-TSHON-SNYING-PO OR SNGAGS-'CHANG HŪM-NAG-ME-'BAR

PROPHECY

"When from the Indian villages Ghanru and Binasa two or three *Paṇḍitas* will come to Tibet in order to worship the *Jo-bo Śākyamuni* in Lha-sa, an omen will appear that the Treasure hidden at Lho-kong-lho-byang should not remain any longer there, but should be taken out. There will come a man called O-rgyan-las-'phro-gling-pa."[295]

BIRTH

At lBa-ru-gnam-tshal in the country of Kong-po[296] in the year 1585 on a day of the star *rGyal*[297] he was born to Chos-skyong-mgon-po, his father, and to Nam-langs-bu-khrid, his mother. From his tender age onwards he was inclined to the Buddha-Doctrine.

YOUTH

Las-'phro-gling-pa studied the ten arts and in particular

medicine. In his youth he already attempted to embody the Buddha-Doctrine and to abandon unsatisfactory ambitions.

EDUCATION AND TEACHERS

Mi-pham bKra-śis-blo-gros, Las-'phro-gling-pa's first teacher, bestowed on him the vows of a novice and gave him the name Ngag-dbang-chos-rgyal-dbang-po. From this teacher he heard many instructions on empowerments (*dbang*), commentaries (*khrid*), and oral traditions (*lung*) which all belonged to the Tantrayāna. He heard also many Sūtras, Tantras, and Pronouncements (*bka'-ma*) from the teachers below listed: *Źabs-drung* Nor-bu-brgyan-pa, 'Brug-pa Thams-cad-mkhyen-pa, and Lha-rtse-ba. The latter bestowed on Las-'phro-gling-pa the monastic vows.

PRACTISING THE WAY OF YOGA

For seventeen years Las-'phro-gling-pa lived in a hermitage whose entrance remained blocked all the time. Simultaneously he received many prophecies about the Concealed Teachings.

DISCOVERING CONCEALED TREASURES

Las-'phro-gling-pa found his first Concealed Treasure on the tenth day of the first month in the year 1620. This Treasure was shaped like the mythical bird *Khyung*. Inside this figure he discovered a list of hiding places in the handwriting of Ye-śes-mtsho-rgyal. Further he discovered the *dKon-mchog-spyi-'dus* at Hom-'phrang-lcags-kyi-sgo-mo in Brag-lung, the *Thugs-rje-chen-po*, *rTa-phag-yid-bźin-nor-bu*, *Źi-khro-nges-don-snying-po*, *Tshe-sgrub-gnam-lcags-rdo-rje*, *rDo-rje-gro-lod*, *dPal-mgon-ma-ning-skor*, and a guide to the holy places of Padma-bkod (*Padma-bkod-kyi gnas-kyi-lam-yig*) in the locality of Kong-po Bu-chu at the *Byang-phreng-mdses* called door of the lJon-pa-lung temple in sNye-mo-lha-ri,[298] Kong-'phrang-dge-'dun and in the dBu-ru źva temple.[299] He unearthed the *dKon-mchog-spyi-'dus* in secret, while most of the books he took out in public.

MIRACLES

Las-'phro-gling-pa had gained the ability of doing miracles. For example, when he was about to discover the Treasure hidden in sNye-mo-lha-ri the governor of Kong-po forbade it and posted warriors in front of the hiding place. Thereupon Las-'phro-gling-pa was dismayed but he did not give up his intention: He mounted his horse, and went at full gallop over the mirror-surfaced rocky walls of a deep gorge, grasped the Concealed Treasure, and sought safety in flight. At this moment the warriors lost their prowess, and they were totally upset. Las-'phro-gling-pa helped and benefited Tibet when he prevented the 'Final Wars' (*mtha'-dmag*) from her.

EDUCATING HIS DISCIPLES

To his talented and qualified disciples he showed the right and pure way by teaching them many theories contained in the Pronouncements (*bka'-ma*) and Concealed Teachings (*gter-ma*) of both the Old (*rNying-ma-pa*) and the New Schools (*gSar-ma-pa*).

FOUNDATION OF A MONASTERY

At a deserted place he founded the meditation college (*sgrub-sde*) Bang-ri-'jog-po which still exists by the support of his successors.

SUCCESSORS

Las-'phro-gling-pa's prominent disciple was sGam-po *Žabs-drung* Nor-bu-brgyan-pa. Many other disciples were *Karma-pa Žva-dmar*,[300] and *Karma-pa Žva-nag*, rGyal-tshab Grags-pa-don-grub, 'Bri-gung Chos-kyi-grags-pa,[301] 'Brug-pa dPag-bsam-dbang-po, rDor-brag Rig-'dsin Ngag-gi-dbang-po, rTse-le sNa-tshogs-rnag-grol, Lha-btsun-nam-mkha'i-'jigs-med,[302] Rig-'dsin Phrin-las-lhun-grub, bKa'- 'gyur-ba mGon-po-bsod-nams-mchog-ldan, sPu-bo rBa-kha sPrul-sku Rig-'dsin Chos-kyi-rgya-mtsho, sDe-dge Grub-thob Kun-dga'-rgya-mtsho, gTer-chen bDud-'dul-rdo-rje,[303] and Ta-bla Padma-mati. Some of his disciples and adherents gained the body of Radiant Light (*'od-lus*).

DEPARTURE

He died at the age of seventy-one in the monastery Bang-ri-'jog-po which he himself had founded.

DISSEMINATION OF HIS TEACHINGS

Although this Discoverer did not have all the auspicious signs the prophecy had stated, his teachings spread far and wide. sKong-sprul Padma-gar-dbang studied all the Discoverer's scriptures and composed a commentary (*khrid-yig*), a guide for meditating through mystic formulas (*bsnyen-yig*), and the *Ži-khro-nges-don-snying-po* together with an appendix as well as several other treatises.

17. SUMMARY OF THE HAGIOGRAPHY OF BDUD-'DUL-RDO-RJE (1615-1672)

BIRTH

In the village dNgul-phu-nang situated in the sDe-dge[304] district, in the year 1615, bDud-'dul-rdo-rje was born to kLu-sgrub, his father, who was a member of the gLing family and a renowned authority in medicines, and to Bo-mu-la, his mother.

BECOMING A NOVICE

sDe-dge *Grub-thob* Kun-dga'-rgya-mtsho[305] (an incarnation of Rig-'dsin rGod-ldem-can 1337-1409)[306] bestowed on him the vows of a novice and gave him the name Kun-dga'-bsod-nams-chos-'phags.

STUDIES

First he studied the theories of the *Sa-skya* School. dKon-mchog-rgyal-mtshan taught him *rDsogs-chen* philosophy. In central Tibet Nyang-po *Grub-chen* bKra-śis-tshe-brtan imparted to him many empowerments (*dbang-bskur*) and instructions.

Later he went to the Ngor[307] monastery in gTsang to deepen his former studies on the cause-effect situation. From Bang-ri *Rig-'dsin-chen-po* 'Ja'-tshon-snying-po[308] he heard many Concealed Teachings (*zab-gter*), empowerments (*dbang*), commentaries (*khrid*), and instructions (*man-ngag*).

MYSTIC EXPERIENCES

At sPu-bo[309] bDud-'dul-rdo-rje realized through meditation *Vajrakīla* (*phur-ba sgrub-pa*) according to the Ratna-gling-pa system.[310] He had visions of Padmasambhava who bestowed on him empowerments, instructions, and a prophecy on Concealed Treasures (*gter-lung*). These events the Discoverer himself wrote down in his book *Dag-snang-dbang-gi-rgyal-po*. Later O-rgyan-bstan-'dsin appointed him *rDo-rje-slob-dpon* (i.e. Tantric Teacher). He also refrained from taking coarse nourishment, but relied only upon essences (*bcud-len*) for maintenance. Further he practised the Yoga of creative motility (*rtsa-rlung-thig-le'i rnal-'byor*).[311]

MARRIAGE

He made Rigs-ldan-padma-skyid his consecrated consort (*Las-rgya*).[312]

DISCOVERING CONCEALED TREASURES AND TEACHINGS

First bDud-'dul-rdo-rje found a profound Concealed Book (*zab-gter*) in gYu-mtsho Rin-chen-brag,[313] as stated in the list of hiding places (*kha-byang*). His most important profound Concealed Book (*zab-gter*)—the *dGongs-pa-yongs-'dus*—he discovered in the grotto'Dong-chu bDe-chen-gsang-ba-phug in sPu-bo. The books below listed he made into supplements of the two works above : The *sPrul-sku-snying-thig-bka'-srung-źing-skyong-dang-bcas-pa* originated from Tsha-ba sGro-brag;[314] the *Zab-don-gsang-ba-snying-thig-dpal-bde-mchog*, and the *bKa'-srung-phyag-bźi-pa'i-skor* from Dvags-rdsong-phug in sPu-ri; the *sNying-thig-tshe-yang-phur-gsum* and the *Srung-ma Ekajaṭī mug-byung-rgyal-mo'i-skor* from Śel-gyi-yang-sgrom which is also situated in sPu-ri; a 'Guide to the Holy Places of the Hidden Country Padma-bkod' (*sBas-yul-padma-bkod-pai-gnas-yig*) from 'Dong-chu'i-byang-ngos-byis-brag in sPu-bo; the *Yi-dam-dmar-nag-'jigs-gsum-gyi-skor* from Khrom-zil-khrom-dkar-yag in sDe-dge (mDo-Khams); the *dPal-mgon-gdong-bži-pa-dan-lha-chen-sgrub-thabs from* Bya-phu-lcags-phur-can; the *bLa-ma-rig-'dsin-'duspa* and the *Tshe-sgrub-tsha-ba-dmar-thag-bka'-srung-žan-blon-dang spom-ra* from the upper storey of the main temple (*dBu-rtse*) in bSam-yas; the *sNyan-brgyud-gtsug-rgyan-yid-bžin-nor-bu*-from the upper storey of an out-house of the Ra-śag-'phrul-snang (i.e. the Jo-khang) temple in Lha-sa. The lost four tractates he had not revised.

There were also two other treatises that were offered to him by the Yogi Dung-phreng-can: *sGyu-phrul-ži-khro-dang-bka'-brgyad-skor-bka'-srung-bcas* (unearthed at bDud-ri-gnom-leags-'bar-ba in sPu-bo), and a ritual on Mahākāla riding on a tiger (*dPal-mgon-stag-gžon*) (unearthed at the stone Stūpa in Ra-stag).[315] It also happened that bDud-'dul-rdo-rje discovered some profound Concealed Teachings in gYu-mdtsho gŚin-rje'i-don-kha, Rig-'dsin-gsang-phug, bSe-rag-cog, Na-bun-rdsong, and rTa-śod-dkyil-'khor-thang. He also unearthed many figures, ritual objects, and one hundred sacred buildings.

FOUNDATION OF TEMPLES

The Discoverer founded many temples in Central Tibet and the border regions, in particular in the Hidden Country of Padma-bkod.[316]

TRAVELLING THROUGHOUT TIBET

Many times bDud-'dul-rdo-rje was invited by high ranking *bLa-mas* and officials; thus he met sDe-dge *bLa-ma* Byams-pa-phun-tshogs from the Khu-dbon family,[317] the King of gLing, gNam-chos-mi-'gyur-rdo-rje at the locality of sPor-ne-brag; he also visited the famous centres of the Old School, such as Kaḥ-thog-rdo-rje-gdan;[318] he also went to Bar-khams, sPa-stod, Bar-ma-lha-steng, and Ri-bo-che.[319]

HIS RESIDENCES

For a long time he resided at bDe-chen-thang in sPu-stod,[320] and at gYu-ri-sgang-'go.

DEPARTURE

While many miracles were appearing he died in 1672 when he was fifty-seven.

DISCIPLES

Masters of the Doctrine (*Chos-bdag*): Lha-btsun-chen-po Nam-mkha'-'jigs-med,[321] Rig-'dsin kLong-gsal-snying-po, rBa-kha *sPrul-sku* Chos-kyi-rgya-mtsho,[322] rDsogs-chen Padma-rig-'dsin, Kun-bzang-khyab-brdal-lhun-grub, and Grub-chen Padma-nor-bu.

Rig-'dsin kLong-gsal-snying-po's son, rGyal-sras bSod-nams-lde-btsan, possessed the lion-throne of the monastery Kaḥ-thog-rdo-rje-gdan, so also did his descendants.

18. HAGIOGRAPHY OF LHA-BTSUN NAM-MKHA'-'JIGS-MED (1597—ca 1650), THE GREAT YOGI

BIRTH

(DC+Tt) *Lha-btsun*[323] Nam-mkha'-'jigs-med was the very incarnation of the compassion of Paṇ-chen Vimalamitra and of Kun-mkhyen Dri-med-'od-zer.[324] In the year 1597 he was born in the Lha-btsad-po family in the southern range of Byar-yul.[325]

AUSPICIOUS SIGNS

He possessed many auspicious signs, for example there appeared the letter AH between his two eye-brows, at the tip of his tongue and at the tip of his nose.

NAMEGIVING

When Nam-mkha'-'jigs-med had taken the vows of a novice O-rgyan-dpal-'byor, an incarnated being, gave him the name Kun-bzang-rnam-rgyal at the hermitage gSung-snyan.

EDUCATION

He started studying every theory that was taught at Thang-'brog College (*grva-tshang*).

(DC) From many Tantric teachers (*rDo-rje-'dsin-pa*) he later received many oral instructions (*lung*) and empowerments (*dbang*) of the profound teachings of the Pronouncements (*bka'-ma*) and Concealed Books (*gter-ma*), such as the Eight Pronouncements (*bKa'-brgyad*) and *dGongs-'dus*. While he was earnestly practising meditation by means of mystic formulas and visual realization (*bsnyen-sgrub*) of his individual guiding deity (*lhag-pa'i lha*)[326] he completely gained spiritual potency and charismatic activity. In particular he heard the whole instruction of the sNying-thig literature by rDsogs-chen-pa bSod-nams-dbang-po, who had been his teacher for seventeen years. Because he practised this doctrine his knowledge became firmly established.

PRACTISING THE MYSTIC WAY OF YOGA

While he was practising in secret, he heard the whole instruction on 'The Path of Desire' (*chags-lam*)[327] from the venerable Ngag-dbang-mi-bskyod-rdo-rje. As he conceived of his body (*lus*) as 'Fitness of Action' (*thabs*)[328] and of the body of the other one (i.e. his consort) as 'Inspiration' (*śes-rab*), through a union with her (*phyag-rgya'i rnal-'byor*)[329] he endeavored to gain the primary awareness of the identity of nothingness and bliss (*bde-stong-gi ye-śes*), and when the recognition of the four types of delight[330] as what they are, had come and faded by itself, the whole of reality (i.e. all that is seen and heard) matured (i.e. reached its highest peak) in the radiant light of spontaneous (i.e. the 'concrete' co-emergent with the 'open') delight.

The three places of Byar, Dvags[331] and Kong[332] and the three districts of dBu,[333] gYor and gTsang[334] are only examples of (DC+Tt) all the famous holy places of Tibet that he visited, and where he practised spiritual asceticism in order to gain the highest stage of spiritual potency (*siddhi*). After the knots of the throat focal point (*mgrin-pa'i rtsa-mdud*) had been unravelled, whatever he said was to the point and positive.

DISSEMINATING THE DOCTRINE BY THE CONVERSION OF HERETICS AND THE FOUNDATION OF TEMPLES

Having converted a heretical king in India he guided him

by the Buddha-Doctrine. [Lha-btsun Nam-mkha'-'jigs-med] asked the demons and deities of Tibet for help, and restored the decayed buildings of bSam-yas. When the large mountain Tsā-ri was about to precipitate, he flung it back by a banishing glance and by pointing his forefinger at it. In this manner he gained authority over these unimaginable miracles.

(DC) DISCOVERING A CONCEALED TEACHING THROUGH MEDITATION

When he was composing his mind to perfect rest for meditation at the holy places of Zab-bu-lung,[335] of Rin-chen-śel-ri-smug-po'i dga'-tshal, of Padma-'ja'-'od-śel-rdsong, and at the heavenly bower of Yar-lung-śel-ri, many overwhelming visions appeared to him. Then, from the dynamic sphere of his [Buddha-] intentionality (*dgongs-pa'i klong-mdsod*) there came forth the essence of all Concealed Teachings, the goal of all oral traditions, the exalted *rDo-rje-snying-po-sprin-gyi-thol-glu'i-chos-skor*, which is conducive to deliverance by merely seeing, hearing, remembering or touching [it]. After having received the text Nam-mkha'-'jigs-med transmitted it orally (*snyan-brgyud*) to some extraordinarily gifted disciples.

(DC+Tt) FOUNDING THE MONASTERY LHA-RI-'OD-GSAL-SNYING-PO IN BHUTAN

When he was fifty years old he followed the entreaties of Rig-'dsin 'Ja'-tshon-snying-po[336] and gTer-chen bDud-'dul-rdo-rje (1615-1672)[337] and opened the doors (i.e. he founded) of the holy place Lha-ri-'od-gsal-snying-po[338] in Bhutan ('Bras-gśongs) where he had arrived there on foot; this was done for the benefit of the Tibetan country. In accordance to the prophecy he built a monastery and a meditation-college (*sgrub-sde*).[339]

OBTAINING CONCEALED TEACHINGS THROUGH VISIONS OF SPIRITUAL BEINGS

According to the prophecy of the Spiritual Beings (*mKha'-'gro-ma*) he was staying inside the 'Grotto of Ḍākinīs' Heart'

(*Da-ki-snying-gi phug-pa*) near Brag-dkar-bkra-śis-sdings when he perceived in a vision the instructions on *A-ti-bla-med-snying-thig*, particularly, on *Rig-'dsin-srog-sgrub-kyi-chos*. He wrote down the theory and delivered it to talented disciples by the ways of empowerments (*dbang*) and oral injunctions (*lung*).

(DC) TRANSMISSION OF HIS TEACHINGS

Later when he actively disseminated the *rDsogs-pa-chen-po* Doctrine it became well-known as the *rDsogs-pa-chen-po* of Bhutan (*'bras-ljongs-rdsogs-pa-chen-po'i ring-lugs*) to which we also adhere. This is known everywhere. It is also known that there did not appear after him a Mystic (*Grub-thob*), who equalled him in attaining the goal of ascesis. The teachings of *Rig-'dsin-srog-sgrub* and *sPrin-gyi-thol-glu* exist up to this day undiminished by ways of empowerments (*dbang*), oral injunctions (*lung*) and instructions (*man-ngag*). The effect of his teachings spread all over Tibet, in particular it was propagated in the Hidden Country (*sbas-yul*) Bhutan.

(Tt states, that Padma-gar-dbang had heard the *Rig-'dsin-srog-sgrub-kyi chos-skor*).

19. HAGIOGRAPHY OF RDO-RJE-THOG-MED-RTSAL, ALIAS BLO-BZANG-RGYA-MTSHO (1617-1682) THE FIFTH DALAI LAMA

(DC+Tt) BIRTH

It is well known that many prophecies in the 'Old and New Concealed Books' (*gter-kha gsar-rnying*) state that the Fifth Dalai Lama[340] whose secret name is rDo-rje-thogs-med-rtsal—will be born as the very incarnation of the compassion of *Avalokiteśvara* who is the Lord of the Snowland, while he will also be the incarnation of the charismatic activity (*Phrin-las-kyi sprul-sku*) of the religious King Khri-srong-lde-btsan (755-797). He was born in the royal family of Za-hor of 'Phyong-rgyas-stag-rtse. His father was the ruler (*Mi-dbang*) bDud-'dul-rab-brtan and his mother Kun-dga'-lha-mdses was a daughter of the leader of ten-thousand men (*Khri-dpon*) of Yar-'brog. He was born as their son in the year 1617 while auspicious signs became visible.

A LIFE-PROTECTING CEREMONY

In the very year of the Fifth Dalai Lama's birth the adherent of the 'Northern Treasure' (*byang-gter*),[341] Rig-'dsin Ngag-gi-dbang-po bestowed on him a life-protecting empowerment connected with *Gur-gyi-mgon-po* (*tshe-gur-gyi dbang*), thus he was endowed with the auspicious signs of bliss from the beginning.

ENTHRONEMENT

Paṇ-chen bLo-bzang-chos-kyi-rgyal-mtshan[342] (1567-1662) recognized him as the incarnation of the Fourth Dalai Lama Yon-tan-rgya-mtsho (1589-1617) and invited him to the famous monastic college (*chos-sde*) of 'Bras-spungs. When he had offered the hair of the crown of his head (i.e. he had become a novice) he was given the name bLo-bzang-rgya-mtsho and was enthroned on the lion-throne.

(DC) EDUCATION

gLing-smad-pa dKon-mchog-chos-'phel who had been prophesied by the Great Teacher (Padmasambhava) to be an incarnation of rNgog Lo-tsā-ba instructed bLo-bzang-rgya-mtsho in philosophy and logic, the most important disciplines (*gźung pod-chen*).[343] The young Dalai Lama had no difficulties in mastering all of them. He heard many empowerments (*dbang*), oral injunctions (*lung*) and instructions (*man-ngag*) by the Paṇ-chen Rin-po-che. He studied poetry (*snyan-ngag*), grammar (*sgra*), versification (*sdeb-sbyor*), semantics (*mngon-brjod*) from sMon-'gro Paṇḍita and his disciples, astronomy according to the Indian and Chinese systems and rain-making (*dbyangs-'char*) from lDum-po-pa and Zur-chen. Since he studied so many subjects and was well versed in the ten arts he became a great scholar (*Mahāpaṇḍita*). When he was twenty-one he received the monastic vows according to the bLa-chen [dGongs-pa-rab-gsal's][344] tradition by Paṇ-chen Rin-po-che. To the Dalai Lama's name the title *Ngag-gi-dbang-phyug* ('master of eloquence') was added.

(DC+Tt) TEACHERS AND FURTHER PURSUITS

bLo-bzang-rgya-mtsho had many very educated and special

teachers[345] like Pha-bong-kha-pa 'Khon-ston dPal-'byor-lhun-sgrub, Žva-lu bSod-nams-mchog-grub, Zur-chen Chos-dbyings-rang-grol, sMan-lung-pa bLo-mchog-rdo-rje and *Chos-bdag* gTer-bdag-gling-pa.[346] He studied most of the commentaries on the Sūtras and Tantras, and various doctrinal traditions of the Tantric empowerments (*dbang*), oral injunctions (*lung*) and instructions (*man-ngag*) which existed at that time in Tibet and which were accepted by the three Schools, the Old one (*rNying-ma-pa*) the *dGe-lugs-pa* and *Sa-skya-pa*. What he had studied there filled four volumes of his *gsan-yig*.[347] All people believe in that.

YOGA PRACTICE

While he was practising meditation his power of abandonment and reflection became accomplished.
(DC) In the meantime he practised every kind of contemplation of the fierceful forces and had the signs of success.

(DC+Tt) DISCOVERING CONCEALED BOOKS AT BSAM-YAS

Now, the method of gaining the Pronouncements (*bka'-ma*) of the profound visions (*zab-mo-dag-snang*): It is stated in the Prophecy on Concealed Books (*gter-lung*) by dPal bKra-śis-stobs-rgyal : "The twenty-five doctrinal treatises and, in particular, the five Concealed Teachings that will be discovered by intuition (*thugs-gter*) and be taken out by one of the five incarnations whose prayers (*smon-lam*) will be pure; you yourself, King of the Black-Heads (i.e. the Tibetans) will be one of these incarnations." Although the auspicious signs of discovering Concealed Books became actually visible when the Fifth Dalai Lama arrived at the holy places of bSam-yas, he did not take out the Concealed Books because the powers of the locality, the time and the circumstances were against it. Later on, when he had envisaged the three main roots of spiritual maturation (*rtsa-gsum*)[348] and many Buddhas, and when he had received a prophecy and an empowerment (*dbang-bskur*) he wrote down [the revised fragments discovered by himself]. He named the twenty-five treatises *gSang-ba-rgya-can*. He composed supplements which fill two further volumes. The Fifth Dalai Lama handed down these books (*gter-ma*) to *Chos-rgyal* gTer-bdag-gling-pa and Rig-'dsin Padma-phrin-las. In this way he bestowed all empowerments and oral injunctions on the assembly of the best preservers of our own system of 'Ancient Translations' (*snnga-'gyur-gyi ring-lugs*). Therefore it still exists with no loss to it and is disseminated far and wide.

POLITICAL EVENTS

Now, the political part! At the age of twenty-four the three main regions of Tibet (*chol-kha gsum*[349] were entrusted to him by Guśri bsTan-'dsin-chos-rgyal, the ruler of the [Qoshot] Mongols.[350] Formerly Guśri Khan had conquered [these regions] by war and, now, he presented the laity and clergy as subjects to the Fifth Dalai Lama. After these events the great sovereign (*Gong-ma-chen-po*)[351] of the eastern direction (i.e. the Chinese Emperor) invited him to Peking. He offered the Dalai Lama a seal with gold letters. Thereby he was titled 'Lord of the Doctrine, the *Vajra*-holding *Tā-la'i bLa-ma*." (Tt does not refer to this inscription but states): He offered the Dalai Lama a seal with gold letters together with a crystal ink pot. He was worshipped by the Chinese Emperor as *Ti-śri* or *Ācārya*.

(DC) At this time the relationship between the officiating priest (*mchod-gnas*) i.e. the Dalai Lama and the householder who employs the priest (*yon bdag*) (i.e. the Chinese Emperor) was established. Then the Fifth Dalai Lama had the great Potala palace built on the top of the hill dMar-po-ri. As had been stated in an unerring, lasting prophecy, that during this evil time the Tibetan country would be guided by a royal *Bhikṣu* who is the authentic being of the 'Noble Lord of the World' i.e. *Avalokiteśvara*, and of *Mañjuśrī* and Khri-srong-lde-btsan; so [the Dalai Lamas] have well protected the whole Tibetan Kingdom by means of the two methods (i.e. by religion and reign) till our times.

(DC+Tt) PROPAGATION OF THE DOCTRINE

As to the Doctrine, the Fifth Dalai Lama has promulgated countless religious cycles of the Tantras, Sūtras—according to the New and Old Schools (*gsar-rnying*)—of the Pronouncements (*bka'-ma*) and Concealed Teachings (*gter-ma*).

DISCIPLES

Almost all Tibetan dignitaries became his disciples (*Źal-slob*), such as the great *bLa-mas*: The venerable *Sa-skya-pa* hierarchs and their successors; the hierarchs of the *'Bri-gung-pa, sTag-longs-pa* and *'Brug-pa*; the famous incarnation of the Paṇ-chen [Rin-po-che], the dGa'-ldan Khri [Rin-po-che] and his predecessor who is still alive; but particularly the great preservers of the 'Ancient Translations' system (i.e. the Old School), who are like a great vehicle, such as *Chos-rgyal* gTer-bdag-gling-pa (1646 ?-1714) and Rig-'dsin Padma-phrin-las, Lho-brag Thugs-sras bsTan-'dsin-'gyur-med-rdo-rje etc., further many persons who supported the [four] philosophical schools (*grub-mtha'*) of Buddhism. The Doctrine of the 'Ancient Translations' (*snga-'gyur*) was aided in unimaginable ways by the Dalai Lama and his successors.

(DC) Further on from the banks of the Ganges in India to the country Tong-ku (Tongkin ?) in the east all spiritual and worldly dignitaries had become his disciples.

FOUNDING MONASTERIES

In the Tibetan provinces of dBus, gTsang, and Khams, as well as in China and Mongolia he founded countless new religious colleges (*chos-sde*).

LITERARY ACTIVITIES

He composed lucid commentaries on the main worldly arts. They are included in the esoteric and exoteric parts of his marvellous collected works (*gsung-'bum*) which run into thirty volumes. As to the New School (*gSar-ma-pa*) he thought only 'Jam-dbyangs-mkhyen-brtse to be trustworthy, as to the Old School (*rNying-ma-pa*) only the system of Byang-pa (bKras-stobs).[352]

RESTORING THE POLITICAL POWER OF TIBET

In particular, when the auspicious signs of sMin-grol-gter-chen as Master of the Doctrine (*Chos-bdag*) and of the Fifth Dalai Lama as a patron (*mchod-yon*) had joined according to the prophecy, he laid the foundation for the establishment of the government of *dGa'-ldan-pho-brang* (i.e. the Tibetan clerical kingship).

DEPARTURE

Thus, at the age of sixty-five when he had wholly accomplished and perfected the three spheres of explaining (*bśad*), realizing (*sgrub*), and studying-contemplating (*thos-bsam*) by means of his exoteric, esoteric and mystic life he departed happily on the twenty-fifth day of the third month in the great Potala palace. This happened when he performed the charismatic action of overpowering (*dbang-gi phrin-las*)[353] by directing his mind towards the female *Bhagavatī Rig-byed-ma*.

SUCCESSORS

His next incarnation was born in the family Pad-gling in the Mon country. From Rig-'dsin Tshangs-dbyangs-rgya-mtsho to the great Fourteenth Dalai Lama of our times, who is the Lord of the whole Buddha-Doctrine on earth and who is enjoying himself alive, the Dalai Lamas appeared one after another. This is well known in the entire world.

20. HAGIOGRAPHY OF GTER-BDAG-GLING-PA, ALIAS PADMA-GAR-DBANG-'GYUR-MED-RDO-RJE (1634 or 1646-1714), DISCIPLE AND LATER TEACHER OF THE FIFTH DALAI LAMA

(Tt) THE PROPHECY

"The country will be full of men who fail in their vows, pervert the Doctrine and spoil the moral rules. Their ill repute will fill the divine and human world. At this instant a sign will appear that the Treasure Concealed (*gter-kha*) at Śa-'ug-stag-sgo shall not remain longer there but shall be taken out. A man will come with the name O-rgyan gTer-bdag-gling-pa".[354] This one is the great Discoverer of Concealed Treasures (*gTer-*

chen) gTer-bdag-gling-pa alias Padma-gar-dbang-'gyur-med-rdo-rje. He is an authentic being of the communicative nature (*gSung-gi sprul-pa*) of the great Translator (*Lo-tsā-ba*) Vairocana.

BIRTH

At the Buddhist monastery Dar-rgyas-chos-sdings[355] in dBus gYo-ru [gTer-bdag-gling-pa's] body unfolded like a lotus flower in the family mThing-ma-myos in the year 1634. His father was Rig-'dsin Phrin-las-lhun-grub, who was like a sun to the Doctrine of the Old Translations i.e. the Old School (*snga-'gyur bstan-pa*) and an incarnation of gNubs-chen Sangs-rgyas-ye-śes,[356] his mother was Lha-'dsing-dbyangs-can-sgrol-ma, an incarnation of Śel-dkar-rdo-rje-'tsho.

(DC starts) Rig-'dsin gTer-bdag-gling-pa alias Padma-gar-dbang-'gyur-med-rdo-rje was the authentic being of the communicative nature (*gSung-gi sprul-pa*) of the great Translator Vairocana. When in his former existence his mortal body had entered the sphere of radiant light[357] (*'od-gsal-gyi dbyings*), the Spiritual Beings (*mKha'-'gro-ma*) of cognitive harmony admonished him through their songs to be useful to the beings. Therefore the very being of his primary awareness (*ye-śes-kyi sku*) took the shape of a *Heruka*[358] and entered his mother's womb. gTer-bdag-gling-pa's father was a Tantric Teacher of the family gNyos by name gSang-bdag Phrin-las-lhun-grub and his mother Lha-'dsin-dbyangs-can-sgrol-ma of good descent. A son was born to these two at the monastery Dar-rgyas-chos-gling in Grva-nang on the tenth day of the second month in the year 1646 while many miracles such as earthquakes and rainbows were witnessed.

AUSPICIOUS CEREMONIES AND MIRACLES

At the very moment of the birth [*gTer-bdag-gling-pa's*] the venerable father performed a blessed empowerment (*dbang-bskur*) to bestow [his son's] mind with indication of acuteness and to prevent obstacles to him. Hitherto, a Yogi of bluish complexion and with knotted hair together with three beautiful women worshipped him during three years. Thus, in later days he remembered exactly the places and the events as they had taken place.

MEDITATIVE TRAINING

From early childhood onwards he used to have the ability of concentrative absorption (*samādhi*). Even when he indulged in child-like plays he made the intelligent ones to be faithful [towards himself] through the goodness that is the manner of an 'awakened' person (*dam-pa'i rigs-sad-pa*). When he was four years old he took part in the empowerment-ritual of *bKa'-brgyad-gsangs-rdsogs* performed by his venerable father; he impressed everything visible with the *Maṇḍala* of the [*bKa'-brgyad gsangs-rdsogs*). He realized the main deity (i.e. *Che-mchog*) and the *bLa-ma* to be identical and thus the seed of the four empowerments was planted in [gTer-bdag-gling-pa's] mind. When he was nine years old, during the autumn of the year 1655, while he had been attending an empowerment of the *bDe-gśegs-'dus-pa* cycle and realizing the radiant light (*'od-gsal-du snang-bar*) he became aware of the great master Padmasambhava who bestowed an empowerment on him and blessed him. By virtue of this blessing his vision increased and by virtue of practising the flask-empowerment (*bum-dbang*) he recognized the visible world to be like an apparition (*sgyu-ma*).[359]

STUDIES

By this time he studied the meditative realization rituals (*sgrub-thabs*), mystic circles (*dkyil-'khor*), empowerments (*dbang-bskur*), permission for attending an empowerment (*rjes-gnang*), and consecration ceremonies (*rab-gnas*) of his own school (i.e. the Old School). He knew by heart these rituals (*cho-ga*) and ceremonial instructions. Without any difficulty he was well-versed in all school-systems. When he had taken over his father's duties he did his best to perform them properly.

BECOMING A NOVICE

When he was ten he offered the hair of the crown of his

head to the all-knowing Fifth Dalai Lama at the wonderful [monastic university] 'Bras-spungs.[360] Thus, he was given the name Ngag-dbang-padma-bstan-'dsin.,

(Tt continues) He felt particularly relieved because [the Fifth Dalai Lama] had recognized auspicious signs for the future. Through his father's kindness he took the three vows[361] (*sdom-pa gsum*). The father poured on his son like from a full jar all the profound theories (*zab-chos*).

(DC continues) At the same time, a self-originated (*rang-byung*) figure of a noble deity arose for the first time at sKyid-grong.[362] Thereupon the Fifth Dalai Lama admonished [gTer-bdag-gling-pa] with pleasure : "This is an auspicious omen !" The figure seemed to smile gently and from its heart a ray emerged and entered deeply into [gTer-bdag-gling-pa].

THE FIFTH DALAI LAMA BECOMES THE TEACHER OF GTER-BDAG-GLING-PA

When [gTer-bdag-gling-pa] at the age of sixteen met the Fifth Dalai Lama at bSam-yas, he knew him to be *Avalokiteśvara*. The great all-knowing Fifth [Dalai Lama] and [gTer-bdag-gling-pa's] venerable father gSang-bdag Phrin-las-lhun-grub kindly gave him a spiritual education, not only by the wonderful means of their personalities but also by their primary awareness. On behalf of these essential blessings [gTer-bdag-gling-pa] had two comparelessly merciful basic teachers (*rtsa-ba'i-bla-ma*).[363] Further he had sixteen important teachers from whom he heard empowerments, oral injunctions and profound methods (*zab-lam*). Altogether he had thirty-five teachers from whom he heard various and profound theories.

FULFILLING THE VOWS

At seasonable times and opportune places he took all the *upāsaka*-pledges and the three ways of the Bodhisattva-vows as well as [the vows appropriate to] the empowerment of the *bKa'-brgyad-yongs-rdsogs* cycle; the meaning and content of which he had appreciated at the very moment of hearing it for the first time. Thus, he took these three vows as a firm basis.

FURTHER STUDIES ON LITERATURE

He heard the Sūtras: *sGyu-'phrul*, the three systems

of *Sems-sde*, further the *mNyam-sbyor*, *Yang-dag*, *Phur-pa*, *gŚed-skor* and all the Pronouncements (*bka'-ma*) which had been translated in ancient times, and are still existing today. He heard the Concealed Teachings (*gter-ma*) : *bLa-rdsogs-thugs-gsum*, treatises of 'The Section of Meditative Realization' (*sgrub-sde*), and many ordinary and particular Pronouncements. The above is only a small portion of all the available works he had studied. He also heard the 'New Tantras' (*gsar-ma*) : *rDo-rje-phreng-ba*, 'One-hundred Meditative Realization Rituals' (*sGrub-thabs-brgya-rtsa*), the ordinary Pronouncements (*spyi-bka'*), further the *bDe-mchog*, *dGyes-rdor*, *Dus-'khor*, *gSang-'dus*, *gŚed-skor*, *Krīyā-yoga* and the special Pronouncements (*zur bka'*). Of the Sūtras he heard many that dealt with the empowerments (*dbang*), guidances (*khrid*), and oral instructions (*bśad-lung*). As he had studied countless doctrinal treatises of *Tripiṭaka* (*bKa'-'gyur-ro-cog*),[364] it is hard to list even their names. When he was thirteen he learnt by heart the fundamental texts and commentaries of *rTsa-rgyud gSang-ba-snying-po*, *rGyud-bla-ma*, *Sems-nyid-ngal-gso*,[364a] and *Yid-bźin-mdsod*. He obtained their appropriate explanations from his venerable father. He studied the scriptures of gNubs, Zur, Rong-zom and Sa-skya Paṇḍita's (1182-1251) *sDom-pa-gsum-gyi-rab-tu-dbye-ba*[365] and bCom-ldan-rigs-pa'i-ral-gri's *sPyi-rnam* and also the religious treatises of Rang-byung-źabs. In particular he ardently studied the scriptures of the great all-knowing [kLong-chen-rab-'byams-pa] (1308-1363), and had no difficulty in becoming a great scholar. Therefore he removed all imputations as to the nature of relative truth (*ji-snyed-pa'i chos*).[366] He heard empowerments, instructions, and declarations, which were linked with sealing ceremonies (*gtad-rgya*),[367] final ceremonies of an empowerment (*mtha'-brten*) and life-preserving empowerment (*tshe-dbang*) of the four rivers (i.e. the four empowerments) that took their origin from the forty-five *Maṇḍalas* (*dkyil-'khor*) which are based on the *Dus-pa-mdo'i-dbang-chog-rin-chen-phreng-ba*. He heard also the empowerments (*dbang*) oral injunctions (*lung*) and instructions (*gdam-ngag*) of the *dBang-chog-sbrang-rtsi'i-chu-rgyun*, in these ceremonies the twenty-one *Maṇḍalas* painted on cotton (*ras-bris*) were used. Further many times, he heard from rDo-rje-brag Rig-'dsin-padma-phrin-las the empowerment (*dbang*), instructions (*gdams-ngag*), and declaration (*bśad-lung*) of *dBang-chog-rin-chen-phreng-ba* from the beginning. At first he had been using a cotton painting of the fundamental *Maṇḍala* that summarized the twenty-seven ones, but then he used the mere focal points (*tshom-bu*) of the *Maṇḍala.*[368] Both teachers gave him the name 'Gyur-med-rdo-rje-rtsal.

DISCOVERING CONCEALED TREASURES

When his prayers (*smon-lam*) became effective he thoroughly mastered the Buddha-Doctrine (*bka'-bab-pa*) but only in relationship to the profound Concealed Treasures (*gter-ma*) [that he might discover]. At the age of seventeen he took out the text *Rig-'dsin-thugs-thig* from gYa'-ma-lung[369] on the tenth day of the fifth month in the year 1663. At the age of twenty-one he obtained the *gŚin-rje-gśed-dregs-'joms* from Śel-brag on the eighth day of the eighth month in the year 1667, while many miracles were seen; at the age of thirty he obtained the cycles of *Gur-drag* and *rDor-sems* from O-dkar-brag[370] on the fifteenth day of the eleventh month in the year 1676; at the age of thirty-four he publicly took out the cycle of *Thugs-rje-chen-po-bde-gśegs-kun-'dus* from Śa-'ug-ltag-sgo[371] on the twenty-ninth day of the sixth month of the year 1680.[372]

PRACTISING MEDITATION FOR ATTAINING THE DEVELOPING STAGE

He retreated for meditative exercises (*mthsams*)[373] to many holy places, be they ancient or new ones, such as Brag-dmar mChims-phu, gYa'-ma-lung, the rooms in old or new residences [of famous *bLa-mas*], or other meditation-rooms. He did so either for two years, for six, three or at least for one month, practising meditation by means of uttering mystic formulas, and by visual realization (*bsnyen-sgrub*) of the thirty-five *Yi-dam* in the cycles of *bLa-ma-źi-drag*, *rDor-sems*, *bKa'-brgyad*, *Thugs-rje-chen-po*, *Yang-phur-gśin-rje-gśed*, *rTa-mgrin*, *mKha'-spyod* etc. When he had had the deep experience of the *rDsogs-pa-chen-po* pure mystic state (*khregs-chod*)[374] he also experienced as to time and essence the would-be mystic state (*thod-rgal*) and the ways of motility (*rlung*)[375] and so was firmly established in the Developing Stage [*bskyed-rim*] in which the impure appearance [of the world] ceases to operate and he could easily perform any one of the four charismatic activities (*phrin-las*).[376]

ATTAINING THE FULFILMENT STAGE

When in the Fulfilment Stage the movement of the *rtsa* (structural pathways), *rlung* (the motility moving along them), and *thig-le* (the creative spark) had become subtle and pure in the central pathway (*avadhūti*), an awareness of pulsating bliss blazed forth [in the shape of] *jñānamudrā*, and when his spiritual attitude had become thus that there were no longer any differentiations and the absolutely real appeared by itself in all its completeness and perfection (*rdsogs-pa chen-po*), the distinctive features of a subject and an object dissolved (lit. : became free in their own place, i.e. they lost their compulsive character). He could control a concentration in which the radiant light shone incessantly and without differentiation between a concentrative and post-concentrative state. He perceived all appearances and activities as a play of the primary awareness (*ye-śes-kyi rol-pa*).

Thereupon the Great Master Padmasambhava, Vimalamitra, Hūṃ-mdsad,[377] Sangs-rgyas-gsang-ba,[378] Vairocana, Ye-śes-mtsho-rgyal, Nyang-ral Nyi-ma'od-zer,[379] Kun-mkhyen Chos-rje and[380] many other Indian and Tibetan Scholars and Mystics appeared to him due to their being-in-the-primary-awareness (*ye-śes-kyi sku*) and they created a magic circle of authentic beings (*sprul-pa'i dkyil-'khor*). They bestowed on him the empowerments (*dbang-bskur*) of many Pronouncements (*bka'-ma*) and Concealed Teachings (*gter-ma*); first they bestowed on him all the essentials of the instructions concerning the profound method (*zab-lam*). After he had realized the countenance of many divine powers of *Yi-dam*,[381] such as *rDo-rje-gźon-nu*, *rDor-sems*, *Yang-dag*, *Thugs-rje-chen-po*, *Źi-khro*, *rNal-'byor-ma*, they blessed him by bestowing empowerments upon him. He gained authority over the completely purified meditation on the realm of Buddha-activity (*yong-su 'byong-pa'i ting-nge-'dsin*)[382] after he had proceeded to *Sukhāvati* and *rNga-yab-dpal-ri* for many times. Without creating any obstacle the Spiritual Beings and the Protectors of the Doctrine (*Chos-*

skyong) furthered his actions; he displayed countless wonderful abilities, such as making prophecies and other miracles. Because of his clairvoyance (*mngon-śes*) that penetrated all that was hidden his prophecies on the later events proved true, but, I shall not discuss the arguments for the trustworthiness of his prophecies here. Even before he had reached his thirty-first year the ability to mature had been deeply implanted in his spiritual being, and it grew gradually. When he experienced [what is meant by] the jar-empowerment, all objects were to him like an apparition, radiant and yet nothing (*gsal-stong*); and since this was the time to act on behalf of others by way of his 'body' (*sku*, i.e. his 'personality') it so happened that when he travelled north and south to many places such as Śood-chen and sKyid-lung, by merely seeing his Body *Maṇḍala* (*sku'i dkyil-'khor*, i.e. his personality) in countless beings, without any discrimination, the seed of liberation was planted. Thus, these beings put a termination to *Saṃsāra* as perceived by themselves.

During the first month of the year 1677 when he was thirty-one his awareness (*rang-rig*) turned into a state of being radiant and open (*gsal-stong*), and [the duality of] percept and percipient (*gzung-'dsin*) dissolved in reality itself. This happened because he had experienced the mystic empowerment (*gsang-dbang*).[383] At this time he was helpful to others through his communicative abilities (*gsung*), therefore without any interruption he continued to declare and explain the Buddha-Doctrine to all people, regardless of whether they had high, medium, or small [cognitive capacities].

In 1683 during the eighth month when he was thirty-seven he experienced the melting bliss (*źu-bde*) while he was practising the Method of Messenger (*pho-nya'i lam*),[384] which illustrates the operation of the primary awareness of reality (*don-gyi ye-śes*), enhancing the four types of delight (*dga'-ba-bźi*) in his mental responsiveness (*thugs-rgyud*). [These four types are marked as] intrinsic perception (*rig-pa*), nothingness (*stong-pa-nyid*), utmost delight (*bde-ba-chen-po*), spontaneity (*lhan-skyes*), and unchangingness (*mi-'gyur-ba*). These experiences he deepened by exercising them. Then [gTer-bdag-gling-pa] was helpful to others by means of his mental responsiveness (*thugs*); as he had done with himself so he liked to bring [his disciples'] spiritual nature to maturity by means of specific methods, although he continued preaching the common theories unbiasedly. He thought it to be his responsibility to have his talented and qualified disciples realize the very manifestation of the self-originated primary awareness (*rang-'byung-gi ye-śes*).[385] For this purpose he used strict methods. Thus, he himself, in his real essence, became the three undiminishable aspects of the being of all Buddhas (i.e. aesthetic, *sku*; communicative, *gsung*; and responsive presence, *thugs*).[386] At this time he helped others by his charismatic activity which spread equally wide and all-pervading. Therefore in all his doings he was set free from being attached to his own interests. He strove only for the advantage of other beings and of the Buddha-Doctrine. He spent his whole time zealously to propagate the Doctrine by oral explanations, meditation, and rituals.

THE GREAT TEACHER

[gTer-bdag-gling-pa's] teaching activity: Above all, the Fifth Dalai Lama heard [from gTer-bdag-gling-pa] various doctrinal explanations, such as the precious Hundred Thousand Tantras that had been translated long ago (*sNga-'gyur rgyud-'bum*). Therefore the Dalai Lama appointed him 'Imperial Master' (*Ti-shih*).[387] Uncomparable in his zeal he declared and explained, clarified and deepened the Doctrine; thus he opened many approaches to the Doctrine of the Pronouncements and Concealed Teachings, the New Tantras (as transmitted in the Kanjur), to the various treatises on the Sūtras, to empowerments, guidances and oral traditions and explanations. He did so in accordance with each disciple's intellectual ability, be this very high or low. Talented and faithful disciples came from dBus, gTsang, Khams, Kong-po, Lho-ka, the Mon country, mNga'-ris ; among them were the high ranking dignitaries of *Sa-skya*, *Phag-mo-gru*, *'Bri-gung*, *sTag-lung*,[388] officials such as the 'Master of the Ten-Thousands (*dPon-chen*) and 'Master of Transport' (*dPon-skya*),[389] his own sons who were teaching the Doctrine, and many other venerable disciples. So that the Doctrine might last long he practised meditation, gave empowerments, and constructed *Maṇḍalas* on the basis of the Pronouncements. He also elaborated many rituals, in particular, in connection with the Old Concealed Teachings (*gter-rnying*) but also the Earlier and Later Concealed Teachings (*gter-kha gong-'og*), that had not existed previously, and writings accounted to thirteen volumes.

HIS MEDITATIVE ACTIVITY

As gTer-bdag-gling-pa stayed motionless in the meditation of mystic illumination and in the subsequent presentational knowledge (*mnyam-rjes khor-yug-gi-ting-nge-'dsin*)[390] he did not treat the students who strove after meditation and explanation, with mere verbiage, rather, he showed them the real nature of intrinsic perception (*rig-pa*).[391] When he was celebrating an empowerment ritual he forced the primary awareness to take effect in the disciples' mind. Visual and auditory realization [of divine powers] in meditation was not only taught, but also practised by him many times.

HIS VIRTUOUS DEEDS

gTer-bdag-gling-pa did not lock up in a treasure-house with iron doors the presents and offerings he had previously received from the Gong-ma Źabs-yas-phyin[392] and the faithful people. He prefered to offer cushions, drawings, figures and books (*rten-gsum*)[393] as well as objects needed for the rituals and for the four season festivals to the three-hundred monks of O-rgyan-smin-grol-glin. These monks had recently arrived and spent the whole time expounding the Doctrine and meditating. They observed three different vows (those of a *Bhikṣu*, a Bodhisattva, and a Tantric). [Because of gTer-bdag-gling-pa's donation] they did not lack anything. Further, he had made many paintings and moulded many holy figures ; more than five hundred books he had printed, among them the Kanjur in gold and silver [letters]. He also had carved many blocks [for printing] commentaries and other books of the Old School. He had moulded a hundred-thousand figures of the great *Tārā* who delivers when looked at. In order to complete the preparatory path through meritorious deeds and knowledge (*tshogs-gnyis*),[394] he generously and without prejudice gave alms to everybody who needed them. He thought himself responsible for the beings and the Buddha-Doctrine. This [feeling of responsibility] is the great miracle in his life.

DEMISE

After gTer-bdag-gling-pa had done all these works that surpasses one's imagination he seemed to fall ill. This happened in the first month of 1714 when he was nearly sixty-eight. In particular, from the twenty-fifth day onwards gTer-bdag-gling pa gave special advices and instructions to his nephew (*Khu-dbon*). Then the people who had assembled to pray for him (*źabs-rim-du gnas-pa*) thought the sweet sound of a flute to be heard outside the western wall of his house]; simultaneously the smell of camphor was perceived both inside and outside the bedroom. In the morning of the second day of the second month he said : "It is necessary to go seven steps to the east !" When he had done so he sat down with crossed legs (*vajrāsana*). "Visual, auditory, and intrinsic perceptions turn into divine powers (*lha*), mystic formulas, and the nature of noetic being (*chos-sku'i ngang*). Out of the intimate relationship between noetic being (*chos-sku*) and primary awareness (*ye-śes*) there emerges the endless variety [of the world], but to the Yogi who has a profound and mystic experience [this variety] is without any distinction. The potentiality of responsiveness (*thugs-kyi thig-le*) is the single essence [of the Yogi's existence]." This was his bequest at the very point of his demise. "Now the Spiritual Beings have arrived to call on me." With these words he moved his hands as if he were beating a small *Ḍamaru* drum and ringing the bell, and his eyes shone with dignity. At this instant many miracles happened and countless marvellous events resulted. Thus he demonstrated his demise to the purified sphere Radiant Lotus, the Realm of Spiritual Beings (*mKha'-spyod-padma-'od*).

THE PROPHECY ABOUT HIS DISCIPLES

The prophecy in the Concealed Teachings (*gter-lung*) says about his disciples and sons, representing either his responsiveness (*Thugs-kyi-sras*), or his communicative being (*gSung-gi sras*): "His disciples and sons, the venerable authorities of his teachings, the rulers, fathers and sons of the present will all be reborn as kings, and their followers will reach at least one of the ten levels of spirituality[395] (*sa-bcu*). Thirty-five [disciples] will help other beings. One-hundred-and-eight will deliver themselves. Two-thousand will be attached to his teachings. Fifty-thousand will be involved withh is prayers. Sixty-seven will be connected with his activity. Seven high-ranking persons will have an umbrella[396] as a sign of power and will worship him on their knees. Three rulers, will support him."

HIS OWN, MOST FAMOUS DISCIPLES

The Fifth Dalai Lama and the regent (*sDe-srid*) Sangs-rgyas-rgya-mtsho[397] who were like sun and moon, like patron and the receiver of gifts (*mchod-yon*), both tasted [gTer-bdag-gling-pa's] nectar-like teachings. rDo-brag Rig-'dsin Padma-phrin-las, Sa-skya Khri-chen Kun-dga'-bkra-śis, rTse-gdong Źabs-drung Khu-dbon, the high ranking persons of the Upper and Lower residence, Tre-hor mChog-sprul, the rGyal-tshab (i.e. the representative of the hierarch himself) of mTshur-phu, who was a reputable authority on the teachings of the *Karma-pa* School, 'Bri-gung dKon-mchog-phrin-las-bzang-po, sTag-lung-pa bstTan-'dsin-srid-źi-rnam-rgyal,' Brug-pa Thams-cad-mkhyen-pa dPag-bsam-dbang-po,sGam-po-mchog-sprul bZang-po-rdo-rje together with his successors. Chab-mdo rGyal-ba-phags-pa-lha, Ngag-dbang-mchog-gi-sprul-sku, mDo-khams-pa Ngag-dbang-kun-dga'-bstan-'dsin, Ta-bla-gong-'og, Kaḥ-thog rGyal-ba and his successors, rDsogs-chen-gnyis-pa 'Gyur-med-theg-mchog-bstan-'dsin: They all are other renowned and high ranking *bLa-mas* who as preservers of the Doctrine worshipped him truly. But the only 'spiritual' (*thugs*) disciple was gCung Lo-tsā-ba Dharmaśri, an incarnation of gYu-sgra. His 'physical' disciples (*sku*) were Padma-gyur-med-rgya-mtsho, Źabs-drung Yid-bźin-legs-grub, Drin-chen-rin-chen-rnam-rgyal, the venerable Mi-'gyur-dpal-sgron, and also the *Bhikṣus* bLo-gsal-rgya-mtsho, sNgags-rab-'byams-pa, O-rgyan-chos-grags, 'Bum-rab-'byams-pa, and O-rgyan-skal-bzang, all of them attending [gTer-bdag-gling-pa]. All these disciples knew him presonally and upheld the Doctrine. This great assembly of renowned (scholars) spread the teaching far and wide by their explanation and meditation.

EFFICACY OF GTER-BDAG-GLING-PA'S ENDEAVOUR

Not only was this great Discoverer devoted to the theories of the Old and the New Schools (*gsar-rnying bstan-pa*), but prompted by others and being himself so inclined, he revived the theories and methods of the minor Schools, such as the *Jo-nang-pa*, *Śangs-pa*, *Żi-byed-gcod-yul-pa*, and *Bo-dong-pa.*[398] In particular, when our own system which is founded on the Pronouncements (*snga-'gyur rnying-ma bka'-ma*), translated long ago, together with its three main theories (the *mDo-sgyu-sems-gsum*) founded by King Khri-srong-lde-btsan (754-797) and the religious people he patronized, was about to disappear like the flame of a lamp without oil, then with undiminished zeal and strength he re-established the endangered Doctrine by explanations, meditations, and rituals. In brief, due to the activities of the venerable [gTer-bdag-gling-pa] himself, his brothers, and successors, the mystic traditions of the Old School were harmonized both in names and content. (The Tt reports: The Earlier and Later Concealed Teachings and the Old Concealed Teachings were harmonized.) This tradition still continues without error or detriment. Therefore, nobody can claim to be his equal in helpful activity and lineage. Those who join this School in later times should not only rely on the profound rituals (*cho-ga*) and ceremonies (*phrin-las*), they should much more study this system as a whole and disseminate it zealously.

(The Tt gives an abridged report of gTer-bdag-gling-pa's life but does not add any new facts)

21. SUMMARY OF THE HAGIOGRAPHY OF 'JIGS-MED-GLING-PA (1729-1798), THE MASTER OF THE *SNYING-THIG* AND EDITOR OF THE *RNYING-MA-PA* TANTRA

FORMER LIVES

'Jigs-med-gling-pa's previous existence was Rig-'dsin-Chos-rje-gling-pa in whom Pan-chen Vimalamitra, King Khri-srong-lde-btsan, and rGyal-sras Lha-rje together were incarnated.

BIRTH

As indicated in the prophecies of Guru Chos-dbang, Sangs-rgyas-gling-pa[399] and Rva-ston, in the district 'Phyong-rgyas, near the monastery dPal-ri-dgon-pa[400] and south of King Srong-btsan-sgam-po's tomb, 'Jigs-med-gling-pa was born in the twelfth month of 1729. It seemed to be an auspicious omen that his birthday was the day of kLong-chen-rab-'byams-pa's (1308-1363) death.

ENTERING THE BUDDHIST ORDER

When still very young he understood the ancient stories of the great Discoverers of Concealed Teachings Sangs-rgyas-bla-ma[401] and Chos-rje-gling-pa.[402] When he was six he entered the monastery dPal-gyi-ri-bo and became a novice under the guidance of Ngag-dbang-blo-bzang-padma, who was the manifestation (*sPrul-sku*) of Ye-śes-mtsho-rgyal and who gave 'Jigs-med-gling-pa the name Padma-mkhyen-brtse'i-'od-zer. Later he took the monastic vows from gNas-gsar-ba Ngag-dbang-kun-dga'-legs-pa'i-'byung-gnas.

PURSUIT OF MYSTIC KNOWLEDGE

'Jigs-med-gling-pa listened to the *Grol-tig* and the *bLa-ma-dgongs-'dus* taught by the *Sthavira* Kun-bzang-'od-zer. When he was twelve he heard the *Phyag-rgya-chen-po* treatise *Ye-śes-mthong-grol* from Rig-'dsin Thugs-mchog-rdo-rje who became 'Jigs-med-gling-pa's—basic Guru.[403] He heard the ancient Pronouncements (*snga-'gyur bka'-ma*, the Earlier and Later Concealed Teachings (*gter-kha gong-'og*) and also some treatises of the transmission of the New School (*gSar-ma-pa*) from gTer-chen Dri-med-'od-gling-pa, Żang-sgom Dharmakīrti, sMin-gling-grub-dbang Śrīnātha, bsTan-'dsin Ye-śes-lhun-grub, Thang-'brog-dbon Padma-mchog-grub, and Mon rDsa-dkar-bla-ma Dar-rgyas. Not only did 'Jigs-med-gling-pa study Buddhist mysticism and philosophy he also busied himself with Indian astrology (*dkar-rtsi*), calligraphy and other arts.[404]

EXPERIENCES OF YOGA AND VISIONS

In his own monastery of dPal-ri'i sGog-khang-thig-le-ngag-gcig, when he was twenty-eight in 1757, he fulfilled the vow of seclusion (*bcad-rgya*) for three months. He gained authority over the Old and New Traditions (*ring-brgyud* and *nye-brgyud*) in reference to the *Grol-tig-dgongs-pa-rang-grol* which is a Concealed Teaching of gTer-chen Śes-rab-'od-zer[405] (the Tt calls him Chos-kyi-rgyal-po 'Gro-'dul-gling-pa). While he was attempting the Development (*bskyed-rim*) and the Fulfilment Stages (*rdsogs-rim*) he gained the capacity of mystic heat (*drod-rtags*).[406] 'Jigs-med-gling-pa realized many divine powers (*lha*) and, thus, became a mature Knowledge-Holder[407] (*rnam-par-smin-pa'i rig-'dsin*). As he had perfectly accomplished the Yoga of 'Pathway-Motility-Potentiality' (*rtsa-rlung-thig-le rnal-'byor*)[408] he gained mastery over the center of communication in his own mind. For that reason the letter which symbolizes the communicative ability, located in the throat focal point of the central pathway, dissolved like a cloud. Thereupon he was an expert at eloquence. He had many visions of *Hayagrīva*, Padmasambhava, and 'Jam-dpal-bśes-gnyen, the famous master of the *rDsogs-chen* tradition. During such a vision a Spiritual Being symbolizing the primary awareness (*ye-śes-kyi mKha'-'gro*), guided him to the Nepalese Stūpa Bya-rung-kha-śor[409] where she offered him a list of Concealed Teachings and a key for understanding them. Thereupon he wrote down his famous treatises of the sNying-thig of kLong-chen-rab-'byams-pa which is one of the basic works of the whole *rDsogs-chen* system. kLong-chen-rab-'byams-pa, the author of the *sNying-thig*, appeared to him several times in bSam-yas.

TEACHING ACTIVITY

Because of his spiritual and essential contacts with kLong-chen-rab-'-byams-pa he became the chief supporter of the *rDsogs-pa-chen-po sNying-thig* literature. At first 'Jigs-med-gling-pa taught the *sNying-thig* theories to fifteen qualified disciples. But later many disciples eager to hear the Old and New Tradition of the *sNying-thig* (i.e. the *sNying-thig* of Vimalamitra and of kLong-chen-rab-'byams-pa),[410] came from every region in Tibet.

BENEFICIENT DEEDS

Due to a prophecy in the *mKha'-ri'i-zus-lan* he travelled to his native place in Phyong-rgyas.[411] There, at a place south of the tomb of King Srong-btsan-sgam-po (627-649) in the upper part of the Don-mkhar valley[412] in the dell of sKung, he built the hermitage Tshe-ring-ljongs Padma-'od-gsal-theg-mchoggling. At this secluded place 'Jigs-med-gling-pa spent all his time. He was a mediator between convicts and official authorities and often rescued the criminals from death. He gave alms generously to everybody without thinking of a reward. To temples (for instance bSam-yas) he made offerings. When the Gurkhas invaded the border regions of Tibet (1788)[413] he prevented them from capturing the whole country. For this act he was rewarded by the Tibetan government.

RE-ESTABLISHING THE OLD SCHOOL TEACHINGS

As he could not bear the idea that the Old School teachings might disappear he collected all the books available in sMin-grol-gling and those that were included in the Old School Tantras (*rNying-ma rgyud-'bum*) in order to revive the Old School traditions. He had copied part of these books in gold, silver and other precious things. The main bulk he had published in the ordinary way.

HIS WORKS

For the first time he composed a catalogue and a history (*'Jam-gling-tha-grug-khyab-pa'i-rgyam*) of the Old School Tantras, thus continuing the attempts of Ratna-gling-pa (1403-1479) who collected the Tantras, that were scattered in other works. Jigs-med-gling-pa is also famous for composing the basic text (*gzung*) of the *kLong-chen-snying-thig* and for some treatises related to it. On the basis of the *kLong-chen-snying-thig* he wrote a 'Stages of the Path' (*lam-rim*) with the title *Yon-tan-rin-po-che'i-*

mdsod. His collected works amount to nine volumes, all of them printed in sDe-dge.

DISCIPLES

His important disciples: Grub-dbang-'jigs-med-phrin-las-'od-zer, 'Jigs-med-rgyal-pa'i-myu-gu, mKhas-grub 'Jigs-med-kun-grol who was a native from the Mon country. He also had the following disciples and students: Sa-skya Khri-chen Ngag-dbang-dpal-ldan-chos-skyong and his brother, both incarnations from the 'Bri-gung-pa monastery,[414] Rig-'dsin-mchog-gi-sprul-sku from the monastery rDo-rje-brag,[415] the incarnation of the communicative ability (*gSung-gi sprul-sku*) of Lho-brag-pa and his disciple, sByor-ra sPrul-sku who preserved the *Bo-dong-pa* Doctrine,[416] both the venerables (*Chos-rje*) from the Eastern and Western College of the dGa'-ldan monastic academy[417] and rTse-le-sprul-sku from the monastery mTsho-sna-dgon in the Mon country.

EFFECT OF HIS TEACHINGS

Most of the Old School scholars who lived during the 18th and 19th century as well as the scholars of our times adhere to his teachings. Thus, 'Jigs-med-gling-pa's teachings still exist through the whole realm of Tibetan Buddhist culture.

DEMISE

In the residence Tshe-ring-ljong, which is part of the hermitage rNam-grol-yang-rtse, on the third day of the ninth month in 1798, he departed at the age of sixty-nine.

22. SUMMARY OF THE HAGIOGRAPHY OF MCHOG-GYUR-BDE-CHEN ŹIG-PO-GLING-PA (1829-1870), THE FAMOUS DISCIPLE OF MKHYEN-BRTSE'I DBANG-PO AND THE MASTER OF THE SEVEN CURRENTS OF PRONOUNCEMENTS

PREVIOUS LIVES AND PROPHECIES

Źig-po-gling-pa is stated to be an incarnation of the royal son Dam-'dsin-mu-rub-btsad-po Ye-śes-rol-pa-rtsal.[418] He was styled a renowned master of the Concealed Teachings in the prophecies of O-rgyan-dri-med-kun-dga', Ratna-gling-pa, and Rong-ston Padma-bde-chen-gling-pa.[419]

BIRTH

In the southern part of the country Yer-pa which is a subdivision of Upper mDo-Khams at the village sGom-sde, which belongs to the district of Grva-nang he was born on the tenth day of the sixth month in 1829. His father was called 'The Tantric of sGom-sde' (*sGom-pa sNgags-'chang*) Padma-dbang-phyug. This family held the rank of a minister (*bLon-po*) under the rule of Nang-chen Ching-hu, who was also called A-lcags-gru. Źig-po-gling-pa's mother had the name Tshe-ring-rgya-mtsho. The child was first called Nor-bu-bstan-'dsin.

BECOMING A NOVICE AND PURSUING HIS STUDIES

When Zig-po-gling-pa was twelve in a vision he saw Padmasambhava who prophesied him to become a notable scholar-saint in the field of Buddhism. He received the novice-vows from sTag-lung Ma Rin-po-che. His first teacher was Chos-skyi-rgyal-po, the Eighth *dPa'-bo-gtsug-lag*,[420] who instructed him in the *bLa-ma-dgongs-'dus-thugs-sgrub* cycle; in particular he was taught the texts *Tsha-ba-dmar-thag* and the ritual-instruction (*las-byang*) *Me-tog-phreng-mdses*. Then Źig-po-gling-pa received instructions from the hierarch of the *Karma-pa* School, the hierarch of the *'Brug-pa-bka'-brgyud* School and their main disciples, from the mChog-sprul of the *'Bri-gung-pa* School, the abbot (*mKhan-po*) and the Tantric Master (*rDo-rje-slob-dpon*) of the Zur-mang[421] residence. Apart from the main branches of the Buddhist Doctrine he also studied the arts of the ritual dance (*gar*), the drawing of *Maṇḍalas* (*thig*), ritual songs and music (*dbyangs*).

When he was twenty-four he met Si-tu Padma-nyin-byed-dbang-po in dPal-spungs monastery.[422] When Źig-po-gling-pa offered Padma-nyin-byed-dbang-po the text *Phur-ba-dbang-chen-bśad-pa*, the latter praised and encouraged him to strive for the Concealed Teachings.—From mKhan-chen Byang-sems-zla-bzang (alias Zla-sprul Karma-nges-don-bstan-pa-rab-rgyas) he received instructions in the Enlightened Attitude (*byang-chub-kyi sems*) and from 'Jam-mgon bLo-gros-mtha'-yas in the *Thugs-rje chen-po-bde-gśegs-Kun-'dus*, the *sGyu-'phrul-źi-khro*.

PROPHECY ABOUT ŹIG-PO-GLING-PA

The *rTen-'brel-mdo-chings* provides us with a prophecy about Źig-po-gling-pa, which will be given below. This prophecy is highly reliable because the revival of the Old School in the 19th century is based on this prophecy. Other prophecies with equal content are mentioned throughout the 19th century literature of the Old School. The prophecy runs as follows: "The profound and Concealed Teachings are hidden in the cosmic treasury. Individuals who are endowed with special prayers (*smon-lam-can*) will not let them remain there but will take them out. Listen, royal son, when your last existence is to come, most of the Translators (*Lo-tsā-ba*) and Scholars (*Paṇḍita*) of the ancient time, King Khri-srong-lde-btsan and his entourage, will congregate. In particular when you, royal son (i.e. now King Mu-rub-btsad-po who will be later born as Źig-po-gling-pa) will meet the ruler (i.e. now Khri-srong-lde-btsan who will be later) mKhyen-brtse'i-dbang-po, you will be useful to each other and cause *Karma* gradually to become exhausted. At last you will realize my (i.e. Padmasambhava's) instructions. During your pure visions you will actually meet me. You will demonstrate the pure method (*dmar-khrid*) of the practice of Tantric tradition! Through your own attempt you will effortlessly gain spiritual potency. You will have many disciples who also will gain spiritual potency."

MEETING HIS TEACHER MKHYEN-BRTSE'I-DBANG-PO (1820-1892)[423]

In the ninth month of the same year (probably 1853) he met 'Jam-dbyangs-mkhyen-brtse'i-dbang-po. The latter bestowed on Źig-po-gling-pa the empowerments (*dbang*) of the cycles *Phur-pa-yang-gsang-spu-gri*, *mKhon-lugs Phur-pa*, and the *Yang-tig-yid-bźin-nor-bu*. At this instant Źig-po-gling-pa realized mKhyen-brtse'i-dbang-po to be identical with the great scholar Vimalamitra.

HIS VISIONS

When Źig-po-gling-pa had a vision of Ekajaṭī[424] she prophesied that he would gain the utmost spiritual power, that is, he would recognize the three *rDsogs-pa-chen-po* sections; also *bLa-ma Heruka* appeared to him. Thereupon he had an intrinsic perception (*rig-pa*) in all its nakedness (*rjen-pa*). The knots of the central pathway of the heart (*snying-ga'i rtsa-mdud*) were loosened. Now, he was able to read and recognize the symbols (*brda'-yig*) of the *Thugs-sgrub-bar-chad-kun-sel* which in its main features was like the *Thugs-sgrub-bde-gśegs-'dus-pa* composed by mKhyen-brtse'i-dbang-po.

HIS TEACHERS

Źig-po-gling-pa himself stated that he had had four teachers : sTag-lung-pa Ngag-dbang-bstan-pa'i-nyi-ma taught him the monastic rules (*Vinaya*) ; Zla-sprul Karma-nges-don-bstan-pa-rab-rgyas, who had the academic rank of a *dGe-ba'i-bśes-gnyen*, instructed him in the Enlightened Attitude (*byang-chub-kyi sems*); sKong-sprul Padma-gar-dbang-blo-gros-mtha'-yas[425] introduced him into the Tantras; and his 'root' *bLa-ma* Padma-'od-gsal-mdo-sngags-gling-pa (alias mKhyen-brtse'i-dbang-po) showed to him the final and certain reality (*mthar-thug-nges-pa don*).

ŹIG-PO-GLING-PA, A RENOWNED AUTHORITY OF THE 'NEW CONCEALED TEACHINGS' AND MASTER OF THE SEVEN CURRENTS OF PRONOUNCEMENTS

mKhyen-brtse'i-dbang-po authorized Źig-po-gling-pa to teach the New Concealed Teachings ; but according to a prophecy in the *rDsogs-chen-sde-gsum* he was also authorized to gain power over the Seven Currents of the Pronouncements (*bka'-babs-bdun*). This authorization he shared with his teacher mKhyen-brtse'i-dbang-po.

THE FIRST CURRENT

He studied the three main subjects of spiritual training

according to the Pronouncement method, the *mDo-sgyu-sems-gsum*, and disseminated these theories.

SECOND CURRENT

This is built up by books and treasures he had unearthed (*sa-gter*). In 1841 when he was twelve he unearthed in Brag-dkar-rdsong-chung twenty-four meditation guides, such as the *Lha-sras-thugs-dam* and *dGongs-'dus-bka'-rtags-rdo-rje-thog-pa-ma-long*. In 1867 when he was thirty-eight he discovered in rTsi-ske-nor-bu-spun-gsum seven cycles about *Dam-chos-nor-bu*, a figure of Padmasambhava, and the ceremonial ornaments of Seng-ge-sgra-sgrogs after he had received the list of hiding places (*kha-byang*) from mKhyen-brtse'i-dbang-po. In sGrags Yang-rdsong he found seven cycles of the *Źi-byed* method, other lists of hiding places (*kha-byang*, *yang-byang*, *gnad-byang* and *snying-byang*), and many sacrificial objects (*rdsas-gter*). But the most important Concealed Treasures are the following ones: *Thugs-sgrub-bar-chad-kun-sel* from Zla-nyin-kha-la-rong-sgo; *Thugs-rje-chen-po-padma-gtsug-dor* from Na-bun-rdsong; *Thugs-dam-zab-pa* from the backside of 'Og-min Karma; some commentaries based on the oral tradition of the books listed above; and the *rTsa-ba'i-thugs-sgrub-dgongs-pa-kun-'dus* from Ye-rgyal-mkha'-mdsod; *Dam-chos-rdsogs-pa-chen-po-sde-gsum* from sMar (or sMad) Śod-dsam-nang-padma-śel-phug; *Dam-chos-śog-sde-drug* from Seng-chen-gnam-brag-gi-ri; *Thugs-rje-chen-po-padma-sgyu-'phrul-drva-ba* and *Thugs-rje-chen-po-'khor-ba-dong-sprugs* from mKha'-'gro-'bum-rdsong; *Ma-mo-spyi-bsdus* from Karma'i-dpal-de'u; *Thugs-sgrub-yid-bźin-nor-bu* which resembles the oral explanation of the Pronouncements as delivered by mKhyen-brtse'i-dbang-po, from Ke-la-nor-bu-sprin-gsum; *bKa'-brgyad-bde-gśegs-kun-'dus* and *Zab-pa-rdsogs-chen-gser-źun* from gYu-'brel-brag in the south of Ye-rgyal; the five cycles of *Thugs-sgrub-rdo-rje-drag-rtsal-dang-snying-po* from Rong Me-dkar-mo-stag-tshang; *bDe-mchog-sangs-rgyas-mnyam-sbyor* from Ru-dam-gang-khrod. In addition to these books he found a list of hiding places in mDo-Khams entitled *mDo-byang*, under a rock named dPa'-bo-dbang-chen-brag. But he also discovered many figures and ritual objects.

THIRD CURRENT

The twice hidden Concealed Teachings (*yang-gter*). Źig-po-gling-pa gained authority over the following Concealed Teachings and re-established their tradition: The *Gur-drag-hūṃ-dmar-snying-thig*, the first discovered by gTer-chen Sangs-rgyas-gling-pa;[426] *Ma-rgyud-gsang-ba-lam-khyer* first discovered by gTer-ston mKha'-'gro-ma-kun-dga'-bum-pa.[427]

FOURTH CURRENT

The Concealed Teachings concerning the (Buddha) intentionality (*dgongs-pa'i gter*): Stimulated by a vision of *Tārā* he composed the *sGrol-ma'i-zab-thig*.

FIFTH CURRENT

The Concealed Teachings revealed by remembering (*rjes-dran-gyi gter-kha*): Źig-po-gling-pa remembered his former existences as gNubs Khu-lung-pa Yon-tan-rgya-mtsho and Sangs-rgyas-gling-pa. On this basis he composed the last will of gNubs and instructions for drawing of *Yantras* (i.e. geometrical and symbolic figures) due to the system of Sangs-rgyas-glingpa.

SIXTH CURRENT

The Concealed Teachings shown in visions (*dag-snang-gi gter-kha*) : When he opened the approach to the holy locality Ri-bo-dbang-źu he recognized Vimalamitra sitting there. Thereupon Źig-po-gling-pa wrote down the *Vimala'i-zab-thig*.

SEVENTH CURRENT

The Concealed Teachings recognized by hearing (*snyan-brgyud-gi gter-kha*): When he saw Padmasambhava in a vision he was taught the *A-ti-zab-don-snying-thig*.

BENEFICIENT ACTIONS

Źig-po-gling-pa appeased the protecting deities and spirits, celebrated auspicious rituals at crucial points of the country (for example at bSam-yas Has-po-ri[428] and dPal-chu-bo-ri[429] and prevented the final wars (*mtha'-dmag*).

TEACHING ACTIVITY

He and his successors disseminated special teachings while bestowing empowerments (*dbang*) and transmitting oral traditions (*lung*) to the hierarchs of all the other Schools of Tibetan Buddhism (*Karma-pa*, *'Brug-pa*, *'Bri-gung-pa*, *Sa-skya-pa*, and *sTag-lung-pa*) and to the prominent masters of the main lineages of the Old School (i.e. *sMin-ling-pa*, *Kaḥ-thog-pa*, *dPal-yul-pa*, *Je-chen-pa*, and *rDsogs-chen-pa*).

DISSEMINATION OF HIS TEACHINGS

His basic theory, the *Thugs-sgrub-bar-chad-kun-sel*, spread far and wide. In several monasteries ('Og-min-mtshur-phu,[430] dPal-spungs, Kaḥ-thog, and rDsogs-chen)[431] he started the performance of miracle plays.

FOUNDING TEMPLES

At his own residence (gNas-brtan-sgang and rTsi-ske-'dus-mdo) he founded temples, installed figures and established a philosophical and a mystical college (*bśad-sde* and *sgrub-sde*) in order to teach the Sūtras and Tantras.

DEMISE

In 1870 when he was forty-one he fell ill. When he had had some visions of the field of Buddha-Activity (*buddha-kṣetra*), miracles appeared and he dissolved in the sphere of calm (*źi-ba'i dbyings*).

SUCCESSORS

His 'spiritual' disciple (*Thugs-sras*) 'Gyur-med-tshe-dbang-grags-pa succeeded him. He was prophesied to be an authentic being of gNubs Nam-mkha'-snying-po. 'Gyur-med-tshe-dbang-grags-pa had completed the buildings of Żig-po-gling-pa's residence rTsi-ske-nor-bu-gling, and he had his corpse deposited in a high and gilded Stūpa.

mKhyen-brtse'i-dbang-po who saw his former disciple in a vision, and sKong-sprul Padma-gar-dbang were particularly attracted by Źig-po-gling-pa's teachings.

23. HAGIOGRAPHY OF 'JAM-DBYANGS MKHYEN-BRTSE'I-DBANG-PO PADMA-'OD-GSAL-MDO-SNGAGS-GLING-PA (1820-1892), THE FIFTH DISCOVERER-KING

(DC) FORMER EXISTENCES

'Jam-dbyangs mKhyen-brtse'i-dbang-po,[432] the fifth Discoverer-King (*gTer-ston-rgyal-po*) was an authentic manifestation (*sPrul-sku*) of Paṇ-chen Vimalamitra, the religious King Khri-srong-lde-btsan, rGyal-sras Lha-rje, and he was thirteen times consecutively born as a Discoverer of Concealed Teachings.

BIRTH

mKhyen-brtse'i-dbang-po's father, Rin-chen-dbang-rgyal, was an official (*Drung-chen*) and belonged to the family gNyos; his mother, Rin-chen-dbang-rgyal, was a Mongolian princess (*Sog-bza'*). In sDe-dge (mDo-Khams), the country of Concealed Treasures, at the village Dil-mgo near the mountain dByar-ru-kyhung-chen-brag mKhyen-brtse'i-dbang-po was born, on the fifth day of the sixth month in the year 1820 while many miracles were happening.

YOUTH

Whenever mKhyen-brtse'i-dbang-po thought of the Protector of the six-armed Primary Awareness (*Ye-śes-mgon-po*) and of *Ekajaṭi*, the guardians of the Tantras, they protected him. Sometimes he remembered his former existences. Already in his youth he was strongly attracted to the Mahāyāna method because he only strove after entering the monastic community (*Saṅgha*). His cognition and abilities were uncomparable; he learned to read and to write without any effort. He had to read the books only once, to recognize the words and their meaning.

EDUCATION

When he was twenty he received the monastic vows from Rig-'dsin-bzang-po who held the rank of an abbot (*mKhan-po*) in O-rgyan-smin-grol-gling.[433] Sa-skya-pa rDo-rje-rin-chen and other teachers taught him the Enlightened Attitude (*bodhi-citta*) and appropriate theories according to the system of Asaṅga and Nāgārjuna.[434] He heard the *Hevajra*-cycle and the *Saṃvara* cycle from the brother of Thar-rtse *mKhan Rin-po-che*; the *Yang-dag*[435] according to the *So*-system and the *Rig-'dsin-thugs-thig* from Sangs-rgyas-kun-dga', the *Khri-chen* in the monastery sMin-gling; the empowerments (*dbang-bskur*) of the *sGyu-'phrul-źi-khro* from Źe-chen-pa 'Gyur-med-mthu-stobs-rnam-rgyal. These became the fundamentals of his own Tantric vows.

mKhyen-brtse'i-dbang-po refused to boast of his incarnate status, of his family or of his wealth, rather he underwent many difficulties. With great zeal and endeavour he learned from the *bLa-mas*, Tantric scholars (*rDo-rje-'dsin-pa*), academic scholars (*dGe-ba'i-bśes-gnyen*), and the scholars of the worldly arts in the provinces dBus, gTsang, and Khams. He studied medicine, *Arthaśāstra*, grammar, logic, and the remaining theories of the ten arts. In the field of philosophy he heard the *Vinaya* (i.e. monastic conduct and ethics), the *Abhidharmakośa*, the *Mādhyamika* theories, the *Prajñāpāramitā* essentials and thoroughly practised these teachings. Also he participated in all empowerments (*dbang*) and oral injunctions that belonged to the pure teaching-system such as the Pronouncements and Concealed Treasures of the Old School (*rNying-ma bka'-gter*), the Old and New Teachings of the *bKa'-gdams-pa* School, the teachings of the *Sa-skya-pa* and *Ngor-pa* School, the *Tshar-pa* School, the *bKa'-brgyud-pa* School, the *'Bri-gung-pa*, *sTag- lung-pa*, *'Brug-pa-bka'-brgyud*, *Jo-nang-pa*,—*Źa-lu-pa* and *Bo-dong-pa* Schools.[436] As to the Tantras he heard every explanation of the *sGyu-'phrul-gsang-ba-snying-po*, *Kālacakra Cakrasaṃvara*, *Hevajra*, and *Guhyasamāja*, in particular, the traditions of the precious Kanjur (*bKa'-'gyur*), the Hundred-Thousand Ancient Tantras (*rNying-ma-rgyud-'bum*), and the Tanjur (*bsTan-'gyur*), but also the unprejudiced expositions of the various Tibetan Schools were taught him. He had gone through about seven-hundred volumes reading and hearing oral explanations. In brief, for thirteen years he only strove after studying. He heard most of the expositions of his own School as for instance the theories of the Famous Ten Columns of the Doctrine (*ka-chen-bcur grags-pa-rnams*) (i.e. ten famous authors). mKhyen-brtse'i-dbang-po thoroughly understood the meaning by a mere perusal of the books because he possessed the mystic formula (*Mantra*) of never forgetting [what one has read].

PRACTISING THE BUDDHA DOCTRINE

He was not content with merely listening to the Buddha Doctrine, but, in order to educate later [generations of disciples], he lived it by practice and meditation. Thus he completed the essentials which each theory insists upon as well as the doctrinal visions and the conduct appropriate to the several Schools. He did not confuse the reliable and unreliable teachings of this or that School because he had the ability of seeing without being deluded, cognizant of reality (*mkhyen-pa'i chos-spyan rdul-med*). Neither the best individuals nor the common people could challenge him. Many times [mKhyen-brtse'i-dbang-po] taught the Sūtras, Tantras, and commentaries which he had heard and about which he was certain through empowerments; there was not a single text which he had not taught once. Without taking any reward, he gave appropriate instructions to everybody who aspired to [such theories] regardless whether they were poor people or rich and noble persons; thus he acted for the sake of the Doctrine. Hence he did not heap up wealth by pretentious actions, performed by a prayer-drone (*Grong-chog-pa*) who might call his job "advantageous to the beings." Through his three brilliant and three comprehending qualities[437] he effortlessly amassed great wealth, but he did not squander it on unworthy matters.

INSTALLING FIGURES, PUBLISHING BOOKS, AND FOUNDING TEMPLES

mKhyen-brtse'i-dbang-po bequeathed about two thousand gilded copper figures. In order to support the promulgation [of the Buddha Doctrine] he had published almost forty volumes; together with manuscripts and other printed matters these works make about two thousand [volumes].

In order to give support to the spiritual responsiveness (*thugs-rten*) he founded a hundred gilded Stūpas of copper, apart of the great Stūpa of Lhun-grub-steng.[438] He had carefully prepared thirteen small and large temples to shelter [these figures and Stūpas]; there he also started the rituals [which have to be performed] every day and on festivals. Due to the adverse and troublesome circumstances he could not very well furnish the new monasteries and temples, but he made donations of thirty thousand tea-loads (*ja-sgrom*) to restore the monasteries which had been damaged in the previous civil riots in lower and upper Amdo. mKhyen-brtse'i-dbang-po asked the rulers of Tibet and China, the religious king (*Chos-rgyal*) of sDe-dge, and the royal ministers for support and because of his entreaty they had the ruined sacred edifices re-established or re-built. mKhyen-brtse'i-dbang-po gave aid to the performance of rituals and, according to the circumstances, he showed his grace to these monasteries through his admonitions. He bequeathed an amount of four thousand tea-bricks to several monasteries of different size in order to recite the mystic formulas (*Mantras*) and to read the holy books every year. In general he attempted the two precious methods of the Enlightened Attitude (i.e. to aid other beings in attaining Buddhahood, and to strive after it oneself).

DISTINGUISHED AS WELL AS COMMON PEOPLE WERE HIS DISCIPLES

Because of his truly unprejudiced (*ris-med*) and righteous attitude towards the [various] doctrinal currents, trusting and venerating every School, he had countless disciples and he did not differentiate the well-known dignitaries of the *Sa-skya-pa*, *bKa'-brgyud-pa*, Old or *dGe-lugs-pa* School, academic scholars (*dGe-ba'i-bśes-gnyen*), hermits or even the narrow-minded religious people or the believers in the *Bon*-religion. Countless nobles (*dPon-chen*) of Tibet and China used to congregate daily [at his residence]. There was not a single person for whom mDo-sngags-gling-pa did not care by the blessing of protective rituals (*rkyen-sel*) and empowerments. He bestowed the Doctrine on each individual according to his desire. Due to his liberation from the eight fetters of worldly attachment[439] mKhyen-brtse'i-dbang-po had renounced all fictitious forms of human behaviour and showed many examples of helpfulness and apprehension to the high and low alike; he conducted himself as a royal ascetic who had cast away the cares of daily life. He spent about thirteen years in realizing the special divine powers (*lha*) of the Tantric cycles of the New and the Old School by means of mystic formulas and visualization. He thoroughly practised what is contained in a hundred commentaries, the *gTso-bor-gyur-pa'i-zab-khrid* of rJe-btsun Grol-mchog. Because of the vows his life cannot be compared with that of others. The above is his short exoteric hagiography (*phyi'i-rnam-thar*), dealing with his exercises of meditations, studies, and rituals (i.e. *khor-lo gsum*).

MKHYEN-BRTSE'I-DBANG-PO, AN ECLECTIC SCHOLAR-SAINT

With heart and soul and without thinking of his own hardship mKhyen-brtse'i-dbang-po accepted all doctrinal matters and traditions which existed hitherto uninjured and uninterrupted. They are listed as follows: The Old System of Ancient Translations (*snga-'gyur-rnying-ma-pa*) which is known in Tibet as the Eight Great Operating Methods of Meditative Tradition (*sgrub-brgyud-kyi śing-rta-chen-po brgyad*) and which had been founded by the grace of the abbot (Śāntarakṣita), the teacher (Padmasambhava), and the religious King (Khri-srong-lde-btsan); the *bKa'-gdams-pa* system which was founded by the venerable Atīśa and which includes the Seven Divine Doctrines (*lha-chos bdun-ldan*);[440] the instructions in the Method and Effect theory (*lam-'bras*) which was founded by the Great Mystic Virūpa and is now transmitted by the hierarchs of the *Sa-skya-pa* School and their main disciples; the theories of the eight minor and eight major *bKa'-brgyud-pa* Schools which were transmitted as the Instructions in the Tradition of the Four Pronouncements (*bka'-bźi-brgyud-pa'i gdams-ngag*) by Mar-pa, Mi-la-ras-pa, and Dvags-ston;[441] the golden theory of the venerable *Śangs-pa-bka'-brgyud* School which was founded by mKhas-grub-Khyung-po; the sixfold Yoga (*sbyor-ba yan-lag drug, ṣadaṅgayoga*) which forms part of the Diamond Yoga of the Fulfilment Stage (*rdsogs-rim rdo-rje'i rnal-'byor*) according to the King of all Tantras, the *Kālacakratantra* of the system of the Great Mystic Dam-pa Sangs-rgyas; the venerable *Źi-byed-pa* School which liberates from suffering and its special section of the *gCod-yul* theory ; and also the tradition of the meditation by visual and auditory realizations of the Three Undiminishables (*rdo-rje-gsum-gyi bsnyen-sgrub*) which *rDo-rje-phag-mo* (*Vajra-vārāhī*) had actually bestowed on Padmasambhava, the master of Uḍḍiyāna. With great zeal and without fault mKhyen-brtse'i-dbang-po heard all empowerments and oral traditions from the teachers (*Yongs-'dsin*) who upheld the essential traditions of the appropriate Schools. After he had practised meditation on these teachings, he abandoned every doubt.

VISIONS

When he was reflecting upon and thinking about these various teachings he perceived by means of visions or dreams the scholars (*mKhas-pa*) and Mystics (*Grub-thob*) of India and Tibet, the tutelary deity (*yi-dam*) *rGyal-ba-źi-khro* the assembly of the Spiritual Beings which are staying in the three realms;[442] they blessed him with three mysteries and instructed him in the New Transmission (*nye-brgyud*). Every moment he had countless pure visions. But that is only a mere hint because he never spoke of visions and super-natural knowledge (*mngon-śes*) in the manner of a boastful *bLa-ma*. He mainly relied on both stages of the Eight Operating Methods (*śing-rta brgyad*). For this reason he was not spoiled by any error or falseness when he was explaining, discussing, or composing. Thus he accepted the talented aspirants to become his disciples. This is the nucleus of his esoteric hagiography (*nang-gi rnam-thar*).

MKHYEN-BRTSE'I-DBANG-PO A PROPHESIED AUTHORITY

In the prophecy of the great Mystic Thang-stong-rgyal-po it is particularly stated : "In the country mDo-Khams after seven hundred years in a dragon-year a son will be born to the family sGa that belongs to the gNyos clan (*rigs*). He will not be different from me and will be endowed with the five signs. He will show the behaviour of a hero because of his 'year element' which is 'iron' (according to Tibetan astrology). He will gain authority over the Seven Currents of Pronouncements (*bka'-babs-bdun-ldan*) due to the blessing of Padma-rgyal-po [and he will have the name] mDo-sngags-gling-pa. He will be the undiminishable authentic being of the Radiant Light (*'od-gsal-sprul-pa'i rdo-rje*) because of the blessing of Vimalamitra. He will be styled a noble friend of the Buddha-Doctrine because of the blessing of mNga'-bdag ['Jam-dpal-bśes-gnyen] who is an authentic being of *Mañjuśrī*. He will appear as a being of Illusion (*Māyā*)." According to this prophecy of the *rDsogs-chen-sde-gsum* he gained authority over the Seven Currents of Pronouncements. He helped and benefited the Doctrine and the beings. He was highly praised in many prophecies.

IMPORTANT VISIONS

When he was just eight years old he fell ill and suffered great pains, at this instant he perceived the appearance of the Precious Teacher (Padmasambhava) and [his consort] Ye-śes-mtsho-rgyal. They both blessed him and bestowed an empowerment (*dbang-bskur*) of the *Vajrakīla Maṇḍala* on him. Afterwards he received instructions to overcome all troublesome obstacles.

When he was fourteen, he had the vision of going to the nine storeyed main pagoda (*ke'u-tshang*) of Vajrāsana (today Bodh Gaya) in India. When he slowly went upstairs he perceived in the eighth storey the great Teacher 'Jam-dpal-bśes-gnyen who looked like an Indian Scholar sitting between heaps of books at his right and left side. mKhyen-brtse'i-dbang-po worshipped him faithfully and addressed him humbly. Then 'Jam-dpal-bśes-gnyen took a book from the heap at his left and showed it to mKhyen-brtse'i-dbang-po : It was the Indian edition of the *Śer-phyin-sdud-pa*. 'Jam-dpal-bśes-gnyen laid the book on his head and directing his mind [towards mKhyen-brtse'i-dbang-po] he declared : "You will complete all philosophical theories by means of their fundamental Pronouncements (*bka'*) and their oral traditions (*lung*)." When he took a book from his right side it seemed to be the *rDsogs-pa-chen-po-rdor-sems-snying-gi-me-long* Tantra. He laid this book also on mKhyen-brtse'i-dbang-po's head and directing his mind towards the latter he said : "You will gain full authority over the words, the meaning, and the blessing of the common and special ways of the Vajrayāna, and of the *rDsogs-pa-chen-po-sde-gsum*. After ['Jam-dpal-bśes-gnyen] had made several prophecies he seemed to be pleased and dissolved in a mass of light. This light penetrated mKhyen-brtse'i-dbang-po. For a short time mKhyen-brtse'i-dbang-po realized a non-discursiveness meditation (*mi-rtog-pa'i ting-nge-'dsin*). When he awoke and was about to go outside a mighty fire blazed at the door. Powerlessly he went into it and his coarse body was burnt till nothing remained. He thought he had become Vimalamitra and had spontaneously become a being of Radiant Light (*'od-gsal-kyi sku*). At this moment the master of all Mystics, Thang-stong-rgyal-po, showed his own countenance to mKhyen-brtse'i-dbang-po and blessed him in a dream. Thang-stong-rgyal-po gave instructions and other advices that were to be obeyed in later times; then mKhyen-brtse'i-dban-po only composed a treatise for the meditative realization of one's own Guru (*bla-sgrub*). Later when he was relieved of the seal of secrecy (*bka'-rgya*) he revised these instructions and composed the *rDsogs-rim-drug-gi-rtsa-tshig*, the *sGrub-skor-lnga*, the *Khrag-thung-bde-gśegs-'dus-pa* which all belong to the *Grub-thob-thugs-tig* cycle. He saw the Protector of Deathlessness (*'Chi-med-mgon-po*) in union with his consort (*yab-yum*). After they had blessed him he clearly apprehended their meaning and he revised the *Tshe-yum-caṇḍalī-rtsa-ba*. Many times he had visions of the Three Roots [of religious practice] (*rtsa-gsum*, i.e. the *bLa-ma*, the *Yi-dam*, and the Spiritual Being). mKhyen-brtse'i-dbang-po used to keep all this secretly in his mind, none [of these mysterious revelations] were known by others.

MKHYEN-BRTSE'I-DBANG-PO'S OPINION ON PROPHECIES

It seemed that prophecies had occurred in various times [so that mKhyen-brste'i-dbang-po declared his own opinion on this matter.] Due to the statement in the Pronouncements that a Discoverer of Concealed Treasures becomes poor by prophecies, he declared : "A prophecy means to practise what is said by abandoning [evil] and by attempting [good], but nobody will do so. By not practising [the advice in the prophecy] one proves not to be reliable. If one talks a lot about this the devil will come into one's words." For this reason he never made any prophecy and when somebody else made a prophecy he was not at all pleased. This is a very important statement.

MKHYEN-BRTSE'I-DBANG-PO'S AUTHORIZATION OVER THE SEVEN CURRENTS OF PRONOUNCEMENTS

THE FIRST CURRENT (Authorization)

When he was sixteen years old mKhyen-brtse'i-dbang-po had a vision before sunrise on the tenth day of the fourth month: He went to [the purified sphere of] *rNga-yab-padma-'od*. In the midst of a quiet mountain-range was a charming white cloud; he recognized the Guru mTsho-skyes-rdo-rje (i.e. Padmasambhava) surrounded by groups of Spiritual Beings. The Guru blessed mKhyen-brtse'i-dbang-po mentally, bestowed a symbolical empowerment (*brda'i dbang-bskur*) on him, and gave him assurance that he would be endowed with the Seven Currents of Pronouncements; finally the Guru looked at him in a special manner : "You are not tainted while perceiving the objects (*gzung-ba'i yul*), and you are not spoiled in intuiting [the objects] (*'dsin-pa'i rtog-pa*). Reflect on intrinsic perception (*rig-pa*) as 'nothing' (*stong-pa*) and 'naked' (*rjen-pa*). This is the very intentionality of the Buddhas." With these words the Guru together with his entourage dissolved in the body of the venerable [mKhyen-brtse'i-dbang-po]. The latter realized that he had now become inalienably fused with the Guru's own thoughts. From this moment onwards mKhyen-brtse'i-dbang-po was firmly established in the primary purity (*ka-dag-gi gnas-lug*) through his awareness of being-itself (*rang-bźin*). Delight rose in his heart and he addressed his prayers only to Padmasambhava, the Precious Guru. He tried every treatise and theory that is a renowned Sūtra, Tantra, be it of the Old or the New School, a Pronouncement or a Concealed Treasure, an empowerment or a ritual which completes the empowerment (*rgyab-rten*), even if the transmission had become scarce. Without difficulties he practised every theory and elucidated them through his explanations. So he kindled the flame of the Doctrine. This is the first part of his authorization over the [Seven Currents of] Pronouncements.

SECOND CURRENT

The unearthed Concealed Books (*sa-gter*) : At the age of nineteen when he went to Brag-dmar mGrin-bzang the Spiritual Being of Primary Awareness (*Ye-śes-kyi mkha'-'gro*) offered him a treasure chest (*gter-sgrom*). Therein mKhyen-brtse'i-dbang-po found the treatise *Thugs-rje-chen-po-sems-nyid-ngal-gso'i chos-skor*, and relics of twenty-one Brahmans. *gNyan-chen-thang-lha*[443] took the *bLa-ma-sku-bźi 'i-sgrub-thabs-kyisk or* and relics of the tooth of the Precious Guru [Padmasambhava] from 'Dam-śod-snying-drung and offered mKhyen-brtse'i-dbang-po everything. Through their magical power the Spiritual Beings let the *rTsa-gsum-sgyu-'phrul-dra-ba'i skor* appear at the lake Si-ngu-gyu-mtsho and the *rTsa-gsum-spyi-'dus-skor* at gTer-klung-padma-śel-ri; they offered him both texts. With the exception of the basic text (*rtsa-ba*) no further treatise about these theories was revised by mKhyen-brtse'i-dbang-po. He admonished mChog-gyur-gling-pa to take out the Concealed Book *Thugs-sgrub-yid-bźin-nor-bu* which had been hidden at rTsi-ske-nor-bu-spun-gsum, and a figure of dNgos-grub-dpal-'bar which was a true image of the latter. After the Concealed Book was unearthed both mKhyen-brtse'i-dbang-po and mChog-gyur-gling-pa revised it. It seems that the *bLa-sgrub-skor-bźi-pa* and the *Vairocana'i-thugs-tig-rdsogs-chen-sde-gsum* were composed by them both.

THIRD CURRENT

The tradition of the Once-more Hidden Books re-established by the venerable one (*yang-gter*) : In the year 1859 the Precious Guru (Padmasambhava) appeared to him in the shape of the Great Discoverer Sangs-rgyas-gling-pa,[444] gave him a book and blessed him. Thereupon mKhyen-brtse'i-dbang-po had pure visions. He gained a clear cognition of all the hagiographies (*rnam-thar*) of the earlier Discoverers of Concealed Teachings (*gTer-ston*) and their theories (*gter-chos*). Therefore he received the actual word and the interpretation of the Seven Currents of Pronouncements. Most of the basic scrolls (*śog-ser*) which had been hidden for a second time (*yang-gter*) in earlier days by several Discoverers of Concealed Teachings were taken out by the Spiritual Being of Primary Awareness (*Ye-śes-kyi mkha'-'gro*). She offered [these scrolls] to mKhyen-brtse'i-dbang-po and afterwards he translated the symbols (*brda' bsgyur-ba*).—Some of these treatises written in symbolical characters he revised and clarified without efforts, because he had realized their meaning by a mere glance of them. During this time the Precious Guru (Padmasambhava) appeared to him in the appropriate shape of each Discoverer of Concealed Teachings and bestowed on him empowerments and oral traditions in a perfect way. 'Jam-mgon-blo-gros-mtha'-yas (alias sKong-sprul Padma-gar-dbang) begged him to revise every Old Concealed Theory whose tradition was lost. Thereupon many more Concealed Teachings of the New Transmission (*nye-brgyud*) emerged and he included all of them in the Precious Treasure of Concealed Teachings, the *Rin-chen-gter-mdsod*.

FOURTH CURRENT

Concealed Teachings revealed by his profound intentionality (*zab-mo-dgongs-pa'i gter*) : In 1848 when mKhyen-brtse'-i-dbang-po was twenty-eight and on the way to the central province of dBus he performed the Congregation Ritual of the Tenth Day (*tshe-bcu'i tshogs-mchod*) in the country of the Virtuous King of the northern herdsmen (*byang-'brog dGe-rgyal*). On this occasion the Precious Guru (Padmasambhava) showed him his real countenance and blessed him. When he made his worship beneath the figure of mTsho-skyes-rdo-rje (which belonged to the Concealed Treasure of Nyang-ral Nyi-ma-'od-zer) in bSam-yas this figure actually turned into mTsho-skyes-rdo-rje himself and bestowed blessings and instructions on mKhyen-brtse'i-dbang-po. Due to these events he started on the mystic meditative realization of the three cycles of *bLa-sgrub*, forming part of the *mTsho-skyes-snying-thig* (*bLa-sgrub-skor-gsum-gyi-gsang-sgrub-mtsho-skyes-snying-thig-gi chos-skor*). In the twelfth month of 1854 when he was thirty-four and about to perform the visual and auditory realization (*bsnyen-sgrub*) of '*Chi-med-yid-bźin-*

'khor-lo (i.e. the *Maṇḍala* of the white *Tārā*) he perceived the Noble *Tārā* with the ten syllables of her *Mantra*, afterwards she blessed him. Later on when three teachers of the meditative realization of the Deathless (*Tārā*) had also blessed him, he apprehended the cycle *'Phags-ma'i-snying-thig*. The origin of the *Grub-thob-thugs-tig* cycle and other cycles has been discussed above. These are his best works on the Concealed Teachings revealed by intentionality (*dgongs-gter*) and indiscernible from the Tantras; they are like imperishable verses beyond the cognitive capacity of common people.

FIFTH CURRENT

The Concealed Teachings revealed by remembering (*rjes-dran*) : Travelling to central Tibet, one day when he wandered through the 'U-yug valley in gTsang he remembered all the circumstances of lCe-btsun-chen-po's[445] attainment of the Light-Body (*'od-lus*), and composed the *lCe-btsun-snying-thig*. When he remembered the ancient place Lang-gro-dkon-'byung he composed a Life Securing Meditation Ritual, (*tshe-sgrub*) which belonged to the *Vairocana-thugs-tig* cycle. He also wrote the *Seng-gdong-dkar-mo'i bcud-len*.

SIXTH CURRENT

The Concealed Teachings as shown in visions (*dag-snang*): The *'Chi-med-thugs-tig-gi-tshe-yum-Caṇḍalī'i-gdams-skor*, the *kLong-chen-snying-thig-gi-bla-sgrub-thig-le'i-rgya-can-gyi-yig-cha*, and the *mChog-gling-bla-sgrub-sku-gsum-rigs-'dus*, cited above are examples of the many treatises [revealed to him in visions], but only those mentioned above were written by him.

SEVENTH CURRENT

The Concealed Teachings recognized by hearing (*snyan-brgyud*) : When he stayed at the holy place of rDsong-śod bDe-gśegs-'dus-pa he had the vision of himself going to the Stūpa bDe-byed-brtsegs-pa. There the eight individual appearances of the Precious Guru (*guru mtshan-brgyad*)[446] were sitting in the eight cardinal points and the all-compassing main appearance (*kun-'dus*) of the Precious Guru (Padmasambhava) in the centre. They bestowed on him the essentials of the oral tradition (*snyan-brgyud*) and the empowerments of the *sGrub-chen-bka'-brgyad* and the *sGyu-'phrul-źi-khro* cycles. Afterwards he revised these cycles.—This is the summary of his secret hagiography (*gsang-ba'i rnam-thar*).

DEMISE

mKhyen-brtse'-i-dbang-po had shown many miracles and had completed [all actions] during his lifetime. In 1892 when he was seventy-two in the morning of the sixth day in the second month he scattered flowers and spoke many prayers. Afterwards he stayed in deep meditation, his coarse body died and he dissolved in the mental sphere (*dgongs-dbyings*) of the great teacher Vimalamitra. In later days there appeared five excellent authentic beings (re-incarnations of mKhyen-brtse'i-dbang-po's being) at the holy mountain of the Wu-tai-shan where his basic being (*sprul-gźi*) (i.e. *Mañjuśrī*) resides. This happened as had been prophesied. In this way mKhyen-brtse'i-dbang-po had made many efforts to advance the Doctrine and to help the beings. He continues doing so.

NOTES TO PART II

[1] *'Phags-pa-klu'i-rgyal-po rgya-mtshos zus-pa źes-bya-ba theg-pa-chen-po'i mdo*= *Ārya-sāgaranāgarāja-paripṛcchā nāma-mahāyāna-sūtra*, *TTP*, vol. 33, no. 820, p. 103, 3. 6-8. There are a few minor differences between the statement in *DC* and the text in *TTP*.

[2] *'Phags-pa bsod-nams-thams-cad bsdud-pa'i ting-nge-'dsin ces-bya-ba theg-pa-chen-po'i mdo*=*Ārya-sarvapuṇya-samādhi-nāma-mahāyāna-sūtra*. *TTP*, vol. 32, no. 802, p. 140, 2.1-2.

[3] For a full explanation of this essential term cf. Guenther, *Naropa*, p. 112 n.2.

[4] For example, Nāgārjuna obtained the whole *Prajñāpāramitā-Sūtra* from the realm of the *Nāga*-spirits like a *gter-ma*.

[5] Ratna-gling-pa's hagiography cf. pt. II p. 144.

[6] *Byang-chub-sems-dpa'i spyod-la-'jug-pa*=*Bodhisattva-caryā-avatāra-saṃskāra* *TTP*, vol. 99, no. 5272, p. 261, 5.4-5; i.e. the tenth chapter.

[7] *'Phags-pa bsod-nams-thams-cad bsdus-pa'i tin-nge-'dsin ces-bya-ba theg-pa-chen-po'i mdo* (cf. pt. II n. 2) *TTP*, vol. 32, no. 802, p. 140, 1.7-2.1.

[8] The disciple's mind is trained by meditation on the Guru, i.e. his individual teacher, the *Yi-dam*, i.e. the individual and appropriate form of spiritual powers and abilities, and the *mKha'-'gro-ma*, i.e. the wisdom and primeval awareness bestowing 'functions' of the being-in-itself. These three roots are called *rtsa-gsum*, i.e. the three roots.

[9] "The Tibetan term......*thugs* never refers to concrete phenomena, but rather to their significance. Genetically speaking......*thugs* (is) present even before there (is) ...a mind in the conventional sense of this word. On the otherhand, (itis) no Platonic idea either. Hence whenever philosophical exactness becomes necessary the ordinary linguistic translation will not do and must be replaced by others." (Guenther, *Naropa*, p. 119 n.1).

[10] The *Padma-bka'-thang-yig* was translated into French by G. Ch. Toussaint, (*Le dict de Padma*, 1933); for further informations cf. *TPS*, p. 110 ff. The list of *gTer-stons* enumerated in the *Padma-bka'-thang-yig*, is given in *TPS*, p. 258 f; vide also the list of the *gTer-stons* in the appendix.

[11] For the folio number of the passages under discussion of DC and Tt see the concordance list in the appendix.

[12] La-stod is called a district south of the river gTsang-po and east of Mang-yul; for further informations cf. Ferrari, *Guide*, p. 66. 103 n. 542.

[13] gLo-bo-dge-skar belongs to the province mNga's-ris in the west of Tibet. The country gLo-also kLo or bLo written—is the area of present day Mustāngbhot near the banks of the river Kāli-Gandakī. (Snellgrove, *Four Lamas of Dolpo*, vol. 1, p. IX and p. 286 and the map of Dolpo).

[14] Sangs-rgyas-bla-ma's name is included in the list of the *gTer-stons* (*TPS* p. 258); he is also reported to be one of the former incarnations of mKhyen-brtse'i-dbang-po (1820-1892). (Macdonald, *Mañjuśrīmūla*, p. 94).—The

Prophecy on Sangs-rgyas-bla-ma is reported in the *Padma-bka'-thang-yig* (Toussaint, *Le dict de Padma*, p. 376).

[15] rGyal-sras Lha-rje alias rGyal-sras mChog-grub-rgyal-po (*TM*, vol. Ka, Tt fol. 185b.).

[16] Rin-chen-bzang-po lived from 958 A.D. till 1055 (Hoffmann, *Religionen*, p. 110). Thus, Sangs-rgyas-bla-ma was born between 958 and 1006.

[17] It was a custom to combine several ways of vows by one person. If some vows overlapped a separate treatment was applied. Our text states that Sangs-rgyas-bla-ma followed the vows of a Tantric and a *Bhikṣu* equally. For the three ways of Buddhist vows (of the *Bhikṣu*, the Bodhisattva, and the Tantric) cf. *Rang-bźin-rdsogs-pa-chen-po'i lam-gyi cha-lag sdom-pa-gsum rnam-par nges-pa źes-bya-ba'i bstan-bcos* by mNga'-ris Paṇḍita Padma-dbang-gi-rgyal-po.

[18] For the connection of Tibetan Buddhism with Chinese Buddhism cf. pt. I chapter 1.2 and 2.3, further Tucci, *MBT*, II, p. 44 ff and Neumaier, *bKa'-brgyad in ZDMG* 1970, p. 131 ff.

[19] Tsā-ri mTsho-dkar: This may be a lake within the mountain range of Tsā-ri ('White Lake') in the Lho-ka province. This mountain range is a holy place to which a pilgrimage takes place every twelve years (Ferrari, *Guide*, p. 51 and 127 n. 262).

[20] Chos-rje-gling-pa alias O-rgyan-rog-rje-gling-pa is said to be the twelfth incarnation of rGyal-sras Lha-rje and, thus, also an incarnation of Sangs-rgyas-bla-ma. Chos-rje gling-pa's father was called rDo-rje-grags-pa and he was born at kLu-mkhar-gdong in Dvags-po. Chos-rje-gling-pa's intimate spiritual son was Rva-ston sTob-ldan-rdo-rje (*TM*, vol. Ka, Tt fol. 69b).

[21] Sangs-rgyas-'bar: "This Discoverer of Concealed Treasures Sangs-rgyas-'bar was born to the family of Sangs-rgyas-bla-ma." (*gter-ston sangs-rgyas-'bar ni/ sangs-rgyas-bla-ma'i rgyud-du 'khrungs/*) He unearthed Concealed Treasures at Kha-chu in La-stod and at Thang-'bar in gLo-bo (*TM*, vol. Ka, Tt fol. 98a).

[22] cf. *SCD*, p. 974.

[23] Padma-'od-gsal-mdo-sngags-gling-pa (1820-1892) was the fifth and last one of the Five Discoverer Kings; he became famous by his incarnation-name mKhyen-brtse'i-dbang-po. (Ferrari, *Guide*, Introduction p. XIXf; Macdonald, *Mañjuśrīmūlakalpa*, appendix p. 91 ff; G. Smith, Introduction p. 28 ff and 53 ff of Kontrul's *Encyclopaedia of Indo-Tibetan Culture*, ed. by L. Chandra).

[24] Most of the Concealed Treasures quoted here are collected in the *Rin-chen-gter-mdsod* that was arranged by sKong-sprul Yon-tan-rgya-mtsho alias Padma-gar-dbang at the end of the 19th century (Neumaier, *Aspekte ZDMG* Suppl. I, p. 861).

[25] For these sacrificial cakes cf. Nebesky-Wojkowitz, *Oracles and Demons* p. 347 ff.

[26] "I" means sKong-sprul Yon-tan-rgya-mtsho alias Padma-gar-dbang—the name he prefers in the colophons of the *Rin-chen-gter-mdsod*—who arranged the mTshur-phu edition of this voluminous *gter-ma* collection.

[27] For the hagiography of the Discoverer of Concealed Treasures mChog-gyur-bde-chen-zig-po-gling-pa cf. pt. II, p. 190.

[28] Dsing may signify a Mongolian tribe because a Mongolian family with the name Dsing-ger is said to have existed in the first half of the 17th century (*TPS*, p. 655 by reference to the *dPag-bsam-ljon-bzang*).

[29] These three chapels were erected by the three wives of King Khri-sron-glde-btsan (754-797) (Ferrari, *Guide*, p. 44, 114 n. 131).

[30] This prophecy is included in the *Padma-bka'-thang* (Toussaint, *Le dict de Padma*, p. 380); Grva-pa-mngon-śes' hagiography is also rendered in DNg in a slightly different form (Roerich, *Annals*, p. 94-97). Ferrari states his lifetime from 1012 till 1090 (*Guide*, p. 54, 133 n. 321), other sources report 1033 his year of birth; further cf. *TPS*, p. 258.

[31] Śud-bu-dpal-gyi-seng-ge was one of the twenty-four adherents of King Khri-srong-lde-btsan (*rje-'bangs-nyer-lnga*) (cf. pt. I chapter 2.4.2); in former times Śud-bu-dpal-gyi-seng-ge had been acting Minister of the Interior (*Nang-blon*) under the reign of King Khri-srong-lde-btsan (*TM*, vol. Ka, Tt fol. 26b-27b).

[32] The mChims family was one of the eldest noble families in Tibet, most of the Tibetan ministers were appointed out of its members (Tucci, *Religionen*, p. 15).

[33] gYo-ru, also gYu-ru written, "was the more eastern of the two parts in which dBus was traditionally divided." (Ferrari, *Guide*, p. 46, 50).

[34] kLu-mes founded many temples some years before Atīśa went to Tibet; he had been one of the most important men during the Buddhist renaissance in the 11th century (Ferrari, *Guide*, p. 96, 109, 110).—Yam-śud-rgyal-ba-'od is cited in the DNg several times (Roerich, *Annals*, p. 75, 93, 95).

[35] *rGyud-bži*, the four Tantras, is the basic text on Tibetan medicine (Vostrikov, *Literature*, p. 125).

[36] gYu-thog Yon-tan-mgon-po was an eminent Tibetan physician. In his short biography (*TM*, vol. Ka, Tt fol 198b) it is stated that he had visited India six times and that he had been physician of the Tibetan king—but the king's name is not mentioned. In Tt fol 228a it is stated that he had been a contemporary of Sa-skya Paṇḍita Kun-dga'-rgyal-mtshan (1182-1251). This statement contradicts the one by Ferrari (*Guide*, p. 141) that gYu-thog Yon-tan-mgon-po had been the physician of King Khri-srong-lde-btsan (755-797). This famous physician was also worshipped in recent times (cf. Taring, *Tochter Tibets*, p. 13, 17 f).

[37] *Jambhala* is also called *Kubera*. He is the god and protector of property and wealth; therefore, he bestows golden things. His appearances are described at full length by Nebesky-Wojkowitz, *Oracles and Demons*, p. 68-82.

[38] The monastery Gra-thang is also called Grva-nang; it was founded in 1081. It is mentioned in *DNg*, (p. 96), further, by Tucci (*Lhasa*, p. 147) and Ferrari (*Guide*, p. 54, 132).

[39] Its real name is Brag-srin-mo-sbar-rjes and is situated in gTam-śul which is a part of Lho-brag (Ferrari, *Guide*, p. 56, 136).

[40] Padmasambhava prophesied the hiding of the *bDe-gśegs-'dus-pa* at mKho-mthing, mentioned in the *Padma-bka'-thang* (Toussaint, *Le dict*, p. 373). The same passage also gives the prophecy about Nyang-ral Nyi-ma-'od-zer (op. cit., p. 380).

[41] Up to this day, only a few references to this famous scholar-saint of the Old School can be found (*DNg*, p. 445 and 542; *TPS*, p. 114; Ferrari, *Guide*

p. 45 and 115; Tucci, *Religionen*, p. 53). —Nyi-ma-'od-zer's birth year is reported to be 1124 (*TPS*, p. 114), 1134 (according to the *Re'u-mig* cited by *TPS*, loc. cit.), and 1135 (Ferrari, loc.cit). Tt reports that his death happened in 1204 when he was sixty-seven.

The Three Most Important Actual Beings are: Nyang-ral Nyi-ma-'od-zer, Guru Chos-dbang, and dNgos-grub-rgyal-mtshan (*DC* fol. 269 a).

[42] This locality is also situated in gTam-śul country, which forms part of Lho-brag.

[43] There exist four empowerments (*dbang-bskur*): the empowerment by the jar (*bum-dbang*), the mystic empowerment (*gsang-dbang*), the empowerment by the transcending awareness together with and through discrimination-appreciation (*śes-rab-ye-śes-kyi dbang*), and the empowerment by the word (*tshig-dbang*). mKhas-grub-rje offers a commentary on these four empowerments on the basis of the *dGe-lugs-pa's* theory in his treatise *rGyud-spyi'i rnam-pa-gźag-par-brjod* (Lessing-Wayman, *Fundamentals*, p. 309-325).

[44] 'Dsed-phu-gangs-ra may be identical with the locality Gangs-ra-nges-gsang-rdo-rje-gling, which is mentioned by mKhyen-brtse'i-dbang-po (Ferrari, *Guide*, p. 70) to be a residence of a hierarchy of the Old School and to be situated in Rong-chen.

[45] This village is also called sMra-bo-lcogs. There was the residence of mNga'-bdag Nyang-ral Nyi-ma-'od-zer. This place is the eastern part of Lho-brag and the Third Dalai Lama visited it during a journey through this country (Ferrari, *Guide*, p. 56, n. 135; *TPS*, p. 254).

[46] Grva-pa-mngon-śes' hagiography is reported in pt. II, p. 94 ff.

[47] Ra-śag gTer-ston is also renowned by the names Ra-śag Chos-'bar and bSod-nams-rdo-rje-grags. He was famous for making thread-crosses (*mdos*) and for his knowledge of medicine (Tt fol 46b-47a). He was a contemporary of Mi-la-ras-pa (1040-1123) and rNgog-Lo-tsā-ba (Tt fol 227b).

[48] She is one of the consecrated consorts of Padmasambhava.

[49] For the various appearances of *Mahākāla* cf. Nebesky-Wojkowitz, *Oracles and Demons*, p. 38 ff.

[50] This place is also named mChims-phu mKho-mthing and is situated in the Yar-klung valley (Tt fol. 46b).

[51] Dan-ma-rtse, alias lDan-ma-rtse-mang, was one of the twentyfour adherents of King Khri-srong-lde-btsan's entourage (*rje-'bangs-nyer-lnga*) (Tt fol. 26a).

[52] Kha-che Paṇ, the Paṇḍita out of Kashmir, died in 1225 (*TPS*, p. 611). His personal name was Śākyaśrī, he visited Tibet from 1204 to 1213 (*DNg*, p. 103).—Źig-po Nyi-ma-seng-ge was an authority of the *Źi-byed*-School (*DNg*, p. 937). Mal Ka-ba-can (1163-1220) met Kha-che Paṇchen Śākyaśrī when he was forty-six and travelling through the upper parts of dBus (*DNg*, p. 306).

[53] These three significances are noetic being (*chos-sku*), communicative being (*longs-sku*), authentic being (*sprul-sku*). For further informations cf. Guenther, *Saraha*, p . 44 f.

[54] These eight important cremation grounds are always connected with the religious training of the mystics. Thus also Padmasambhava did his

meditative realizations on these eight cremation grounds (Tucci, *Indo-Tibetica col. III*, 2 p. 173 ff; Neumaier, *Mitarah und Ma-mo*, p. 45-64). The cremation ground Śītavana (in Tibetan bSil-ba'i-tshal) was founded by Nandikeśvara (*TPS*, p. 542) and was located near Bodh Gaya. Nowadays a small Tibetan temple exists there.

[55] cf. pt. I chapter 2.4.2.

[56] Jo-'bum-ma was a daughter of Dharmeśvara. By the practice of the sixfold yoga (*ṣaḍaṅga-yoga*) she became purified, having previously engaged in black magic. Thus she attained the Path of Insight (*mthong-lam*) (*DNg*, p. 768).

[57] This Goddess of Medicine (*sMan-gyi-lha-mo*) is not identical with Śrīdevī—as suggested by Gordon (*Ikonography*, p. 57)—but an allegorical figure like *Me-tog-ma.*, the Bearer of Flowers.

[57a] According to Tt he died in the year 1204 (wood-mouse) at the age of seventy-nine.

[58] The mystic formula Hrī holds a central position within the practice of transferring mind to higher spiritual levels (*'pho-ba*): Within the heart focal point of the central structure or pathway (*avadhūtī*) is creative motility (*rlung-gi thig-le*). In the midst of it exists the red formula Hrī which means the discerning capacity (*rig-pa*) of the Yogi. This Hrī becomes dissolved in the heart of *Amitābha*. (*kLong-chen snying-gi-thig-le las/ 'pho-ba-ma-bsgoms-sangs-rgyas-bźugs* fol. lb, 2a).

[59] For further informations on Chags Lo-tsā-ba Chos-rje-dpal (1197-1264) cf. Roerich, *Biography of Dharmasvāmin*, p. XXXIX.

[60] The Tibetan language has different terms for the various kinds of relics. There are *rten*-and *ring-srel*—relics. *rten* signifies relics in the shape of Stūpas or gods that originated from parts of the corpse during the cremation. *ring-srel* denotes some whitish, pill-like stuff that also came from the cremation residues.

[61] Kha-che Paṇ-chen cf. pt. II, n. 52

[62] Śam-po seems to be the name of a mountain. Tucci mentions a mountain which is called Śam-po; it is situated near the Yar-klung valley (p. *TPS*, 728), while our Śam-po mountain must be at the banks of the sKyid chu.

[63] For the hagiography of Guru Chos-dbang vide pt. II, p. 103 ff.

[64] The three Bodhisattvas below mentioned are actual beings of the three action patterns or 'lineages' that guide the beings towards Liberation (*rigs-gsum sprul-pa*). These action patterns are represented and taught by distinct Bodhisattvas. Thus comes about the connection of actual beings with action patterns.

Nyang-ral Nyi-ma-'od-zer
|
'Gro-mgon Nam-mkha'-dpal-ba
(authentic being of *Avalokiteśvara*)
|
mNga'-bdag bLo-ldan
(authentic being of *Mañjuśrī*)
|
mNga'-bdag bDud-dul
(authentic being of *Vajrapāṇi*

[65] gNyos Grags-rgyal died in 1216 (*DNg*, p. 1056); Źig-po-bdud-rtsi (1149-1199) was well experienced by the *rDsogs-chen* doctrine (*DNg*, p. 133 ff); Śākya-'od of sMan-lung was called by his secret name Mi-bskyod-rdo-rje, he was the eldest son of mNyam-med-pa (*DNg*, p. 155 ff.).

[66] 'The hundred thousand Tantras of the first translation period' (*sNga-'-rgyur-rgynd-'bum*) are a collection of Tantras authorized by the Old School.

[67] The basic book of the Eight Pronouncements is the *bKa'-brgyad-bde-gśegs-'dus-pa*.

[68] Also mKhar-chu called (Ferrari, *Guide*, p. 56 f, 137 n. 376).

[69] This prophecy is reported by the *Padma-bka'-thang* (Toussaint, *Le dict*, p. 381).

[70] The four temples which had been founded for the renewed education of the Tibetan people are: Kong-po Bu-chu, Lho-brag mKho-mthing, Byams-sprin dGe-rgyas, and Byang-bra Dum-rtse (Ngag-dbang-blo-bzang-rgya-mtsho, the Fifth Dalai Lama: *rGyal-rabs*, p. 23.3).

[71] La-yag-rdsa-bar is situated in the country of La-yag, possibly near Guru Lha-khang (Ferrari, *Guide*, p. 58, 140 n. 396).

[72] The eight ways of conduct of the celibate monks (*dge-slong-gi sde-brgyad*) are identical with the eight ways of taking vows (*so-thar rigs-brgyad*): 1. those who take the vows for a short time only (*bsnyen-gnas*), 2. and 3. the laity that keeps the vows (*dge-bsnyen pha-ma gnyis*), 4. and 5. the female disciples (*dge-slob-ma*), 7. and 8. the female and male *Bhikṣus*.

[73] 'Bri-gung sKyobs-pa alias 'Bri-khung 'Jig-rten-mgon-po (*PK* fol. 169 a-170a) was born in 1177 (the year fire-bird in the third sexagesimal cycle). He belonged to the hierarchy of the '*Bri-gung-pa* School and reigned in the residence of the Phag-mo-gru-pa for three years. (PJ ed. L. Chandra, *Re'u-mig*, chapter p. 18).

[74] Źang Rin-po-che was born in 1123, already in his childhood and youth he showed signs of aspiring to Liberation (*DNg*, p. 711).

[75] The unborn syllable AH—as it is spoken—is the seed formula of *śūnyatā*, the openness of being (Guenther, *sGam-po-pa*, Foreword by Chögyam Trungpa p. VI).

[76] '*Jam-dpal-ye-śes sems-dpa'i don-dam-pa'i mtshan yang-dag-par-brjod TTP*, vol. I, p. 119, 5.6).

[77] Nebesky-Wojkowitz, *Oracles and Demons*, p. 369 f.

[78] *Pramāṇavārttika* (ed. by Gnoli, 1960); *Abhidharmasamuccaya* (ed. by P. Pradhan 1950); *Bodhisattvacaryāvatāra* (ed. V. Bhattacharya, 1960); *Hevajra-Tantra* (ed. D. L. Snellgrove, 1959).

[79] This is the aim of the *bKa'-brgyud* School (Tucci, *Religionen*, p. 87 f.)

[80] Main theory of the Old School (Neumaier, *ZDMG*, 1970, p. 135 ff).

[81] Tucci, *Religionen*, p. 54.

[82] *DNg*, p. 164, 364, 439, 549.

[83] cf. pt. II, n. 81.

[84] 'Gro-mgon Chos-rgyal-'phags-pa was the teacher of 'Bri-gung sKyobs-pa, for the latter cf. pt. II n. 73.

[85] cf. pt. II, p. 97 ff.

[86] Sa-skya Paṇḍita (1092-1158) of the *Sa-skya* School. He was experienced alike in politics, religion and arts. (*TPS*, p. 9 ff; *DNg*, p. 216ff, and 606 ff; Casinelli-Ekvall, *Principality*, p. 3 f, 13 ff; Tucci, *Religionen*, p. 44, 325).

[87] This *mChod-rten* (Stūpa) overlooks the monastery; a description is given by Ferrari (*Guide*, p. 139).

[88] Hackmann depicts the whole scenery of this holy mountain and the miracles *Mañjuśrī* showed there (*An den Grenzen von China und Tibet*, p. 5-30).

[89] Guenther, *Saraha*, p. 117.

[90] Grva-pa-mngon-śes (1012-1090) discovered several Concealed Books in the main temple (dBu-rtse) of bSam-yas. One of them seems to have been the list of hiding places (*kha-byang*), although it is not included in Grva-pa-mngon-śes' hagiography; cf. pt. II, p. 94 ff.

[91] For some remarks on the *gCod* theory cf. Evans-Wentz, *Tibetan Yoga and Secret Doctrines*, pp. 278-297.

[92] This is the temple Brag-dmar Ke'u-tshang near bSam-yas mChims-phu; for a description of this temple cf. Ferrari (*Guide*, p. 45, 116 n. 146), and for the historical events cf. *MBT*, II, p. 11 and Tucci, *Tombs*, p. 83.

[93] A mythical bird, cf. Tucci, *Religionen*, p. 241.

[94] Brag-dmar mGrin-bzang near bSam-yas (Ferrari, *Guide*, p. 44 113 n. 123).

[95] Perhaps the same locality as rTa-mgrin-gling near bSam-yas (Ferrari, *Guide*, p. 45, 115 n. 142).

[96] A part of Mon-kha (Ferrari, *Guide*, p. 56, 136 n. 367).

[97] The same as Sras-mkhar-dgu-thog, the residence of Mar-pa-who died in 1098 (Ferrari, *Guide*, p. 57, 138 n. 384).

[98] sKya-bo-phug-ring is supposed to be near to sKya-bo-kha-gdong (Ferrari, *Guide*, p. 65).

[99] This term *ārya* refers to a holy figure in the temple of bSam-yas.

[100] mKhar-chu lCags-phur-can is mentioned as a hiding place of Concealed Treasures discovered by Guru Chos-dbang (Ferrari, *Guide*, p. 57).

[101] The monastery Bum-thang sPa-sgro-skyer-chu is called Mon sPa-gro-skyer-chu by kLong-rdol-bla-ma (Ferrari, *Guide*, p. 140 n. 400). Our text combines the two names.

[102] i.e. rTsi-gnas-gsar, this is one of the four temples which were erected for the education of the Tibetan border regions (*mtha'-'dul-gyi lha-khang*). This temple is situated north of 'Brong-rtse (Ferrari, *Guide*, p. 59, 142 n. 419).

[103] This place is situated in the country of Rong (Ferrari, *Guide*, p. 70 f.).

[104] i.e. Has-po-ri (Ferrari, *Guide*, p. 45, 115 n. 140).

[105] Where only the text of *DC* is reported, *Tt* summarizes the content in a few short sentences.

[106] *go-go-des-chog*: this is an expression of a slightly antiquated colloquial language and is similar to the literal expression *klong-cig* 'read!'

[107] Guenther, *Saraha*, p. 72 n.2.

[108] About Pehar cf. Nebesky-Wojkowitz *Oracles and Demons* p.94 ff.

[109] This is the name of a 'purified sphere' (*źing-khams*) where the activity of Padmasambhava becomes evident.

[110] In 1239 Godan, the second son of Ogodai, sent his army with rDo-rta-nag and rGyal-sman as guides into Tibet. They penetrated up to Rva-sgreng and rGyal-lha-khang (*TPS*, p.9). The statement of the year 1264, made by our text, is wrong.

[111] Guenther, *Saraha*, p. 155 n. 62.

[112] Guenther, *Naropa*, p. 269.

[113] *rdo-rje-dam-tshig-chen-po'i gnas=rDsogs-pa-chen-po.*

[114] The use of metaphors which belong primarily to the sexual sphere for denoting distinguished transformation within the man's mind is a common use in Tantric literature. For a detailed explanation cf. Guenther, *Naropa*, p. 202 ff.

[115] The practice of the *thod-rgal* meditation makes clear the apparitional character of *Saṃsāra* while the Yogi has to stare at the sun and to realize the light circlet lacking reality as such.

[116] The Tantrayāna uses the term *dgra-bsgral-ba* 'to kill the enemies of the Buddha-Doctrine' which means to kill their body in order to prevent them from doing more evil, and to free their minds in order to raise them to a higher level of existence.

[117] This is a round diagram which is used for the protection of the dead. The drawing is fixed at the dead person's shoulders, throat, head, and heart.

[118] This is a prayer that claims to transfer one's own karmic merits to another being who still clings to an evil Karma.

[119] *'jigs* is used in a slightly antiquated colloquial language; for example there is still the expression *mi-'jigs-po 'dug* 'he is an awfully good man'.

[120] Guenther, *Saraha*, p. 94 n. 24.

[121] see pt. II n. 116. Only an individual that has attained the Path of Insight (*mthong-lam*) is allowed to do such.

[122] *źo*, i.e. a small weight of gold, a little more than one half of a *tolah* or a rupee (SCD 1076).

[123] The *Jo-nang-pa* School was founded by Śes-rab-rgyal-mtshan (1292-1361) (Tucci, *Religionen*,p. 52).

[124] Bu-ston, a famous scholar of the *Jo-nang-pa* School (Ruegg, *The life of Bu-ston Rin-po che*, p. 1 ff.).

[125] For this important term cf. Guenther, *Naropa*, p. 174 ff.

[126] *bde-chen* or *bde-ba-chen-po* is the highest quality of satisfaction (Guenther, *sGam-po-pa*, p. XIV, and *Naropa*, p. 76 ff, 202 ff).

[127] Mi-bskyod-rdo-rje is also a known authority in the field of the *gCod* doctrine (*DNg*, p. 991 ff).

[128] Ye-śes-mtsho-rgyal is one of Padmasambhava's consorts and is claimed to be a Spiritual Being (*mKha'-'gro-ma*). (Evans-Wentz, *The Great Liberation*, p. 60 and 189 f; *TPS*, p. 582 n. 202).

[129] A name of a year according to the Tibetan calendar (Pelliot, *Le cycle sexagènaire dans la chronologie tibètaine A*, 11 serie, Tome I, no. 3, pp. 633-667).

[130] Ferrari, *Guide*, p. 51, 126 n. 257.

[131] Ferrari, *Guide*, p. 48, 121 n. 203.

[132] For *Vajravārāhī* cf. Evans-Wentz, *Great Liberation*, p. 121, 142; Snellgrove, *Four Lamas*, p. 103, 105, 193, 250, 262, 264 f.

[133] The title of the book is *mKha'-'gro-ma'i gsang-ba kun-'dus*.

[134] They are Yoginīs who have attained the Development Stage (*bskyed-rim*) but not yet the Fulfilment Stage (*rdsogs-rim*). (*Źing-skyes-kyi rnal-'byor-ma* are defined as *bskyed-rim thob-la rdsogs-rim ma-thob-pa'i pho-nya*, *Dagyab*, p. 572).

[135] The *sMan* are she-demons that are worshipped by common folk (Nebesky-Wojkowitz, *Oracles and Demons*, p. 198-202, and Tucci, *Religionen*, p. 238).

[136] For the country of Lho-brag cf. Ferrari, *Guide*, p. 56-58, 135 n. 347. The locality sPang-grong is situated in La-yag and it may be the same as sPa-gro.

[137] cf. Guru Chos-kyi-dbang-phyug's hagiography in pt. II, p. 103 ff.

[138] For an explanation cf. Guenther, *Naropa*, p. 25.

[139] For a detailed analysis cf. Guenther, *Naropa*, p. 270 note F.

[140] Ding-ri was founded by Pha-dam-pa in 1097 and is situated near the Nepalese frontier (Ferrari, *Guide*, p. 66, 154 n. 543 and 544).

[141] gLing-rje-ras-pa's hagiography is reported in the *DNg*, (p. 659ff). His lifetime given there does not fit the lifetime of Jo-mo-sman-mo as told by our sources. Maybe the *DNg*, is wrong in the number of the sexagesimal cycle (*rab-byung*). The *DNg* also tells the story about gLing-rje-ras-pa's relation to Jo-mo-sman-mo; but Roerich is wrong at this point by assuming '*Jo-mo*' to be *Vajravārāhī*, rather she is Jo-mo-sman-mo.

[142] For the hagiography of mKhyen-brtse'i-dbang-po cf. pt. II, p. 197 ff.

[143] This king is Byang-chub-rgyal-mtshan (1302-1373) who founded the *Phag-mo-gru-pa* dynasty (*TPS*, p. 18 ff); Yar-klung is the name of the valley where the ancestral castle of the ancient Tibetan kings had been; mThil refers to gDan-sa Thel or mThil, a monastery founded by Phag-mo-gru-pa (who was a saint-scholar belonging to the royal family) (1110-1170).

[144] Our translation gives only the hidden meaning of the prophecy, but in the Tibetan original there is a play on words. Of one merely makes a word for word translation then the sentence is "The pig (*phag*) uproots the soil (*sa*)." According to the explanation in the historical work *KhG*, (*rNying-ma-pa* chapter Pt. I, p. 258) *phag* signifies the *Phag-mo-gru-pa* ruler, and *sa* is the Tibetan kingdom. For the historical events cf. *TPS*, p. 21 and 635.

[145] Ferrari, *Guide*, p. 51. 128 n. 276.

[146] The connection of historical events (suppression by the Mongols and restoring the national Tibetan power) with the discovery of the Concealed Literature (as the *bKa'- thang-sde-lnga* by O-rgyan-ling-pa) is discussed by Tucci in *TPS* p. 111, 113 ff; see also Ferrari, *Guide*, p. 44, 128 n. 276, 277.—The prophecy on O-rgyan-gling-pa is given in the *Padma-bka'-thang* (Toussaint, *Le dict de Padma*, p. 385).

[147] This location is also called Yar-rje-lha-khang, which was the birth place of Kun-mkhyen kLong-chen-pa and the residence of O-rgyan-gling-pa (Ferrari, *Guide*, p. 55).

[148] Description of bSam-yas see Ferrari, *Guide*, p. 44 ff.

[149] =Yar-klung Śel-gyi-brag-phug (Ferrari, *Guide*, p. 51. 128 n. 271).

[150] cf. Vostrikov, *Tibetan historical literature*, p. 32 ff.

[151] =gYu-sgang-brag of Grva (Ferrari, *Guide*, p. 55).

[152] At this place there are five great *mChod-rten* (Ferrari, *Guide*, p. 46, 117 n. 161).

[153] Ferrari, *Guide*, p. 47, 120 n. 192.

[154] Perhaps a mountain range in Grva-phyi (Ferrari, *Guide*, p. 54, 132 n. 314).

[155] The locality is situated in the Yar-klung valley (Ferrari, *Guide*, p. 50 124 n. 237).

[156] This is Byang-chub-rgyal-mtshan (1302-1373), the founder of the *Phag-mo-gru-pa* dynasty. sNe'u-gdong-rtse is the family's ancestral castle. (Ferrari, *Guide*, p. 49, 123 n. 226).

[157] E-yul: Ferrari, *Guide*, p. 51. 126 n. 257; Dvags-po: op. cit. p. 48, 121 n. 203.

[158] Perhaps near Lo-gdon rTse-thang (Ferrari, op.cit. p. 112 n. 118).

[159] These are relic-pills which deliver from *Saṃsāra* within the next seven lives when one tastes them. These pills originated from the dismembered corpse of a Brahman (Toussaint, *Le dict de Padma*, p. 165 ff; Tt fol. 31b).

[160] pt. II, p. 197 ff.

[161] Demo Thubten Jigme took office as regent in 1810 (Shakabpa, *Political history*, p. 173).

[162] Gung-thang-pa of mGron was the predecessor of Gung-thang Lama (Shakabpa, op. cit. p. 316).

[163] Yong-'dsin Phur-lcog-byams-mgon Rin-po-che guided the committee that was in charge to inquire for the Thirteenth Dalai Lama's incarnation (Shakabpa, op. cit., p. 279).

[164] cf. pt. II, p. 174 ff.

[165] rGya Lo-tsā-ba was contemporaneous with Lha bLa-ma Ye śes-'od (Tt fol. 227a). For his hagiography see Tt fol. 37a-37b.

[166] sNa-nam-rdo-rje-bdud-'joms belongs to the group of the twenty-four religious adherents of King Khri-srong-lde-btsan's entourage (*DNg* p. 184; Ferrari, *Guide*, p. 71, 163 n. 642.

[167] This name signifies a family living on the estate (*gži-kha*) of sNa-mo (*TPS*, p. 634).

[168] This locality is near Zang-zang-lha-brag (Ferrari, *Guide*, p. 65, 153, n, 539).

[169] Neumaier, *ZDMG* 1970 p. 134.

[170] In rGyangs-yon-po-lung there is a meditation grotto of Padmasambhava (Ferrari, *Guide*, p. 66, 155 n. 557).

[171] This fact is mentioned by Ferrari, *Guide*, p. 65, 153 n. 537.

[172] bSod-nams-dbang-phyug: *DNg*, p. 374, 634, 1072.

[172]a The term 'final war' comes from the *Kālacakra*-Tantra. There is told that the last king of Śambhala, Rigs-ldan Drag-po'i-khor-lo-can by name, will subdue all heretics. This big war is called 'final war' (*mtha'-dmag*). But nowadays this word is also applied to wars which the neighbouring countries waged with Tibet.

[173] The illness caused by the *kLu* and *gNyan* demons is dropsy.

[174] The Silver Castle in the country of the *Khyung* bird (dNgul-mkhar in Kyung-lung) was the birth-place of gŚen-rab, the founder of the *Bon* religion (Snellgrove, *Four Lamas of Dolpo*, p. 84; Tucci, *Religionen*, p. 266, 271; Tucci, *Santi e'briganti*, p. 135).

[175] The term *sbas-yul* signifies landscapes of an extremely peaceful and lucky character; they are beneficial to the practice of the Buddha-Doctrine. In order to discover approach to these hidden countries the individual's *Karma* must have reached maturity (*las-sad-pa*) and the individual must have the key (*lde-mig*) to open the door of the hidden country. These hidden countries form part of this transitory world although they, to a certain extent, resemble a Fairyland.

[176] 'Bras-mo-gśongs is the name of one of the seven hidden countries (*sbas-yul*).

[177] cf. Wylie, *ZG*, p. 65; Gung-thang is situated near to the birthplace of Mi-la-ras-pa.

[178] Guenther, *Naropa*, p. 69 ff.

[179] This text was translated into German for the first time by Neumaier (*ZDMG* 1970, p. 131-163).

[180] For the historical background cf. *TPS*, p. 136 ff.

[181] This monastery is mentioned by Ferrari, *Guide*, p. 46, 118 n. 175.

[182] In Tibetan: '*khor-lo gsum* : *bśad-pa*, *bsnyen-pa*, and *sgom-pa*.

[183] Wylie, *ZG*, p. 55 ff.

[184] Dar-rtse-mdo=Ta-chien-lu in Chinese (Wylie, *ZG*, p. 184 n. 636) Eastern Tibet is generally called the Lowland (*smad*), and Western Tibet the Upland (*stod*).

[185] Ru-lag is one of two districts of the province gTsang (Ferrari, *Guide* p. 63).

[186] Ferrari, op.cit. p. 48, 51. 122 n. 210; Wylie, *ZG*, p. 96 f.

[187] Toussaint, *Le dict de Padma*, p. 387.

[188] Brag-gsum rDo-rje-brag is situated in Kong-po near the castle Kong-po Brag-gsum rDsong (Wylie, *ZG*, p. 96 f., 176n. 579).

[189] *DNg*, p. 499, 541.

[190] Rol-pa'i-rdo-rje (1340-1383), the hierarch of the *Karma-pa* School, was a famous figure in the political scene of the fourteenth century during the reign of the Yüan dynasty (Richardson, Karma-pa Sect JRAS 1958, p. 146 f).

[191] Tsā-ri is a mountain-side south of Dvags-po and worshipped as the heart of *Cakrasaṃvara* (Wylie, *ZG*, p. 95-97; Ferrari, *Guide*, p. 51. 127 n. 262).

[192] *dBon-po* : "A nephew of a Lama or a chief of Tibet, in the case of an abbot or Lama of a monastery the *dBon-po* is from his brother's side

and is generally appointed to supervise the monastery; hence the supervisor of a monastery is generally called *dBon-po.*" (*SCD*, p. 913).

[193] This locality is near the castle Lhun-grub-rdsong (Wylie, *ZG*, p. 162 f).

[194] This is a cave near the monastery rTse-chen (Ferrari, *Guide*, p. 59, 142 n.416).

[195] Both localities are situated in the country Long-po near the border of Dvags-po (Ferrari, *Guide*, p. 48, 122 n. 209).

[196] Dri-med-lhun-po: Tt fol. 119a.

[197] This temple was erected by King Srong-btsan-sgam-po in order to educate the border regions (*mtha'-'dul lha-khang*). (Ferrari, *Guide*, p. 67, 156 n. 572).

[198] Ferrari, *Guide*, p. 66, 153 n. 542; Wylie, *ZG*, p. 64.

[199] The small village gŚin-rje'i-rba-dong is located at a pass in the rGya valley (rGya-mda'). (Wylie, *ZG*, p. 176 n. 571).

[200] Ferrari, *Guide*, p. 48, 51, 122 n. 210; Wylie, *ZG*, p. 96.

[201] The term *sgyu-lus* is explained by dByangs-can-dga'-ba'i-blo-gros (*gSang-ba-'dus-pa'i sa-lam*) fol. 12 a) as follows: "*sgyu-lus* is said so because it refers to the body (*lus-yin*) or the existential presence (*sku*) of a divine entity which is nothing but a very subtle motility (*rlung*)-mentation (*sems*) [combination] which is indicated or illustrated by twelve similes such as *sgyu-ma* (apparition) and so on." (*sgyu-lus źes-pa'i sgra-bśad yod-de| sgyu-ma-la-sogs-pa'i dpe bcu-gnyis-kyis mtshon-pa'i śin-tu phra-ba'i rlung-sems-tsam-gyi lha-sku'am lus yin-pas de-ltar brjod-pa'i phyir*).

[202] *Karma Źva-dmar-pa* mKha'-spyod-dbang-po (1350-1405) : *DNg*, 540-545.

[203] The ruler of the castle sNe'u-gdong was the founder of the *Phag-mo-gru-pa* dynasty (*DNg*, p. 591).

[204] *DNg*, p. 316, 591, 634.

[205] gYag-sde Paṇ-chen lived between 1299 and 1378 (*DNg*, p. 310)

[206] *DNg*, p. 507-509.

[207] He succeeded Rol-pa'i-rdo-rje in the dignity of *Karma-pa* hierarch and was invited by the Chinese Emperor Cheng Tsu (Yung-lo) to China (Richardson, Karma-pa Sect, *JRAS* 1958, p. 147).

[208] '*dam*' is the Tibetan abbreviated form of the Mongolian word '*tamga*'. In Tibet this expression is only used for denoting the privy seal of the Dalai Lama.

[209] *bdud-rtsi sman-sgrub* : Through meditative powers medical herbs are transformed to nectar (*bdud-rtsi*), this ritual is called *bdud-rtsi sman-sgrub.*

[210] He was a member of the Bya-khung-bśad-sgrub-gling monastery which is situated on the left bank of the rMa-chu (Huang-ho) river in Amdo (*DNg*, p. 330, 374).

[211] *dgongs-'dus-sgrub-chen* : *sgrub-chen* signifies a ritual realization of a mystic cycle (here the *dgongs-'dus* cycle) that lasts many days or weeks. This realization is effected by the representation of the actual being-in-the world of the divine power (i.e. by theatrical performances as the *Cham*-dances), the representation of its communicative being (i.e. the preaching

of the Buddha-Doctrine), and the representation of its spiritual being (i.e. meditation). In this way the pictorial representation of the *Maṇḍalas* which are shown on the Tankas became embodied in the actors of this ritual performance. Therefore the Tibetan *sgrub-chen* performances resemble the miracle plays of mediaeval Europe.

[212] The *rNying-ma-pa* believe in Padmasambhava's coming on the tenth day of each month. On this day they celebrate a special ritual in honour of Padmasambhava, which is called 'the ritual of the tenth day'.

[213] cf. Guenther, *Tibetan Buddhism without mystification*, p. 25.

[214] Toussaint, *Le dict de Padma*, p. 387.

[215] An ancestor of bSod-nams-rgyal-mtshan who was also a Tantric of the family Khu living in the Gra district is mentioned in the *DNg*, (p. 96).

[216] The district Gra-nang is located to the east of Yar-klungs (Ferrari, *Guide*, p. 54, 132 n. 320).

[217] This is a miracle-performing figure of *Tārā* (Tib. *sGrol-ma*) in the temple of Khra-'brug which was founded by King Srong-btsan-sgam-po (620-649). (Ferrari, *Guide*, p. 50, 124 n. 237, 125 n. 240).

[218] For his hagiography cf. pt. II, p. 103 ff.

[219] 'Taking only essences' (*bcud-len*) is a dietetic method; while practising it the Yogi is not allowed to take any other food except the allowed essence of flowers or stones for example (*me-tog-gi-bcud-len or rdo'i bcud-len*).—gYag-sde Pan-chen (born in 1299) hear the *bCud-len-phreng-ba* from Dharma-svāmin Rang-byung-rdo-rje (*DNg*, p. 532 f).

[220] Bying-mda'-'od-dkar-brag is a meditation place of Padmasambhava (Ferrari, *Guide*, p. 54, 132 n. 313).

[221] This belongs to the whole field of rituals which increase the lifetime (*tshe-sgrub*) by overcoming its obstacles. (cf. Paulson, *Die primitiven Seelevorstellungen der nord-eurasiatischen Volker* and Tucci, *Religionen*, p. 210).

[222] *rNam-thar-thang-yig* or *Padma-bka'-thang-yig* (Vostrikov, *Literature*, p. 32 ff.)

[223] Guenther, *Naropa*, p. 123 n. 1, and *Buddhist Philosophy*, p. 204 ff.

[224] This turquois has a special relation to a man's spirit. When a man falls ill the ritual 'Calling the Spirit' has to be performed. In order to do it properly a small figure of a sheep is put within a bowl of water. The Spirit Turquois is placed outside the bowl. When the water is stirred and the sheep turns to face the turquois it is thought to be an auspicious omen for ending the illness and regaining the man's spirit. This ritual is called *tshe-'gug*.

[225] "This Chu-bo-ri is famous because there is a mountain which gives prosperity to Tibet, with one-hundred and eight springs, one hundred and eight meditation places etc. In front of the iron bridge (*lcags-zam*), which is today very famous, there are the lCags-zam bLa-brang (Palace of the Iron Bridge), a Stūpa, the gZim-phug bLa-brang (Palace of Sleeping Cave) etc." (Ferrari, *Guide*, p. 71).

[226] "East of there on the north shore of the sKyi-chu is the mGon-khang of gNyan Lo-(tsā-ba) which is known as gNyan-mgon-phug." (Wylie, *ZG*, p. 85; cf. also Ferrari, *Guide*, p. 105 n. 101).

227 *gNyan-chen-thang-lha* protects the dMar-po-ri hill where the Potala Palace is erected. This god is also called 'Protector of the Treasures' (*gter-bdag*). (Nebesky-Wojkowitz, *Oracles and Demons*, p. 205-210).

228 *Gangs-dkar-śa-med* is a minor goddess belonging to the group of the twelve *bsTan-ma*. She is of white complexion, holds a blood-stained banner, is dressed in clothes of glacier-ice and her toupet consists of pearls, she rides a three-legged mule, and her residence is rDo-rje-brag-dmar (Nebesky-Wojkowitz, *Oracles and Demons*, p. 186 f.)

229 The eight explanations or songs are dealing with the Eight Pronouncements (*bka'-brgyad*) the Eight Wisdom-Holders (*Rig-'dsin brgyad*) have delivered.

230 Ferrari, *Guide*, p. 69, 160 n. 609.

231 At mKhar-chu which forms part of Lho-brag is a meditation grotto of the famous hierarch of the Old School gNubs Nam-mkha' -snying-po (Ferrari, *Guide*, p. 57; *MBT*, II, p.21).

232 Ti-sgrom is situated in the country of gŹo-stod (Ferrari, *Guide*, p. 44, 112 n. 117).

233 Phung-po Ri-bo-che is a famous and holy place: There Padma-sambhava had meditated, there rGya-źong-khrom discovered a Concealed Treasure, and there the Fifth Dalai Lama founded a monastic college (Ferrari, *Guide*, p. 70, 162 n. 628).

234 A column called Bum-pa-can exists also in the middle storey of the main temple of bSam-yas.

235 The meaning of *Ta-bi-hri-tsa* is not clear.

236 Wylie, *ZG*, p. 54, 93; Ferrari, *Guide*, p. 56 ff.

237 =Mon Bum-thang sPa-sgro-skyer-chu, cf. n. 101 (pt. II).

238 bKra-śis-'byung-gnas is mentioned to be an official of a hierarch on the beginning of the fifteenth century (*DNg*, p. 510).

239 This crematory is shaped like a Stūpa and used only for the cremation of high ranking religious men.

240 These are twelve Discoverers whose names end with '*gling-pa*' (for example O-rgyan-gling-pa) although it is not known which Discoverers form this group.

241 Gru-śul=Gro-śul (*DNg*, p. 864; *TPS*, p. 629; Ferrari, *Guide*, p. 51, 127 n. 260).

242 The country Khyung-po is in the extreme east of Tibet (Wylie, *ZG*, p. 99, 180 n. 602).

243 In the cave dPal-gyi-phug-ring, gNubs Nam-mkha'-snying-po stayed for practising meditation. In this very place he also hid the Chinese Buddhist texts which he had to leave behind before he fled from Tibet. Ratna-gling-pa discovered these texts, revised them and styled them treatises on *rDsogs-chen*. (Ferrari, Guide p. 57, 138 n 377; MBT II, p. 49 f.)

244 *thugs-sgrub* is the abbreviated form of *bla-ma thugs-sgrub*. During this meditation the disciple's Guru represents himself in the aspect of his noetic, communicative, and authentic being (*chos-sku*, *longs-sku*, *sprulsku*).

245 Mount Kailas is called Gans Ti-se by the Tibetans, it forms a prominent spot of the western border of Tibet (Wylie, *ZG*, p. 53, 114 n.3).

[246] Khams and rGyal-mo-rong are the two most eastern parts of Tibet. rGyal-mo-rong was divided into eighteen small kingdoms which were ruled and inhabited by people of Tibetan stock (Wylie, *ZG*, p. 102).

[247] Yoshimura, *The Denkar-ma, an oldest catalogue of the Tibetan Buddhist Canon*; Lalou, *Les texts bouddhiques au temps du Roi Khri-srong-Ide-bcan*, JA tome 241 (1953) p. 313 ff; Pelliot. *Notes à propos d'un catalogue du Kanjur*, JA (1914) p. 27; Tucci *MBT* II, p. 46 n.1.

[248] Zur-'ug-pa-lung was a famous residence of some hierarchs of the Old School in former days. Today it is merely a village. This place is in the upper part of sPan-thag-ma (Ferrari, *Guide*, p. 70, 162 n. 627).

[249] dPal-spungs is a well-known monastery and residence of the Old School which is situated near sDe-dge in Khams (Snellgrove-Richardson, *A cultural history*, p. 137).

[250] 'Gos-Kyi Phag-ri is perhaps near Phag-ri rdsong (Wylie, *ZG*, p. 78, 144 n. 262).

[251] Wylie, *ZG*, p. 64; Ferrari, *Guide*, p. 66, 153 n. 542.

[252] cf. pt. I, p. 55 (chapter 2.6.2).

[253] This locality is mentioned in the *DNg*, (p. 420).

[254] Maṇḍāravā is one of the consecrated consorts of Padmasambhava.

[255] rGyal-ba-don-grub: cf. *TPS*, p. 410. Nang-so signifies an office of the administration of the *Sa-skya* School. Concerning the authority of the *Nang-so* office it was equal to that of the *Nang-blon* (Minister of the Interior) in the royal administration (*TPS*, p. 35).

[256] Beyond the sBrum pass is Lha-lung in west Lho-brag. At first this monastery was a residence of the *bKa'-brgyud* School, but nowadays it is possessed by the incarnations of Padma-gling-pa (Ferrari, *Guide*, p. 58, 139 n. 393).

[257] *TPS*, p. 549.

[258] Cog-ro Lo-tsā-ba kLu'i-rgyal-mtshan was a contemporary of King Khri-srong-lde-btsan (*DNg*, p. 344 f; R Ferrari, *Guide*, p. 51, 129 n. 280.)

[259] *mngon-par śes-pa*: certain gifts of supernatural perception (skr. *abhijñāna*) of which six kinds are enumerated: 1. seeing anything clearly as if with divine sight (*lha'i mig-gi mngon-śes*); 2. divine hearing in a perfect manner (*lha'i rna-ba'i mngon-śes*); 3. knowledge of another's heart (*pha-rol-gyi sems śes-pa*); 4. Knowledge of the four famous miracles (*rdsu-'phrul-gyi bya-ba śes-pa'i mngon-śes*; 5. The power of remembering the acts of one's former existence of life (*sngon-gyi gnas rjes-dran-pa'i mngon-śes*); and 6. the knowledge of the destruction of the three distortions (*zag-pa zad-pa śes-pa'i mngon-śes*) (*SCD*, p. 365 f).

[260] *stong-mchod* : Every kind of offering is presented a thousand times to the deity.

[261] "Thang-stong-rgyal-po (1385-1464) who is famous throughout Tibet as the saint builder of iron bridges. The greater part of the Tibetan bridges is attributed to him and his images are venerated in many temples side by side with those of the Masters of the Law." (Ferrari, *Guide*, p. 90 n. 54; Snellgrove, *Four Lamas*, p. 256; *TPS*, p. 163).

[262] Ferrari, *Guide*, p. 80 ff; Wylie, *ZG*, p. 64, 71, 74 f.

[263] Although he knows all theories and mysteries of Mahāyāna and Tantrayāna he undertakes regular studies in order to be the model for his later disciples.

[264] cf. pt. II, p. 131 and Neumaier, *ZDMG*, 1970, p. 135.

[265] the *Śangs* School was founded by 'Ba'-ra-pa rGyal-mtshan-dpal-bzang alias Śangs-pa (born in 1310) (G. Tucci, *Religionen*, p. 51).

[266] The name of a purified sphere which is attributed to Padmasambhava.

[267] The focal points (me-btsa) are distinctive features within the field of Tibetan medicine. Glowing pills made of medical herbs are set up on these focal points to cure the illness (Burang, *Tibetische Heilkunde*, p. 100 f.). The text here does not deal with a sick person but with the she-demon *Brag-srin-mo*. She is stretched at full length on her back forming the Tibetan realm. On the focal points of her body temples are built. These temples are supposed to cure the fierce character of the she-demon; they are called *mtha'-'dul-gyi gtsug-lag-khang* and *yang-'dul-gyi gtsug-lag-khang* (*KhG*, pt. 4, p. 17,2.6).

[268] see n. 172a (pt. II).

[269] Gram-pa is the name of the region around Lha-rtse-rdsong; in a temple of this place the well-known work Le'u-bdun-ma was discovered (Ferrari, *Guide*, p. 66, 154 n. 553).

[270] Ferrari, *Guide*, p. 57 f, 139 n. 389.

[271] sTag-tshang ('Tiger-cage') is near Mon Bum-thang sPa-sgro-skyer-chu. (Ferrari, Guide p. 140)

[272] dPal-ri-bo-che was also called gCung-ri-bo-che, and was the residence of Thang-stong-rgyal-po (Ferrari, *Guide*, p. 65, 153 n.534).

[273] The term *sku* refers to our philosophical conception of 'existence' which here is synonymous with 'primary awareness' (*ye-śes*). 'Existence' as 'awareness' is the Guru's or Buddha's compassion (*thugs-rje*) as it represents the very fact of intrinsic perception (*rig-pa'i ngo-bo*). This is a homogeneous continuum shared by all Buddhas. Unbiased and undisturbed, this compassion manifesting itself in the Guru's existence, teaches and guides the disciples.

[274] The term *thugs-gter* signifies a Concealed Teaching which reveals itself through the unbiased cognition of the Discoverer.

[275] King of Tibet (born 742), ruled between 755 and 797. He supported the dissemination of Buddhism in Tibet and was the patron of Padmasambhava (Demieville, *Le Concil de Lhasa*, p. 386 with further references of literature).

[276] 'Jam-dbyangs-rin-chen-rgyal-mtshan is mentioned as the teacher of Dharmasvāmin Ratna-guru (*DNg*, p. 633).

[277] Chos-kyi-blo-gros from Mar, alias Mar-pa (1012-1096) was a hierarch and prominent master of the *bKa'-brgyud-pa* School. (Bacot, *La vie de Marpa*; Tucci, *Religionen*, p. 50).

[278] The country gLo-bo is part of mNga'-ris; perhaps is Ma-thang and sMan-thang the same place (Snellgrove, *Four Lamas*, map I).

[279] This is the basic theory of the *Sa-skya* School (*TPS*, p. 91).

[280] gLo-bo Lo-tsa-ba Śes-rab-zin-chen (*DNg*, p. 379, 1046).

[281] bSod-nams-lhun-grub is mentioned to be an adherent of the *Kālacakra* cycle (*DNg*, p. 795).

[282] Sa-skya Paṇḍita (1182-1231), famous scholar-saint and hierarch of the *Sa-skya* School (Tucci, *Religionen* p. 48).

[283] In accordance with Tibetan monastic usage the *mKhan-po, Las-slob, gSang-ston*, and *Kha-bskong* (abbot, master of monastic conduct, secret teacher, and admonisher) are necessary to perform a novice's initiation into the monastic community (*Saṅgha*).

[284] *cod-pa* does not mean 'crown' (Skr. *Mukuṭa*), but is an ear-drop attached to the cap which is adorned with the figures of the five *Dhyāni*-Buddhas (*rigs-lnga*). Tucci calls this ear-drop *dar-dpyangs* (*Religionen*, p. 147).

[285] The Discoverer of Concealed Treasures Śakya-bzang-po, alias Śakya-'od, found a section of the *Maṇi-bka'-'bum* in gLo-'bur. He lived between 1387 and 1446; his short hagiography is delivered in Tt fol. 101b.

[286] In Zang-zang-lha-brag in the province of gTsang rGod-ldem-can discovered a Concealed Treasure (Ferrari, *Guide*, p. 65, 153 n. 537).

[287] gŹung sPre-źing, the residence of rNgog Chos-sku-rdo-rje (1036-1102), was also a famous center of the *bKa'-brgyud-pa* School: There exists a Stūpa with relics of Mar-pa and there Mi-la-ras-pa and rNgog-ston met. (Ferrari, *Guide*, p. 55, 134 n. 334).

[288] Grva-thang=Grva-nang. The place was founded by Grva-pa-mngon-śes (1012-1090) (Ferrari, *Guide*, p. 49, 54, 55, 132 n. 320).

[289] Ferrari, *Guide*, p. 46, 117 n. 162.

[290] cf. pt. II, p. 103.

[291] Ferrari, *Guide*, p. 56-58.

[292] Ferrari, op. cit. p. 44, 113 n. 124 and 125.

[293] Title of this text : *Rig-'dsin-yongs-'dus-kyi-chos-skor-gsol-'debs-le'u-bdun-ma'i-sgrub-thabs*.

[294] A hamlet situated in the 'On district, cf. Ferrari, *Guide*, p. 47, 119 n. 186, 120 n. 192.

[295] Toussaint, *Le dict de Padma*, p. 387 f.

[296] Kong-yul is mentioned in the *DNg*, (p. 495).

[297] *rgyal*=Skr. *tiṣyā, puṣya-nakṣatra* the eighth constellation in Hindu and Buddhist astronomy (*SCD*, p. 310; cf. Petri, *Indo-Tibetische Astronomie* p. 92).

[298] cf. Ferrari, *Guide*, p. 161; in the *Padma-bka'-thang* this locality is mentioned to be a hiding place (Toussaint, *Le dict de Padma*, p. 375).

[299] This locality was founded by Myang Ting-nge-'dsin-bzang-po during the eighth century, in later times the *sNying-thig* manuscripts were discovered there (Ferrari, *Guide*, p. 110 n. 114).

[300] There are two branches of the *Karma-pa* School: the red one (*dmar-po*) and the black one (*nag-po*), also referred to as 'black-hats' and 'red-hats' (Richardson, *JRAS*, 1958, p. 139 ff.).

[301] 'Bri-gung Chos-kyi-grags-pa held the rank of a *sPyan-snga* during the decline of the *Phag-mo-gru-pa* dynasty (*TPS*, 29 ff., 254 n. 69).

302 cf. pt. II, p. 166 ff.

303 cf. pt. II, p. 163 ff.

304 sDe-dge is a region in the eastern part of Tibet (Wylie, *ZG*, p. 103 ff).

305 He was a disciple of Las-'phro-gling-pa (cf. pt. II, p. 188).

306 cf. pt. II, p. 162.

307 For a description of these two large monasteries cf. Ferrari, *Guide*, p. 62-64.

308 i.e. gTer-ston Las-'phro-gling-pa (cf. pt. II, p. 160 ff).

309 =sPo-bo, a landscape at the bending of the Brahmaputra (Ferrari, *Guide*, p. 48, 122 n. 211).

310 cf. pt. II, p. 144 ff.

311 Guenther, *Naropa*, p. 46 n. 1

312 *las-rgya=las-kyi phyag-rgya*, the *Karmamudrā* (Guenther, *Naropa*, p. 207 ff.)

313 gYu-mtsho=Tsa-ri gYu-mtsho (*DNg*, p. 491, 683, 815).

314 The district Tsha-ba-yul is mentioned in the *DNg*, p. 134.

315 Ferrari, *Guide*, p. 73, 167 n. 693.

316 Wylie, *ZG*, p. 98, 177 n. 580.

317 *khu-dbon* means 'uncle and nephew'. Within the social system of clerical hierarchy in Tibet the expression signifies the ruling 'uncle' (i.e. the *bLa-ma*) and his 'nephew' as his secretary and 'right hand'. The latter often belongs to the laity and is a ruler. In this way the spiritual and worldly powers are held by a single family.

318 Kaḥ-thog rDo-rje-gdan is a famous monastery of the Old School (*DNg*, p. 158, 484). This monastery was founded by Dam-pa-bde-gśegs in 1059. Many mystics came from it. Later on it declined in power and wealth. The Discoverer of Concealed Treasures bDud-'dul-rdo-rje and Rig-'dsin kLong-gsal-snying-po restored it. (*Bod-na-bžugs-pa'i-rnying-ma'i dgon-deb*, p. 120).

319 Ri-bo-che=gCung Ri-bo-che. (v. n. 272 pt. II)

320 sPu-stod is a tributary of the Yar-klung river (Wylie, *ZG*, p. 178 n. 591).

321 cf. pt. II, p. 166 ff.

322 He was a disciple of Las-'phro-gling-pa, cf. pt. II, p. 162.

323 *Lha-btsun* was the title of the ancient kings of Guge (*TPS*, p. 26).

324 Kun-mkhyen Dri-med-'od-zer=kLong-chen Rab-'byams-pa (1318-1363).

325 Byar is the valley of the Charchu, a tributary of the Subansiri (Ferrari, *Guide*, p. 127 n. 261).

326 *lhag-pa'i lha* means the very divine power (*lha*) on which the Yogi is relying during many lifetimes.

327 *chags-lam* : This method aims to make the erotic attitude operative on attaining the liberation (Guenther, *Naropa*, p. 202 ff).

328 *thabs* (Skr. *upāya*) refers to 'activity' in Buddhism. "In Buddhism, activity is always viewed in the light of its motivation. This distinguishes Buddhist activity from the modern concept of it, which only sees

the external 'achievements' and overlooks the internal driving-force, whether this be a sense of insecurity or the greed for money and power. Such activity is as the following words of sGam-po-pa explain, 'bondage'; man is really a slave of his passion. But he is free and active (not driven) when he lives by his real nature revealed through discriminating awareness (prajñā)." (Guenther, *sGam-po-pa*, p. 225f.)

[329] cf. Guenther, *Naropa*, p. 222 ff., and *Saraha.*, p. 148 ff.

[330] These four types of Delight are: joyous excitement (*dga'-ba*), ecstatic delight (*mchog-dga'*), absence of excitement (*dga'-bral*), and co-emergence delight (*lhan-skyes-dga'*). (Guenther, *Naropa*, p. 78 n. 2).

[331] Ferrari, *Guide*, p. 48; Wylie, *ZG*, p. 94.

[332] Ferrari, op.cit., p. 48, 51; Wylie, *ZG*, p. 96, 98.

[333] Ferrari, op.cit., p. 37, 39, 44, 54; Wylie, op.cit., p. 64.

[334] Ferrari, op.cit., p. 80 ff.; Wylie, op.cit., p. 71 ff.

[335] Ferrari, op.cit., p. 69, 160 n. 609; Tt reports the place name as lJag-ma-lung.

[336] 'Ja'-tshon-snying-po alias Las-'phro-gling-pa, cf. pt. II, p. 160 ff.

[337] cf. pt. II, p. 163 ff.

[338] Lha-ri-'od-gsal-snying-po in 'Bras-ljongs means a locality in Sikkim (which is also called Mon 'Bras-ljongs, and Su-kham by the Indians). (Wylie, *ZG*, p. 73).

[339] *sgrub-sde* or *sgrub-grva* is the Tantra College within a monastic academy and different from the *bśad-grva* or *mtshan-nyid grva-tshang*, the Philosophical College (Tucci, *Religionen*, p. 131, 148).

[340] The Fifth Dalai Lama Ngag-dbang-blo-bzang-rgya-mtsho is often mentioned to have had a peculiar relationship with the Old School; for further informations cf. Bell, *Tibet past and present*, p. 35 ff.; Schulemann, *Dalai Lamas*, p. 127 ff.; *TPS*, p. 57; Shakabpa, *Tibet—a political history*, p. 100; Snellgrove-Richardson, *Cultural history*, p. 193 ff; Ahmad, *Sino-Tibetan relations in the 17th century* (many quotations cf. Index by Ch. Pedersen).

[341] *byang-gter*, the Northern Treasure, was unearthed by Rig-'dsin rGod-ldem-can (cf. pt. II, p. 131).

[342] Pan-chen bLo-bzang-chos-kyi-rgyal-mtshan, the first Panchen bLa-ma (cf. Shakabpa, *Political history*, p. 97 f.).

[343] According to the *rNying-ma-pa* tradition there are thirteen main subjects to be studied (*gzung-chen*) but the *dGe-lugs-pa* tradition counts only five main subjects. (Tucci, *Religionen*, p. 144).

[344] dGongs-pa-rab-gsal was one of the chief proponents of the Buddhist revival in the tenth century; he received the monastic vows from four Tibetans and a Chinese monk. There are some doubts about the legitimacy of this tradition. (cf. Shakabpa, *Political history*, p. 56; Sum-pa-mkhan-po, *PJ*, p. 68 ff).

[345] Schulemann, *Dalai Lamas*, p. 131.

[346] cf. pt. II, p. 174 ff.

[347] *gsan-yig* means a special section of Buddhist Tibetan literature which includes all treatises and works the author had heard during his studies.

[348] *rtsa-gsum*, the three roots for religious practice are : the teacher (*bLa-ma*), the tutelary deity (*yi-dam*), and the Spiritual Being (*mKha'-'groma*).

[349] *'chol-ka-gsum* are the thirteen-*khri-skor* (*TPS*, p. 66), the three main regions of Tibet. (cf. for detailed information Shakabpa, *Political history*, p. 2).

[350] For Guśri Khan cf. Shakabpa, op.cit., p. 103.

[351] This was the title given by the Tibetans to the Chinese Emperor in reference to the title of the Dalai Lama (*Gong-sa-chen-pa* or *Gong-sa-skyabs-mgon*). This title of the Chinese Emperor as referred to in the Tibetan sources gives no hint at any supremacy of the Chinese Emperor over the Tibetans.

[352] This obviously refers to dPal bKra-śis-stobs-rgyal who had made a prophecy about the Fifth Dalai Lama.

[353] There are four kinds of charismatic activities: peaceful (*źi-ba'i phrin-las*), expanding and enriching (*rgyas-pa'i phrin-las*), overpowering (*dbang-gi phrin-las*), and fierceful (*drag-po'i phrin-las*).

[354] This prophecy is reported in the *Padma-bka'-thang* (Toussaint, *Le dict de Padma*, p. 386), cf. also *TPS*, p. 259, and Ferrari, *Guide*, p. 132n. 319. Tt gives the birth-year 1634 (wood-dog) but this does not fit the year of his death (1714-wood horse) and a lifetime of sixty-eight years.

[355] Dar-rgyas-chos-gling=Dar-rgyas-chos-sdings was the ancient seat of sMin-gling and is located in the country dBu-ru. The family of gTer-bdag -gling-pa (Myos) held the rank of abbot in this monastery by inheritance.

[356] gNubs-chen Sangs-rgyas-ye-śes, cf. Tt fol. 120a.

[357] Guenther, *Naropa*, p. 188.

[358] A Tantric deity, cf. Guenther, *Saraha*, p. 156; Neumaier, *ZDMG* 1970, p. 154 f.

[359] Guenther, *Naropa*, p. 174 ff.

[360] 'Bras-spungs is one of the three most famous monastic academies in Tibet; it was founded in 1416. For a description cf. Ferrari, *Guide*, p. 41 f. and Wylie, *ZG*, p. 79 f.

[361] These are : the vows of monastic conduct (*Vinaya*), the vows of the Bodhisattva-method, the vows of the Tantric method.

[362] sKyid-grong, a district in the south western corner of Tibet (Ferrari, *Guide*, p. 60, 154 n. 552).

[363] "The *rtsa-ba'i bla-ma* as distinct from the *brgyud-pa'i bla-ma* who upholds the school tradition, instructs the pupil whose doubts are thus dispelled. He is set on the way so that by finding himself he may be able to help others." (Guenther, *sGam-po-pa*, p. 9 n.3).

[364] *bKa'-'gyur-ro-chog* means the whole of a Buddha-Word and is identical with *bKa'-'gyur* (Vostrikov, *Literature*, p. 123).

[364] a Recently translated by H. V. Guenther : *Kindly Bent to Ease Us* (Dharma Press, Emeryville 1975).

[365] *Sa-skya-bka'-'bum*, vol. 5, p. 297.1.1; 320.4.5.

[366] *ji-snyed-pa'i chos=kun-rdsob-pa'i-chos*, i.e. the Reality as it becomes manifest.

[367] A method of sealing the Concealed Treasures; cf. Neumaier, *ZDMG*, Suppl. I, pt. 3, p. 858 f.

[368] *tshom-bu* are the focal points within a *Maṇḍala* on which the figures of the deities are placed. (cf. Tucci, *Religionen*, p. 135 f.).

[369] Ferrari, *Guide*, p. 44.

[370] Ferrari, op.cit., p. 54, 132 n. 313.

[371] Sa-'ug-stag-sgo in the Mon country (*DNg*, p. 72, 319, 464, 477).

[372] Tt has the same statements but in different sentences.

[373] *mtshams* means a tight seclusion in order to practise special Yoga exercises. (cf. Tucci, *Religionen*, p. 176).

[374] *khregs-chod*: This is a state of a pure mystic experience and contrasted with that of *thod-rgal*; this latter term refers to the experience which is close to the pure mystic experience. It precedes the 'break-through' while in the *khregs-chod* experience everything is seen after the break-through. (Guenther, *Philosophy*, p. 230 n. 23).

[375] Guenther, *Naropa*, p. 59.

[376] *(phrin-) las-bźi* cf. n. 353 (pt. II).

[377] Hūṃkara was the teacher of Nam-mkha'-snying-po (*TPS*, p. 380).

[378] Sangs-rgyas-gsang-ba was contemporary with King Khri-srong-lde-btsan and taught the *Anuttara-tantra* Padmasambhava (*TPS*, p. 87, 257 n. 156).

[379] cf. pt. II, p. 79 ff.

[380] *Kun-mkhyen Chos-rje* is only a title; I suppose it indicates the Sa-skya Paṇḍita.

[381] Guenther, *Saraha*, p. 115 n. 62.

[382] *Źing-yongs-su-'byongs-pa'i ting-nge-'dsin*: This meditation aims to realize the appropriate field of Buddha-activity (*buddha-kṣetra*). This is done by replacing unpure realms by pure ones; a meditative transformation takes place, which leads from the unpure field to the pure field of Buddha-activity. (for the term of *Buddha-kṣetra* see Lamotte, *L'ensei;nement de Vimalakírti* p. 395 ff; and for this meditation Maitreyanātha, *Abhisamayālaṃkāra-śāstra-kārikā, TTP*, vol. 88, p. 6.3.6.

[383] For an explanation of this essential term in Buddhist Tantras cf. Guenther, *Naropa*, p. 269, note D.

[384] For the explanation of the term '*pho-nya*', messenger, cf. Guenther, *Naropa*, p. 70: "This psychological phenomenon has been recognized in Western psychology and been described by C.G. Jung as the 'anima'. The term 'messenger' is used in a purely psychological context and is a sort of inspiratory force."

[385] Neumaier, *ZDMG*, 1970, p. 136 f.

[386] *rDo-rje-gsum*: *sku'i rdo-rje, gsung-gi rdo-rje, thugs-kyi rdo-rje.*

[387] *Ti-shih* 'Imperial Master': This title was first used by the Mongolian Emperors who conferred it on several Tibetan hierarchs. (*TPS*, p. 31).

[388] For a short outline of the various Tibetan Buddhist Schools vide Tucci, *Religionen*, p. 47 ff.

[389] *TPS*, p. 34 f.

[390] Guenther, *sGam-po-pa*, p. 241.

[391] Guenther, *Philosophy*, p. 96.

[392] Perhaps this expression refers to the Chinese Emperor who is generally referred to by the term *Gong-ma-chen-ma* in Tibetan sources.

[393] *rten-gsum*: *sku'i rten*, *gsungs-gi-rten*, *thugs-kyi rten*.

[394] *tshogs-gnyis*: 'the two acquisitions' are the acquisition of meritious deeds (*bsod-nams-kyi tshogs*) and the acquisition of knowledge (*śes-rab-kyi tshogs*).

[395] Guenther, *sGam-po-pa*, p. 41.

[396] Literally 'Owner of an Umbrella'; the umbrella signifies royal power in the whole area of South and Central Asia.

[397] Sangs-rgyas-rgya-mtsho (1653-1705) became regent in 1679; besides his political activities he was an excellent scholar in the 'History of Buddhism' (*Vaiḍūrya-ser-po*, a history of the *dGe-lgus-pa* School), and 'Astrology' (*Vaiḍūrya-dkar-po*). (*TPS*, p. 74, 77, 136; Snellgrove-Richardson, *Cultural history*, p. 201, 204 ff., 207 ff.)

[398] Tucci, *Religionen*, p. 47 ff.

[399] cf. pt. II, p. 132 ff.

[400] 'Phyongs-rgas dPal-ri was formerly a most important monastic college of the Old School. This place is close to the tomb of King Srong-btsan-sgam-po. Nowadays the monastery is called dPal-ri-dgon, but in former times its name was rDo-rje-smin dPal-ri. The temple shelters a well-known image of the Precious Guru Padmasambhava. It was founded by bSod-nams-stobs-rgyal in the second half of the sixteenth century. (Ferrari, *Guide*, p. 53).

[401] cf. pt. II, p. 92 f f

[402] His hagiography is reported in the Tt fol. 69 b.

[403] cf. Guenther, *sGam-po-pa*, p. 9 n. 3.

[404] The five minor arts are : medicine, astrology and astronomy, calligraphy, eloquence, grammar, and drawing (Tucci, *Religionen*, p. 160).

[405] see Tt fol. 135 a.

[406] *drod-rtags*, 'the sign of heat' marks the successful meditation (*sgrub-rtags*) and it is identical with the word *gtum-mo*, 'mystical heat'.

[407] This is the first stage of further four meditation stages: The knowledge maturation (*rnam-par-smin-pa'i rig-'dsin*), the knowledge of having power over the life (*tshe-la dbang-ba'i rig-'dsin*), the knowledge of transcendent immanence (*lhun-gyis-grub-pa'i rig-'dsin*), and the knowledge of the *Mahāmudrā* (*phyag-rgya-chen-po'i rig-'dsin*).

[408] Guenther, *Naropa*, p. 46, 270 note F.

[409] Bya-rung-kha-śor is a Buddhist temple near Bodhnath in Nepal (Snellgrove, *Buddhist Himalaya*, p. 99).

[410] cf. pt. I, p. 56.

[411] In the valley of 'Phyongs-rgyas are the tombs of the Kings of the Yar-klung dynasty (Bacot, *Introduction à l'histoire*, p. 8 ff; Tucci, *Tombs of the Tibetan Kings*; Haarh, *Yar-luṅ Dynasty*).

[412] In the Don-mkhar valley was the residence of 'Jigs-med-gling-pa, called Tshe-ring-ljongs (Ferrari, *Guide*, p. 53, 130 n. 297); there also are the majority of the tombs of the ancient Tibetan Kings (Tucci, *Tombs*, p. 32).

[413] Shakabpa, *Political history*, p. 158.

[414] Snellgrove-Richardson, *Cultural history*, p. 137.

[415] The monastery Thub-bstan rDo-rje-brag was a well-known center of the Old School (Ferrari, *Guide*, p. 56).

[416] *Bo-dong-pa*: adherents of a small School of Tibetan Buddhism (Tucci, *Religionen*, p. 47).

[417] dGa'-ldan one of the three most famous monastic academies in Tibet (Snellgrove-Richardson, *Cultural history*, p. 181f, 230, 238).

[418] Mu-rug-btsan-po, or Mu-rub-bstan-po, was a Tibetan King of the Yar-klung Dynasty (Haarh, *Yar-luṅ dynasty*, p. 20, 57 f, 68, 339, 392, 395; Tucci, *Tombs*, p. 13).

[419] Rong-ston Padma-bde-chen-gling-pa: his hagiography is given in Tt fol. 165 a.

[420] The hierarch of the *Žva-dmar-po bKa'-brgyud-pa* School is entitled *dpa'-bo-gtsug-lag*.

[421] For the foundation of the Zur-mang monastery cf. *DNg*, p. 511.

[422] Snellgrove-Richardson, *Cultural history*, p. 137.

[423] Macdonald, *Le Mandala*, p. 91 ff; G. Smith, Introduction in Kongtrul's *Encyclopaedia of Indo-Tibetan Culture* (ed. by L. Chandra) p. 34ff.

[424] *Ekajaṭī* is the leader of the *Ma-mo* demons (Nebesky-Wojkowitz, *Oracles*, p. 94). She also is the fierce form of Tārā.

[425] sKong-sprul collected all reliable Concealed Teachings in the 'Precious Treasury of Concealed Teachings', the *Rin-chen-gter-mdsod*

[426] cf. pt. II, p. 132 ff.

[427] His hagiography is reported in the Tt fol. 113 b.

[428] Ferrari, *Guide*, p. 45, 115 n. 140.

[429] op.cit., p. 71, 163 n 646.

[430] op.cit., p. 74.

[431] dPal-spungs in sDe-dge: vide Snellgrove-Richardson, *Cultural history*, p. 137; Kaḥ-thog vide pt. II ,n. 318; rDsogs-chen-ru-dam-bsam-gtan-chos-gling, also a famous monastery of the Old School: vide *Bod-na-bžugs-pa'-rnying-ma'i dgon-deb*, p. 78c.

[432] In the *Rin-chen-gter-mdsod* three different hagiographies of mKhyen-brtse'i-dbang-po are found. The essential points of the three editions are reported in the DC; for this reason only the text of the DC is here translated.

[433] Ferrari, *Guide*, p. 54, 132 n. 318.

[434] The DC only mentions 'the system of the two great charioteers'. The *TM* vol. A gives the name of these two great charioteers, Asaṅga and Nāgārjuna (*TM* vol. A, *mKhyen-brtse'i-rnam-thar* fol. 254b).

[435] Part of the Eight Pronouncements (*bKa'-brgyud*).

[436] Tucci, *Religionen*, p. 47

[437] It is not clear which qualities are implied here.

[438] Ferrari, *Guide*, p. 83 n. 28.

[439] The eight fetters of worldly attachment (*'jig-rten chos-brgyad*): gain and profit (*rnyed-pa*), loss (*ma rnyed-pa*), fame (*snyan-pa*), ill-repute (*mi snyan-pa*), scandal (*smad-pa*), praise (*bstod-pa*), happiness (*bde-ba*), misery (*sdug-bsngal-ba*).

[440] The Seven Divine Doctrines (*lha-chos bdun*) are the cycles of *Śākyamuni*, *Avalokiteśvara*, *Tārā*, and *Akṣobhya*, as well as the *Tripiṭaka* (the Three Collections of Buddha's Teachings). (GT, *bKa'-gdams-pa* chapter fol. 12 a.4).

[441] Mar-pa: Bacot, *La vie de Marpa, le 'traducteur'*; *Mi-la-raspa*: Bacot, *Le poete tibetain Milarepa*; Chang, *The hundred thousand songs of Milarepa*; Dvags-po: Guenther, *sGam-po-pa*, p. IX.

[442] The three realms (*gnas-gsum*)- *sku'i gnas, gsungs-gi gnas, thugs-kyi gnas*.

[443] A mountain god (Nebesky-Wojkowitz, *Oracles*, p 205 ff.)

[444] cf. pt. II, p. 132 ff.

[445] This is a different spelling of the Name Che-btsan-skyes, the master of Bur-za (cf. pt. I, p. 41).

[446] During the various stages of his spiritual transformation Padma-sambhava received eight names. The *PK* has the following list: Śāntara-kṣita, rDo-rje-drag-po-rtsal, Śākya-seng-ge, mKhas-pa bLo-ldan-mchog-sred, Padma-'byung-gnas, Padmasambhava, Padma-rgyal-po, sLob-dpon-gyi sgyu-ma'i-gra-ro, 'Phags-pa Seng-ge-sgra-grogs (*PK* fol. 62 bf). Another list is given by Waddell (*Lamaism*, p. 379): Padma-'byung-gnas, Padma-sambhava, Padma-rgyal-po, rDo-rje-gro-lod, Nyi-ma-'od- zer, Śākya-seng-ge, Seng-ge-sgra-sgrog, bLo-ldan-mchog-sred. For the significance of the Stūpa bDe-byed-brtsegs vide pt. I, p. 19.

APPENDIX

DISCOVERERS THAT WERE AUTHORIZED BY PADMASAMBHAVA'S PROPHECY

Name	Tt	DC
Sangs-rgyas-bla-ma	36a.3	258a.5
rGya Lo-tsā-ba = rDo-rje-bzang-po	37a.5	
sNa-nam-pa = 'Brog-pa sNa-nam-thub-pa-rgyal-po	37b.4	
rGya-źang-khrom rDo-rje-'od-'bar = rDo-rje-'od-'bar	38a.4	
Nyi-ma-seng-ge	39a.4	
dBu-ru-ston-pa Śākya-'od	39b.3	
Bon-po Brag-tshal = rDo-rje-'bar	40a.3	
sNye-mo-źu-yas = gNod-sbyin-'bar	40b.4	
Grub-thob-dngos-grub	41a.4	
gTsug-lag-dpal-dge	41b.6	
Ku-sa-sman-pa = Kun-spangs-zla-'od-sman-pa-padma-skyabs	42a.6	
Bon-po Lha-'bum = Guru rNon rtser	43a.4	
Khyung-po dPal-dge	43b.3	
Śa-mi rDo-rje-rgyal-po	44a.2	
lDang-ma Lhun-rgyal = Lhun-gyis-rgyal-mtshan	44b.4	
Grva-pa-mngon-śes dBang-phyug-'bar	45b.6	259a.3
Ra-śag-chen-po = Ra-śag-chos-'bar = bSod-nams-rdo-rje	46b.5	
Nyang-ral Nyi-ma-'od-zer	47a.6	260a.1
dPon-gsas-khyung-thog	50a.6	
Ra-mo-śel-sman = Ye-śes-bzang-po	51a.4	
Guru Chos-kyi-dbang-phyug	52a.4	263a.1
Guru Jo-tshe = Tshe-dbang-dar-po	55a.4	
Padma-dbang-phyug	56a.3	
Do-ban rGya-mtsho	56b.4	
Rakṣi sTon-pa	57a.4	
Byang-rong E-yi-sman-pa = Nyi-'od-gsal	57b.3	
Gra'-sgom Chos-kyi-rdo-rje	58a.6	
gYag-phyar-sngon-mo = rDo-rje-'bum	58b.6	

Name	Tt	DC
bLa-ma-grum = mKhar-nag	59b.3	
Lha-btsun sngon-mo = Rig-pa'i-rgya-mtsho-glog-gi-phreng-ba	60a.2	
Nyi-ma-grags-pa	60b.5	
Rin-chen-tshul-rdor = Padma-las-'brel-rtsal = Tshul-khrims-rdo-rje	61a.6	
Tshe-brtan-rgyal-mtshan = Guru brTan-rgyal-mtshan = Chos-kyi-blo-gros	62b.5	
Me-ban Rin-chen-gling-pa = Rin-chen-rgyalpo	63b.1	
O-rgyan-gling-pa	65a.3	274a.6
Dri-med-'od-zer = Tshul-khrims-blo-gros	67a.3	
Rog-rje-gling-pa = Chos-rje-'jam-gling-rdo-rje = bDe-ba'i-rdo-rje	69b.4	
gTer-bdag-gling-pa = Padma-gar-dbang-'gyur-med-rje = Ngag-dbang-bstan-'dsin	71b.6	303a.2
Padma-kun-skyong-gling-pa	74b.2	
mDo-sngags-gling-pa mChog-ldan-mgon-po	76b.2	
bsTan-gnyis-gling-pa Padma-tshe-dbang-rgyal-po	78a.5	
(O-rgyan-)rdo-rje-gling-pa	79b.2	282b.3
Rin-chen-gling-pa = Sangs-rgyas-gling-pa	82a.1	279a.3
O-rgyan-padma-gling-pa	85b.4	286a.6
Las-'phro-gling-pa = Rig-'dsin 'Ja'-tshon-snying-po = sNgags-chang Hūm-nag-me-'bar = Ngag-dbang Chos-rgyal-dbang-po	88a.1	293a.2
bSam-gtan-bde-chen-gling-pa	91a.2	
Źig-po-gling-pa Gar-gyi-dbang-phyug = Nam-mkha'-tshe-dbang-rgyal-po	91b.4	
bDe-chen-gling-pa	93b.1	

DISCOVERERS WITHOUT A PROPHECY—ARRANGED IN CHRONOLOGICAL SEQUENCE

Name	Tt
Guru Hūṃ-'bar	96a.3
Lha-btsun Byang-chub-'od	96a.5
Jo-bo-rje Dīpaṃkara = Atīśa	96b.4
Źang-btsun Dar-ma-rin-chen	97a.6
Rong-zom Chos-kyi-bzang-po	97b.2

Name	Tt	DC
rDor-'bum Chos-kyi-grags-pa	97b.4	
Sangs-rgyas-'bar	98a.4	
Se-ston Ring-mo	98a.6	
rGya-phur-bu = Phur-bu-mgon	98b.3	
dGe-bśes Prang-rdo-rje-kun-grags	99a.2	
Lha-rje gNubs-chung	99a.4	
rGya-ston bTson-'grus-seng-ge-dar	99b.1	
Ce-btsun Seng-ge-dbang-phyug	99b.4	
Sar-ban-phyogs-med	100b.6	
gNyan Lo-tsā-ba Dar-ma-grags	101a.2	
sTon-pa Śākya-'od = Sākya-bzang-po	101b.3	
bLa-ma Zangs-ri-ras-pa	102a.1	
gNyal-pa Jo-sras = gNyal ston Nag-po	102a.3	
rGya-gong-ri-pa Sangs-rgyas-dbang-chen	102a.5	
Chu-pho-rtogs-ldan = dGe-'dun-rgyal-mtshan	102b.1	
Ba-mkhar-smug-po	102b.6	
mNga'-bdag Mol-mi-'khyil	103a.5	
Guru Yang-dbang = rDo-rje-bzad-rtsal	103b.3	
Sum-pa Byang-chub-blo-gros = bSod-nams-rgyal-mtshan	104a.4	
sTag-lung-pa Sangs-rgyas-dbon-po = Grags-pa-dpal-'od-zer-bzang-po	104b.3	
gNyal-ba Nyi-ma-śes-rab	105a.4	
Khro-phu Lo-tsā-ba gNubs-byams-pa'i-dpal	105b.2	
gYas-ban-ya-bon	106a.1	
A-hūṃ-'bar, the Nepalese	106a.3	
A-jo-dpal-po	106a.6	
Sum-tshogs	106b.3	
Du-gu Rin-chen-seng-ge	107b.1	
gTsang-pa La-ba-ring-mo	108a.3	
sPrul-sku La-stod dMar-po = Dam-pa-dmar-po	108a.5	
Jo-mo-sman-mo = Padma-mtsho-skyid	108b.4	271b.6
Grub-chen-me-long-rdo-rje	111a.5	
sKal-ldan-byis-pa	112a.3	
Prang-ti-rgyal-nye-mkhar-bu	112b.2	
sGom-chen 'Brug-pa gNyan-ston Jambhala = Don-grub-seng-ge = Padma-grags-pa	112b.5	

Name	Tt	DC
Dung-mtsho-ras-pa, the Elder = Dung-rab-śes-rab-rgya-mtsho = Rin-chen-bzang-po	113a.3	
mKha'-'gro-ma Kun-dga'-bum-pa	113b.4	
Dung-mtsho-ras-pa, the Younger	114b.4	
Vajramati	115a.6	
rGyal-sras-legs-pa	115b.4	
O-rgyan-bzang-po	116b.3	
Śes-rab-me-'bar	117a.3	
Nyi-zla-sangs-rgyas	117b.6	
sNgags-'chang Las-'phro-gling-pa	118a.6	
sPrul-sku bZang-por-grags-pa	118b.3	
Dri-med-lhun-po = rNam-par-snang-mdsod-'od	119a.4	
Dri-med-kun-dga' (-śes-rab-rgyal-mtshan)	120a.6	
Rig-'dsin-chen-po dNgos-grub-rgyal-mtshan = Rig-'dsin rGod-ldem-can	121b.4	277a.4
Lad-po-pa dPal-rgyal-mtshan	123a.5	
Karma-gling-pa	124a.3	288b.2
dPal-ldan 'Jam-dbyangs-bla-ma	124b.3	
Grub-chen Thang-stong-rgyal-po	125a.3	289a.3
mGon-po-rin-chen	126b.3	
Ratna-gling-pa	127a.3	284b.6
sKal-ldan-rdo-rje	128b.1	
mChog-ldan-rdo-rje	128b.5	
Chag-byang-chub-gling-pa	129a.2	
sNgags-'chang Śākya-bzang-po	129a.4	
'Gro-'dul-las-'phro-gling-pa	130a.6	
'Jam-dpal-rdo-rje	131b.1	
mNga'-ris Pan-chen rGyal-rdo-rje = Padma-dbang-rgyal	131b.3	290b.4
Mi-'gyur-las-'phro-gling-pa-kun-dga'-dpal-bzang	133b.6	
gNam-lcags-me-'bar	134a.5	
'Gro-'dul-gling-pa Śes-rab-'od-zer	135a.6	
mNga'-ris Rig-'dsin-chen-po Legs-ldan-rdo-rje	137a.6	
Matiratna	138b.2	
mKhyen-brtse'i-dbang-phyug-mdo-sngags-gling-pa bsTan-pa'i-rgyal-mtshan	139a.6	
Karma-gu-ru = Chos-rgyal-dbang-po'i-sde	140a.6	

Name	Tt	DC
Rig-'dsin Ngag-gi-dbang-po = Ngag-dbang-rig-'dsin rDo-rje-chos-rgyal-bstan-pa'i-rgyal = mtshan-dpal-bzang-po	141b.5	
Gar-dbang-las-'phro-gling-pa	142b.4	
Yongs-'dsin Ngag-dbang-grags-pa	143b.2	
sNgags-'chang bKra-śis-tshe-brtan	143b.5	
Padma-rig-'dsin = Ra-źi gTer-ston	144a.3	
bDud-'dul-gling-pa	144b.5	
Rig-'dsin-chen-po bDud-'dul-rdo-rje = Kun-dga'-bsod-nams-chos-phags	145a.3	295b.5
Rig-'dsin-chen-po kLong-gsal-snying-po	148a.2	
Vol-mo-sprul-sku bsTan-'dsin-nor-bu = Karma-thub-bstan-snying-po-rnam-par-rgyal-bu'i-sde	150b.2	
sPrul-sku bZang-po-rdo-rje-blo-bzang-phrin-las-rnam-rgyal	151b.2	
Gar-dbang-zla-ba-rgyal-mtshan = Padma-gar-dbang-rtsal	153a.2	
Mi-'gyur-rdo-rje-drag-po-nus-ldan-rtsal = Karma-bsam-'grub	154a.4	
Ja-pa gTer-ston Bya-btang-sku-mchog = Ngag-gi-rdo-rje	156b.2	
Guru dPon-gsas-khyung-thog	157a.4	
Rig-'dsin sTag-śam-rdo-rje = bSam-gtan-gling-pa	157b.5	
Rva-ston sTobs-ldan-rdo-rje = Padma-tshe-dbang-rtsal	159b.6	
Khams-pa Rin-po-che Ngag-dbang-kun-dga'-bstan-'dsin	161a.2	
Rig-'dsin-chen-po-Rol-pa'i-rdo-rje = dKon-mchog-lhun-grub	162a.6	
Padma-chos-rgyal	166b.3	
Padma-dbang-phyug	166b.5	
Khyung-grags-rdo-rje = O-rgyan-phun-tshogs	167a.5	
Rig-'dsin Tshe-dbang-nor-bu = Tshe-dbang-nor-bu-rdo-rje-dpal	167b.5	
rTsa-gsum-gter-bdag-gling-pa = Gar-dbang-gnam-lcags-rdo-rje = bKra-śis-phun-tshogs	169a.4	

Rig-'dsin Thugs-mchog-rdo-rje-hūṃ-nag-'gro-'dul = Kun-bzang-phrin-las	170b.5	
Dri-med-gling-pa = Karma-'gro-don-mthar phyin	171b.6	
Kun-bzang-bde-chen-rgyal-po = sMon-lam-rdo-rje	172b.4	
Rog-rje-gling-pa 'Gro-'dul-rtsal	173b.2	
Gar-dbang-'chi-med-rdo-rje = Kun-bzang-'od-zer-gar-dbang-bstan-pa'i-nyi-ma	174a.5	
rDo-rje-thogs-med = bsTan-'dsin-zla-'od-rdo-rje	175a.5	
Zla-ba'i-'od-zer = Rang-grol-ting-'dsin-rgyal-po	175b.5	
mChog-gyur-bde-chen-zig-po-gling-pa = Nor-bu-bstan-'dsind = Kon-mchog-bstan-'dsin	177a.4	314b.4
Rig-'dsin Chos-rgyal-rdo-rje	184b.1	
Padma-'od-gsal-mdo-sngags-gling-pa	185a.4	320b.1

DISCOVERERS OF UNKNOWN LIFETIME

Zla-ban-gzi-brjid	195a.2
Rog-ban-śes-rab-'od	195a.4
'Brom Chos-kyi-snying-po	195a.5
'Od-zer-ston-pa	195a.6
Me-nyag-grags-'byung	195b.1
Zla-ba-rdo-rje	195b.2
gTsang-gi Nyang-ston Ses-rab-grags-pa	195b.2
gCang-stong Chos-'bar	195b.3
Khams-pa Me-zor	195b.3
sNgags-'chang dBang-chen-bzang-po	195b.4
Mar-po-bya'u-mgon	195b.4
sKyes-bu-zangs-gling-dbang-phyug	195b.5
Ri-khrod-pa Seng-ge	195b.6
lCang-sman Don-grub-dar-rgyas	196a.1
'Gos-padma	196a.2
Rang-byung-ye-śes	196a.3
bSe-ban Nyi-ma'i-snying-po	196a.4
Khams-pa 'Brug-sgom-zig	196a.5

Name	Tt	DC
Byang-chub-dpal	196a.6	
Mahāvajra	196b.3	

DISCOVERERS THAT REVEALED CONCEALED TEACHINGS BY MEANS OF VISIONS

Name	Tt	DC
Ras-chung-rdo-rje-drags-pa	198a.3	
Kha-chen Paṇ-chen Śākya-śrī	198b.2	
gYu-thog Yon-tan-mgon-po	198b.6	
sKyer-sgang Chos-kyi-seng-ge	199b.5	
Karma-pa Rang-byung-rdo-rje	200a.3	
Kun-mkhyen Dri-med-'od-zer	200b.4	
Lho-brag Grub-chen Nam-mkha'-rgyal-mtshan = Las-kyi-rdo-rje	200b.6	
Phan-yul-pa dPal-ldan-rdo-rje	202a.6	
Śrī-ba-ratna = dPal-nags-kyi-rin-chen	202b.2	
rGyal-dbang Chos-rje-kun-dga'-dpal-'byor	203b.6	
bSam-gtan-gling-pa'i A-tir-grags = mNyam-mod-nam-mkha'-bsod-nams	204a.4	
Karma-pa drug-pa mThong-ba-don-ldan	204b.3	
Ras-chen-dpal-'byor-bzang-po	204b.5	
rTogs-ldan-sangs-rgyas-mgon-po	205a.3	
Thams-cad-mkhyen-pa Padma-dkar-po	205a.6	
rGyal-sras bsTan-pa'i-'byung-gnas = 'Ja'-tshon-me-'bar-mkha'-'gro'i-dbang-phyug	205b.4	
sNang-gsal Rig-'dsin bKra-śis-rgya-mtsho	206a.2	
Żabs-drung dKon-mchog-rin-chen	206a.3	
'Bri-gung-pa Chos-kyi-grags-pa	206a.5	
Lha-btsun Nam-mkha'-'jigs-med = Kun-bzang-rnam-rgyal	206b.2	298b.5
Rig-'dsin-chen-po gSang-bdag-phrin-las-lhun-grub	207b.3	
rGyal-mchog-lnga-pa = rDo-rje-thog-med-rtsal i.e. the Fifth Dalai Lama	207b.5	300a.6
mNga'-ris Pa-'od-gsal-mchog-ldan	209a.6	
Rig-'dsin Mi-'gyur-rdo-rje	211a.6	
mKhas-grub Karma-chags-med	213a.3	
Rig-'dsin Thugs-kyi-rdo-rje = rDo-rje-drag-po-phrin-las-'dus-pa-rtsal	214a.6	

Name	Tt	DC
rDo-rje-'chang Padma-nyin-byed-dbang-po	215a.4	
dPa'-bo-gtsug-lag Chos-kyi-rgyal-po	218a.3	
Karma-bstan-'dsin-phrin-las	218b.2	
dGe-rgan Padma-dgyes-pa	218b.5	
Kun-mkhyen 'Jigs-med-gling-pa	219a.3	310b.2
Padma-chos-'byor-rgya-mtsho	223a.5	
'Jigs-med-phrin-las-'od-zer	224a.6	
Mi'-gyur-nam-mkha'i-rdo-rje-tshe-dbang-grub-pa-rtsal='Jigs-med mKhyen-brtse'i-dbang-phyug-phrin-las-rnam-rgyal-rdo-rje	226a.3	

MASTERS OF THE OLD SCHOOL

52 A[1]	'Jam-dpal-bśes-gnyen obtains the rDsogs-chen verses from his teacher dGa'-rab-rdo-rje
342	'Jam-dpal-bśes-gnyen's death
?	Śrīsiṃha
467	'Jam-dpal-bśes-gnyen, the Younger is born
496	Jñānsūtra receives the prophecy that he shall discover the hidden sNying-thig books
506	Jñānasūtra's death
ca. 750-780	Vimalamitra was about two hundred years old when he was invited to Tibet Padmasambhava was invited to Tibet Vairocana was banished
ca. 1000-1080	Sangs-rgyas-bla-ma, the first gTer-ston
1012-1090	Grva-pa-mngon-śes
1052	Dseng Dharmabodhi born
1124-1192	Nyang-ral Nyi-ma-'od-zer
1212-1270	Guru Chos-kyi-dbang-phyug
1248-1283	Jo-mo-sman-mo
1318-1363	kLong-chen-rab-'byams-pa

---

1. Note on the chronology : dPa'-bo-gtsug-lag, author of the KhG states that the parinirvāṇa of Śākyamuni occurred in the fifth year after the enthronement of King Ajātaśatru. This statement roughly corresponds to the calculations of western scholars who put the enthronement of Ajātaśatru in the year 493 B. C., eight years before the parinirvāṇa (cf. Lamotte, *Histoire du Buddhism Indien* p. 100). Thus, dPa'-bo-gtsug-lag-takes the year 488 B.C. as the parinirvāṇa of Buddha.

1323-ca. 1360	O-rgyan-gling-pa
1337-1409	Rig-'dsin rGod-ldem-can
1340-1396	Sangs-rgyas-gling-pa
1346-1405	rDo-rje-gling-pa
14th century	Karma-gling-pa
1385-1510	Thang-stong-rgyal-po
1403-1479	O-rgyan-gling-pa, first collection of the Ancient Tantras
1450- ?	O-rgyan-padma-gling-pa
1487-1543	mNga'-ris Paṇ-chen Padma-dbang-rgyal-rdo-rje
1585-1656	Las-'phro-gling-pa
1597-ca. 1650	Lha-btsun Nam-mkha'-'jigs-med
1615-1672	bDud-'dul-rdo-rje
1617-1682	rDo-rje-thogs-med-rtsal, the Fifth Dalai Lama (alias bLo-bsang-rgya-mtsho)
1634?-1714	gTer-bdag-gling-pa
1729-1798	'Jigs-med-gling-pa, revised edition of the kLong-chen sNying-thig and catalogue of the Ancient Tantras
1813-1899	sKong-sprul Padma-gar-dbang Yon-tan-rgya mtsho-blo-gros-mtha'-yas, collector of the gter-ma books
1829-1870	Źig-po-gling-pa
1820-1892	mKhyen-brtse'i-dbang-po Padma-'od-gsal-mdo-sngags-gling-pa
1846-1912	Mi-pham 'Jam-dbyangs-rnam-rgyal-rgya-mtsho

Chronological Table

POLITICAL AND RELIGIOUS EVENTS IN TIBET

173 A.C.	Lha-tho-tho-ri born
233	obtains Buddhist scriptures and figures
609-649	Srong-btsan-sgam-po (627 enthronement)
742-797	Khri-srong-lde-btsan (enthronement 754/5)
755	Construction of bSam-yas
792-94	Debate of bSam-yas; hiding of the rDsogs-chen literature
836	gLang-dar-ma's persecution of Buddhism
842	Assassination of gLang-dar-ma
958-1055	Rin-chen-bzang-po, revivor of Buddhism
1012-1096	Mar-pa
1040-1123	Mi-la-ras-pa
1042	Atīśa arrives in Tibet
1204	Śākya-śrī, the Kashmirian scholar, visits Tibet
1249	Sa-skya Paṇḍita becomes viceroy of Tibet
1290-1364	Bu-ston
1302-1373	Byang-chub-rgyal-mtshan, founder of the Phag-mo-gru-pa Dynasty
1357	Birth of Tsong-kha-pa, founder of the dGe-lugs-pa School
1340-1383	Rol-pa'i-rdo-rje, hierarch of the Karma-pa School
1391	dGe-'dun-grub-pa, First Dalai Lama born
1409	dGa'-ldan, the first dGe-lugs-pa academy founded
1475	Second Dalai Lama born
1543	Third Dalai Lama
1578	He obtains the title 'Dalai Lama'
1589	Fourth Dalai Lama

1653	Fifth Dalai Lama visits Peking
1642	Guśri Khan defeats Karma bsTan-skyong
1683	Sixth Dalai Lama
1708	Seventh Dalai Lama
1758	Eighth Dalai Lama
1806	Ninth Dalai Lama
1816	Tenth Dalai Lama
1838	Eleventh Dalai Lama
1856	Twelfth Dalai Lama
1876	Thirteenth Dalai Lama

CHINESE BUDDHISM AND ITS RELATION TO TIBET

344-413	Kumārajīva born in Kucha (revivor of Chinese Buddhism)
401	Kumārajīva patronized by a Tibetan noble
4th century	East Tibetan tribes come into contact with Chinese Buddhism
384-414	Seng-chao
460-534	Bodhidharma, founder of the Ch'an (Zen) School
538-597	Chih-i, founder of the T'ien-t'ai School
596-664	Hsüan-tsang, founder of the Chinese Vijnāna-vāda ('Consciousness-Only') School
643-712	Fa-tsang, founder of the Hua-yen School
781	Chinese monks sent to Tibet

BIBLIOGRAPHY

1. WORKS BY MODERN AUTHORS

AHMAD, Zahiruddin, *Sino-Tibetan relations in the seventeenth century.* Rom 1970 (Index by Pedersen, Ch.)

BACOT, Jacques, *Introduction à l'histoire du Tibet.* Paris 1962.

—, *La vie de Marpa* Paris 1937.

—, *Le poete tibetain Milarepa.* Paris 1925.

BELL, Charles, *Tibet, past and present.* Oxford 1924.

BHATTACHARYA, V., *Bodhicaryāvatāra.* 1960.

CASINELLI, C.W. and EKVALL, R.B., *A Tibetan principality, the political system of the Sa-skya.* Ithaca 1969.

CHAN, Wing-tsit, *A source book in Chinese philosophy*, translated and compiled by. New Jersey 1970.

CHANG, G. C. C., *The hundred thousand songs of Milarepa.* New York 1962.

CHANDRA, Lokesh, *Kongtrul's Encyclopaedia of Indo-Tibetan culture* pt. 1-3, with an introduction by E. Gene SMITH. New Delhi 1970.

CHATTOPADHYAYA, Alaka, *Atīśa and Tibet.* Calcutta 1967.

CONZE, Edward, *Thirty years of Buddhist studies.* selected essays by. Oxford 1967.

DAGYAB, Loden Sherab, *Tibetan dictionary.* Dharamsala 1966.

DEMIEVILLE, Paul, *Le concil de Lhasa.* Paris 1952.

DODRUP-CHEN : *The biography of Mahā-Paṇḍita Vimalamitra.* Gangtok 1967.

EVANS-WENTZ, W.Y., *The Tibetan Book of the Great Liberation.* Oxford 1954.

—, *Tibetan Yoga and Secret Doctrines.* Oxford 1935.

FERRARI, Alfonsa and PETECH, L., *mK'yen brtse's guide to the holy places of Central Tibet.* Rome 1958.

GNOLI, R, *The Pramāṇavārttikam of Dharmakīrti.* Rome 1960.

GORDON, A., *The Iconography of Tibetan Lamaism.* Tokyo 1959.

GRÜNWEDEL, A., *Tāranātha's Edelsteinmine. das Buch von den Vermittlern der sieben Inspirationen.* Bibliotheca Buddhica XVIII, Petersburg 1914.

GUENTHER, Herbert V., *sGam-po-pa—Jewel Ornament of Liberation.* London 1959.
—, *Tibetan Buddhism without mystification.* Leiden 1966.
—, *The royal songs of Saraha.* A study in the history of Buddhist thoughts, translated and annotated by. Seattle 1969.
—, *Buddhist philosophy in theory and practice.* Baltimore, Penguin Books 1971.
—, *The life and teaching of Naropa.* Oxford 1971. (repr.)
HAARH, Erik, *The Yar-luṅ dynasty.* Kopenhagen 1969.
HACKMANN, H., *Von Omi bis Bhamo, Wanderungen an den Grenzen von China, Tibet und Birma.* Berlin 1907.
HEILER, Fr., *Erscheinungsformen und Wesen der Religionen.* Stuttgart 1961.
HOFFMANN, H., *Die Religionen Tibets.* Freiburg 1956.
JAN, Yün-hua, *A chronicle of Buddhism in China* 581-960 *A.D.* Santiniketan 1966.
LALOU, M., *Contribution à la bibliographie du Kanjur et du Tanjur*
—, *les textes boudhiques au temps du Roi Khri-sroṅ-lde-bcan.* JA tome 241, p. 313, Paris 1953.
LAMOTTE, Etienne, *Histoire du Bouddhism Indien des origines a l'ere Śaka*, Louvain 1958.
—, *L'enseignement Vimalakīrti-Vimalakīrtinirdeśa.* Louvain 1962.
LESSING. F. D. and WAYMAN, Alex, *mKhas-grub-rje's fundamentals of the Buddhist Tantras, rGyud-sde-spyiḥi rnam-par-gźag-pa rgyas-par-brjod.* Paris, The Hague 1968.
LIEBENTHAL, W., *The book of Chao.* Peking 1948.
MACDONALD, Ariane, *Le maṇḍala du Mañjuśrīmūlakalpa.* Paris 1962.
MITSCHERLICH, Alexander, *Auf dem Weg zur vaterlosen Gesellschaft.* München.
NEUMAIER, Eva, *Mātaraḥ und Ma-mo, Studien zur Mythologie des Lamaismus.* Munich 1966. (thesis)
—, *Einige Aspekte der gter-ma Literatur der rNin-ma-pa Schule.* *ZDMG* Suppl.I, p. 849, Wiesbaden 1969.
—, bKa'-brgyad raṅ-byuṅ-raṅ śar, ein rJogs-c'en Tantra. *ZDMG* vol. 120, p. 131 ff, Wiesbaden 1970
PEDERSEN, Christiane, Index to *ZAHIRUDDIN AHMAD Sino-Tibetan relations in the seventeenth century.* Rome 1971.

PELLIOT, P., *Notes à propos d'un catalogue du Kanjur. JA* p. 27, Paris 1914.

—, *Le cycle sexagênaire dans la chronologie tibêtaine.* JA 11e sêrie, tome I, no 3, p. 633-667.

PETRI, Winfried, *Indo-tibetische Astronomie*, Munich 1966. (unpublished typescript)

PRADHAN, Pralhad, *Abhidharmasamuccaya of Asaṅga.* ed., and studied by. Visvabharati, Santiniketan 1950.

RICHARDSON, H. E., *The Karma-pa sect, a historical note. JRAS* 1958, p. 139 ff and 1959, p. 1 ff

ROERICH, G. N., *The Blue Annals*, 2 vols. Calcutta 1949-1953

—, *Biography of Dharmasvāmin.* Patna 1959.

RUEGG, D.S., *The life of Bu-ston Rin-po-c'e, with the Tibetan text of the Bu-ston rnam-thar.* Rome 1966.

SCHIEFNER, Anton, *Tāranātha's Geschichte des Buddhismus in Indien.* Petersburg 1869.

SCHULEMANN, G., *Die Geschichte der Dalai Lamas.* Heidelberg 1911.

SHAKABPA, Tsepon W.D., *Tibet-A Political History.* New Haven 1967.

SIMNONSSON, Nils, *Indo-tibetische Studien.* Uppsala 1957.

SNELLGROVE, D. L., *Buddhist Himalaya.* Oxford 1957.

—, *The Hevajra-Tantra*, 2 vols. London 1959.

—, *Four Lamas of Dolpo*, 2 vols. Oxford 1967.

SNELLGROVE, D. and RICHARDSON, H.E., *A Cultural History of Tibet.* London 1968.

SUZUKI, D.T., *Die grosse Befreiung, Einfuhrung in den Zen-Buddhismus*, Leipzig 1939.

TARING, Rinchen Dolma, *Eine Tochter Tibets, Leben im Land der vertriebenen Gotter.* Hamburg 1972.

THOMAS, F.W., *Tibetan literary texts and documents concerning Chinese Turkestan*, 4 vols. London 1935-1963.

TOUSSAINT, G.Ch., *Le dict de Padma, Padma-thaṅ-yig-Ms. de Lithang.* Paris 1933.

TUCCI, Giuseppe, *Santi e briganti nel Tibet ignoto.* Milano 1937.

—, *Indo-Tibetica*, 4 vols. Rome 1932-41.

—, *Indo-Tibetica* II, Rin-c'en-bzaṅ-po e la rinascita del Buddhismo nel Tibet intorno al mille. Rome 1933.

—, Validity of Tibetan historical traditions. *India Antiqua-*

a volume of Oriental studies presented to J.Ph. Vogel, p. 309 ff. Leyden 1947.
—, *Tibetan painted scrolls*, 3 vols. Rome 1949.
—, *The tombs of the Tibetan kings*. Rome 1950.
—, *To Lha-sa and beyond*. Rome 1956.
—, *Minor Buddhist texts*, 2 vols. Rome 1956, 1958.
TUCCI, G. and HEISSIG, W., *Die Religionen Tibets und der Mongolei*. Stuttgart 1970.
VOSTRIKOV, A.I., *Tibetan historical literature*, translated from the Russian by Harish Chandra Gupta. Calcutta 1970.
WADDELL, L.A., *The Buddhism of Tibet or Lamaism*. Cambridge 1934.
WEIZSACKER, C.F. von and GOPI KRISHNA, *Biologische Basis religioser Erfahrung*. Weilheim 1971.
WIDENGREN, Geo, *Mani und der Manichoismus*. Stuttgart 1961.
WYLIE, Turrell V., *The geography of Tibet according to the'Dzam-gling-rgyas-bshad*. Rome 1962.
YOSHIMURA, S., *The Denkar-ma, an oldest catalogue of the Tibetan Buddhist canon*. Kyoto 1950.
ZÜRCHER, *The Buddhist conquest of China*, 2 vols. Leiden 1959.

2. TIBETAN SOURCES

klong-chen-snying-gi-thig-le-las 'pho-ba-ma-bsgoms sangs-rgyas-bźugs

klong-rdol-bla-ma rin-po-che ngag-dbang blo-bzang-gi gsung-'bum (Tibetan Buddhist Studies I, ed. by L. Chandra. Mussoorie 1963)

mKhas-pa'i-dga'-ston or lho-brag-chos-'byung by dPa'-bo-gtsug-lag (ed. by Raghu Vira. New Delhi 1959-62)

Gangs-ljongs-rgyal-bstan-yongs-rdsogs-kyi phyi-mo snga-'gyur rdo-rje-theg-pa'i bstan-pa rin-po-che ji-ltar-byung-ba'i tshul dag-cing gsal-bar brjod-pa lha-dbang-gyul-las rgyal-ba'i rnga-bo-che'i sgra-dbyangs, abbreviated title : rnying-ma'i chos-'byung by bDud-'joms Rin-po-che (ed. by Dudjom Tulku Rinpochee. Kalimpong 1967)

Gong-sa-rgyal-dbang lnga-pa chen-po-mchog-gis mdsad-pa'i bod-kyi-rgyal-rabs rdsogs-ldan-gzon-nu'i dga'-ston, chronicle of the Fifth Dalai Lama Ngag-dbang-blo-bzang-rgya-mtsho

Grub-mtha'-thams-cad-kyi khungs-dang-'dod-tshul ston-pa-legs-bśad śel-gyi-me-long by bLo-bzang-chos-kyi-nyi-ma-dpal-bzang-po

sGrub-chen-bka'-brgyad bde-gśegs-'dus-pa'i sngags-sgrub nang-ma'i dbang-chog padma-śel-phug-ma-bltas-chog-tu-bsdebs-pa dngos-grub-bum-bzang (*TM*, vol. Pha)

rGyud-kyi-rgyal-po dpal-gsang-ba-'dus-pa'i rdsogs-pa'i-rim-pa-rim-lnga gdan-rdsogs-kyi-dmar-khrid by Tsong-kha-pa (*TTP*, extra vol. 159)

rGyud-spyi'i rnam-par-gźag-par-brjod by mKhas-grub-rje (ed. and translated by Lessing and Wayman)

Chos-'byung-bstan-pa'i padma-rgyas-pa'i-nyin-byed by Padma-dkar-po

'Jam-dpal ye-śes-sems-dpa'i don-dam-pa'i mtshan yang-dag-par brjod-pa (*TTP*, vol. 1)

rJe-btsun-bla-ma thams-cad-mkhyen-cing gzigs-pa 'jam-dbyangs mkhyen-brtse'i-dbang-po kun-dga'-bstan-pa'i-rgyal-mtshan-dpal-bzang-po'i rnam-thar mdor-bsdus-pa ngo-mtshar udumbara'i dga'-tshal by sKong-sprul Padma-gar-dbang (*TM*, vol. A)

sNyan-brgyud phrin-las phur-pa'i gnad-tig-gi smin-grol 'bogs-pa'i lag-len phrin-las-gsang-ba'i-bcud-'dus (*TM*, vol. Khi)

rDor-sems-kyi sgrub-pa'i khyad-par-gyi rdsogs-rim snang-bźi'i man-ngag-gi khrid-yig mngon-sum-'od-gsal-'khor-lo (*TM*, vol. Ga)

'Phags-pa bsod-nams thams-cad bsdus-pa'i ting-nge-'dsin ces-bya-ba theg-pa-chen-po'i-mdo (*TTP*, vol. 32, no. 802)

'Phags-pa klu'i-rgyal-po rgya-mtshos źus-pa źes-bya-ba theg-pa-chen-po'i-mdo (*TTP*, vol. 33, no. 820)

'Phags-yul rgya-nag-chen-po bod dang sog-yul du dam-pa'i chos byung tshul dpag-bsam-ljon-bzang by Sum-pa-mkhan-po Ye-śes-dpal-'byor (ed. by L. Chandra, New Delhi 1959)

Bod-na bzugs-pa'i rnying-ma'i dgon-deb (ed. by Lama Paltul Jampal Lodoe, Dalhousie n.d.)

Byang-chub-sems-dpa'i spyod-la'-jug-pa (*TTP*, vol. 99, no. 5272)

bLa-ma-mchod-pa'i khrid-yig gsang-ba'i-gnad rnam-par-phye-ba snyan-rgyud man-ngag gter-mdsod by Paṇ-chen bLo-bzang-ye-śes

Zab-mo'i gter dang gter-ston grub-thob ji-ltar-byon-pa'i

lo-rgyus mdor-bsdus bkod-pa rin-chen-bai-ḍū-rya'i-phreng by sKong-sprul Padma-gar-dbang (*TM*, vol. Ka)

Rang-bźin rdsogs-pa-chen-po'i lam-gyi cha-lag sdom-pa-gsum rnam-par nges-pa źes-bya-ba'i bstan-bcos by mNga'-ris Paṇḍita Padma-dbang-gi-rgyal-po

Rang-bźin rdsogs-pa-chen-po'i lam-gyi cha-lag sdom-pa-gsum rnam-par nges-pa'i bstan-bcos-kyi tshig don-legs-pa'i-'grel-pa 'jam-dbyangs-dgyes-par-źal-lung by Karma-nges-don-snying-po-gźan-phan-chos-kyi-dbang-phyug

śes-rab-kyi-pha-rol-tu-phyin-pa'i man-ngag-gi bstan-bcos mngon-par rtogs-pa'i rgyan by Maitreyanātha (*TTP*, vol. 88, no. 5184)

gSang-ba-'dus-pa'i sa-lam by dByangs-can-dga'-ba'i-blo-gros

INDEX

TIBETAN PERSONAL NAMES AND TITLES

PERSONAL NAMES IN OTHER LANGUAGES

"t" signifies names derived from Tibetan sources with uncertain orthography

PLACE-NAMES IN TIBETAN

PLACE-NAMES IN OTHER LANGUAGES

TITLES OF CITED LITERATURE

TECHNICAL TERMS

SUBJECTS

DATE DUE

DEC 06 '89	
JAN 6 '90	
NOV 11 '92	
Ret 11/22	
NOV 23 1998	

BRODART, INC. Cat. No. 23-221